The Past Is Not Dead

University of Minnesota Press
Minneapolis
London

The Past Is Not Dead

Facts, Fictions, and Enduring Racial Stereotypes

Allan Pred

A portion of Part II was published as "Unspeakable Spaces: Racisms Past and Present on Exhibit in Stockholm, or The Unaddressable Addressed," *City and Society* 13, no. 1 (2001): 119–59. Reprinted with permission of the American Anthropological Association.

The illustration *A Harlot's Progress, Plate II: The Quarrel with Her Jew Protector* is reprinted with permission from *Hogarth: The Complete Engravings.* Copyright The British Museum.

Published by the University of Minnesota Press
111 Third Avenue South, Suite 290
Minneapolis, MN 55401-2520
http://www.upress.umn.edu

Library of Congress Cataloging-in-Publication Data

Pred, Allan Richard, 1936–
    The past is not dead : facts, fictions, and enduring racial stereotypes / Allan Pred.
        p.   cm.
    Includes bibliographical references and index.
    ISBN 0-8166-4405-5 (hc : alk. paper) — ISBN 0-8166-4406-3 (pb : alk. paper)
    1. Badin, 1747?–1822. 2. Sweden—Race relations—History. 3. Racism—
Sweden—History. 4. Sweden—History—1718–1814. 5. Race discrimination—
Sweden. I. Title.
    DL639.P745 2004
    305.8'009485—dc22

                                                                        2004004957

Printed in the United States of America on acid-free paper

The University of Minnesota is an equal-opportunity educator and employer.

12 11 10 09 08 07 06 05 04   10 9 8 7 6 5 4 3 2 1

The past is not dead. It is not even past.
—*William Faulkner*

Telescoping of the past through the present.
—*Walter Benjamin*

Contents

Part II. The Unaddressable Addressed: A Montage of Racisms on Exhibit

Acknowledgments

The past is not dead. Anybody who reads but a few pages of this work will quickly realize that I am deeply indebted to people long dead, to people whose texts and lives demand being given actuality, demand being brought into constellation with the here and now. Not least of all Walter Benjamin. And the Afro-Caribbean Badin, who died in Stockholm in 1822.

This is a book that may be traced back to numerous of my previous projects, and, consequently, those who have directly and indirectly contributed to its emergence and are deserving of acknowledgment are far too numerous to name. In confining my thanks to those whose impact has been most direct and voluminous, I trust that the many unnamed will know that my genuine appreciation all the same exists.

Expressions of profound gratitude then to:

Ola Larsmo, the Swedish novelist and cultural critic, who, at the very outset, provided support that was both enlightening and enthusiastic, as well as generous access to materials on Badin that he had already collected;

Anna Westerståhl Stenport, who assisted in the gathering of materials held in Stockholm's Royal Library;

Derek Gregory, a true friend and intellectual brother, whose thoughtful advice and encouragement have been valuable beyond words;

Gill Hart, Jean Lave, Donald Moore, Sven Nordlund, Gunnar Olsson, Mark Sandberg, Michael Watts, and the dozens of my seminar students who either have commented constructively upon portions of the manuscript or in other ways have provided sustaining support;

and my wife, Hjördis, who, by way of her remarkably resilient spirit in the face of physical difficulties, has proved the sturdiest of buttresses.

Past and Present Tense: Perpetuations of the Preseen (and Preknown) Previewed

The tradition of the oppressed teaches us that the "state of emergency" in which we live is not the exception but the rule. We must attain to a conception of history that is in keeping with that insight.

Walter Benjamin[1]

In keeping with that insight?
I can only lay forth my intentions.

This is a book that attempts
to show,
by way of telling Swedish example,
    the (con)fusions of fact and fiction,
    the fiFcAtCiTonS,
    through which racializing stereotypes are perpetuated
        and reenacted at dispersed sites;

to show
    the erosion-resistant sediments,
    the entangled webs of horizontal connection
        and situated practice,
    the multiple mundane means
        and contingencies,
    the ever-present structures of power
    through which racializing stereotypes
        and relations of domination and exploitation
    have been (f)actually (re)produced

time and again,
since the eighteenth century (and earlier);

to show
how fiction-laden racializing images,
how images of hypersexuality, the childlike,
and the otherwise negatively charged,
have circulated and connected up unpredictably
in time and space,
have traveled through shifting discursive networks,
have readily flowed back and forth
between
"scientific," literary, political, and popular discourses,
have had their meanings repeatedly recontextualized,
their assumptions somewhat shifted
and occasionally challenged,
and yet—
however complex the process(es)—
have endured to this day,
unevenly reactivated nationally and locally,
over and over recycled, rearticulated, and re-present-ed,
over and over put to new kinds of work,
over and over taking on more or less reshaped forms
that cannot be separated
from the on-the-ground circumstances
they already have helped produce.[2]

It is a book that attempts to deal
with the construction and acquisition of taken-for-granteds
that prescript ways of (not) seeing,
with the forenowness of past image(ination)s,
with the lived consequences of being made invisible
by way of stereotypes that Universalize,
with how pre-envisioned fi¢xtions in (f)act fix upon the body,
epidermically entrap and fix in place,
and thereby place the stereotyped subject in a fix,
with how fictions enter into the everyday life
(f)acts and experiences of the stereotyped,
with how the "dialectics of not seeing"
touch the emotions and sense of self of the stereotyped,
yielding individual and collective identity dilemmas

that demand reworking,
some kind of (f)actual contestation.

It is a book that attempts to confront the unspeakable,
    to undermine the already "known,"
    to destabilize it-goes-without-saying images,
    to disrupt fiction-based stereotypes,
in among other ways
by bringing the collective memory and amnesia
    of those who stereotype
into tension with the personal remembering and forgetting
    of those who are stereotyped,
and by strategically interrupting the text
    with fact-based counterfictions.

—

In the fields with which we are concerned knowledge comes only in
lightning flashes. The text is the long roll of thunder that follows.
    Walter Benjamin[3]

The long roll of thunder that follows?
I can only allude to my textual desires and designs.

The repetitive devices,
the fleeting-pause-forcing indentations,
the meaning-altering parentheses,
the contrived spellings,
while only a start,
already indicate
this is a book that departs from conventional textual strategies.
But here, there is no wordplay for the mere sake of wordplay.
My way with words—my wayward words—
    is not a mere exercise in playful formulation.
For here, with something(s) serious at stake,
    words like re-fuse and re-view are used
    with polysemous, punishing intent.
For here every turn of phrase involves a turn of thought.
For this is not a postmodern pastiche—
    "which sees the jumbling of elements as all there is"[4]—
but the performance of a position.

For here the watchwords are not whimsy and caprice,
but intelligibility and re-cognition.

—

[Benjamin employed a] "micrological procedure," concentrat-
ing on the smallest thing, stilling its historical forces and turning
it into image. The impression, then, is of a close-up—a peering
into material in order to record spatial, temporal, and political dimensions. But this is no new objectivism. It is writing as montage
image, an imaging cut through by time and tingling with the
vibrating struts of social relations that underpin and traverse it.
    Esther Leslie, characterizing Theodor Adorno's take on Benjamin's
"condensed mode of envisioning"[5]

With the close-up, space expands; with slow motion, movement
is extended. The enlargement of a snapshot does not simply render more precise what in any case was visible, though unclear; it
reveals entirely new structural formations of the subject.
    Walter Benjamin[6]

With the close-up? Render more precise?
I can only expand on my critical engagement
with you
briefly.

Leastmost.
The maximum
    about the prescripting of vision
by way of the minimum.
The large picture
    of stereotyping and its consequences
by way of the miniature.
The multiply scaled workings
    of discourse and power relations
    revealed
by way of minute details.
Grand fictions
    stripped naked
by way of the smallest,
    otherwise seemingly inconsequential,
(f)acts.

Widespread conventions of observation
  critically observed
by way of looking over—
  oh so close up—
the overlooked.
Theory shown,
  assembl(ag)ed on the page,
by way of microscopic empiricism
  that is at once delicate and heretical,
  that does not draw back
    from touching raw nerve endings,
    from stirring the reader,
    from rousing feelings
      that may dismay and disgust.[7]
Broad subject matter
  illuminated
by way of a single subject who matters.

> Isn't it that one wants a thing to be as factual as possible, and
> yet at the same time as deeply suggestive or deeply unlocking
> of areas of sensation other than simple illustration of the object
> that you set out to do? Isn't that what art is all about?
>   *Francis Bacon*[8]

—

> The historical projected into the intimate.
>   *Walter Benjamin*[9]

> There is a delicate empiricism which so intimately involves itself
> with the object that it becomes true theory.
>   *Goethe, as quoted by Walter Benjamin*[10]

While not in any sense a biography, much of this book centers on the life of
a single figure. As much due to Benjamin-inspired strategic intent as initial
accident . . . Unforewarned, devoid of anticipation, I found myself standing
there before the pastel portrait. I was fascinated immediately, if not transfixed, by the play of Swedish summer sunlight on his eyes, his smiling lips,
his feathered attire, the chess piece in his right hand. And by his startling
difference. It was my first visual encounter with the young Afro-Caribbean

who, in 1775, had been captured by a painter to the royal court. As a person of color he stood out there, distinctly alone amid countless others, hanging on the wall of the National Portrait Gallery, sharing the space of a magnificent Renaissance castle with national "heroes" and the textbook famous, an unexpected presence in this Who's Who in Swedish History, in this fortress of national identity construction. It was the summer of 1985, and the presence of this figure—heretofore only vaguely known to me— took on especial significance in the context of ongoing events. Sweden, as yet, possessed what was arguably the world's most generous refugee policy. Since the early 1970s there had been a rapid influx of Middle Easterners, Africans, Latin Americans, and Southeast Asians, especially into the Stockholm area; and now, in an effort to stem the metropolitan concentration of those Muslims and non-Europeans of color, the government had recently introduced a Whole of Sweden Strategy, designed to spread newly admitted refugees of obvious Difference to smaller municipalities throughout the country that lacked any previous history with that kind of migrant Otherness. Also, at that very moment, with Middle Eastern war refugees showing up at the borders in unprecedented numbers, the country was in the midst of a media-induced moral panic—replete with racist undertones—regarding the "invasion" or "uncontrolled flood" of non-European and Muslim arrivals.[11]

Thereafter, I renewed my acquaintance with the portrait annually, as the National Portrait Gallery was a more or less compulsory stop on the local tour offered friends who were visiting our summer home—and with each repeated encounter the man portrayed, who was called Badin, took an ever-firmer grip on my imagination. By the fall of 1999, after having completed a book on the burgeoning of cultural racism in Sweden during the past decade, after having just visited a Stockholm museum exhibit where the long-standing stereotype of black hypersexuality was rendered in an absolutely unspeakable manner, and after having read two 1996 novels in which Badin was the principal character, I could not avoid assigning a central role to him in my next project. Even though the writing of the just finished book had proved a personally painful experience, I felt compelled to address issues of stereotyping and (hyper)sexuality that were there left largely unaddressed. Like it or not. Badin's portrait, and every mention of him, left my mind crowded with questions. Questions that were not spatially and temporally confined to Sweden.

> Indeed, the most intense point of a life, the point where its energy
> is concentrated, is where it comes up against power, struggles
> with it, attempts to use its forces and to evade its traps.
> *Michel Foucault*[12]

[For Benjamin] the most a writing dealing with the biographical
sphere of a subject can . . . strive to accomplish is to give a sense
of the infinite and infinitely mediated set of complex relations
that constitute the fiber of the text of the subject's life.

    Gerhard Richter[13]

What can be shown about the complex of power relations, representations,
and practices through which Badin came to be "known" and seen during
his life, through which his subjectification became? How did he view the
ways in which he was (not) known and (not) seen, and the concrete everyday
consequences thereof? How did he attempt to escape the traps strewn across
the path of his existence? Could these initial questions be dealt with in such
a manner as to enable Badin to be "'blasted' out of history's continuum and
made 'actual' in the present"?[14] Was there some way in which Badin, as a
historical subject, as an object of focus, could be superimposed upon "barbaric present reality,"[15] upon ongoing on-the-ground injustices and sufferings? Was there some way in which he could be imag(in)ed into the spaces of
this current "moment of danger,"[16] in Sweden and far beyond? Some way in
which the particulars of his life, and subsequent representations of those particulars, could step into our lives? Some way in which his textual traces could
be seized, montaged into relational complexity, and put to critical use? Some
way in which he could be given voice? Be enabled to address the present?
Shockingly? To speak to the unspeakable? To counter the current propensity
for collective amnesia? To tell and show the absence of any stable boundary between fact and fiction? To enter into conversation with contemporary
voices? To thereby facilitate a constellation, a stunning image of forgotten
histories juxtaposed with the present? Or was he to remain no more than
a pastel portrait, hanging in a palace where he once trod, existing in fact
as little more than a fiction, languishing in dead silence—unre(dis)covered,
unre-deemed, unreimag(in)ed—and denied his political potential?[17]

> Historicism contents itself with establishing a causal connection
> between various moments in history. But no fact that is a cause
> is for that very reason historical. It became historical post-
> humously, as it were, through events that may be separated from
> it by *[hundreds or]* thousands of years. A historian who takes
> this as his point of departure stops telling the sequence of events
> like the beads of a rosary. Instead, he grasps the constellation
> which his era has formed with a definite earlier one.
>
>   *Walter Benjamin*[18]

—

> Benjamin was at least convinced of one thing: what was needed
> was a visual, not a linear logic. The concepts [*of his* Arcades
> Project] were to be imagistically constructed, according to the
> cognitive principles of montage.
>   *Susan Buck-Morss*[19]

Walter Benjamin is a specter who walks the pages of this work, an invisible figure present in every one of its montaged elements.[20] His street-
roaming, flaneuring footsteps echo throughout this assemblage of disjointed
(geographical-hi)stories, this collection of jagged-edged partial narratives,
this set of anecdotes and other fragments that are meant to fall into place(s)
with one another. His voice is put to work, is time and again given an afterlife, in this set of tales in which the past and the present—the then-there and
here-now—are shown to be discontinuously and complexly enfolded within
one another. As they always are. Inextricably.

> [The Arcades Project] is supposed to liberate the enormous ener-
> gies of history that are slumbering in the "once upon a time"
> of classical historical narrative. The history that was bent on
> showing things "as they really and truly were" was the strongest
> narcotic of the nineteenth century.
>   *Walter Benjamin*[21]

> [T]he aphorism, the illuminating aside, the quotation, the imag-
> istic fragment, became his preferred—indeed, essential—mode
> of expression. In presenting and representing the everyday in a
> new light, observing it from an unexpected angle, such minia-
> tures were intended to catch the reader off guard (like a series of
> blows decisively dealt, Benjamin once observed, left-handed).
>   *Graeme Gilloch*[22]

While Benjamin's ghost haunts these pages, while he is quoted on numerous
occasions, there is no effort here to provide yet another exegesis of his works,
to provide yet another "authoritative" reading of writings that are often "no-
toriously elusive" and "contradictory,"[23] to explicate what he possibly meant
in the "Theory of Knowledge, Theory of Progress" portion of *The Arcades
Project,* in his "Theses on the Philosophy of History," or in any other of his
here-relevant writings. I am not a "Benjamin scholar" in that sense, and I
do not pretend to be one—I do not aspire to say anything new or profound
about any portion of his oeuvre. . . . Among the places where the presence of
Benjamin's specter makes itself most evident is in my effort to bring images
of the past and present into constellation with one another so as to unsettle,

in my effort to juxtapose temporally distant (dis/con)junctures with those of the present so as to disrupt. This tactic of attempting to make the past contemporary and the contemporary past is meant to "catch the reader off guard." And thereby throw open the possibility of a momentary insight, of a "flash" of re-cognition that is one with re-remembering and reimag(e)ining, one with reviewing the preseen and refusing the preknown. The presence of his specter is thereby evident in the absence of any "classical narrative" held together by neatly sutured causal connections, of any supposedly exhaustive account reciting "the sequence of events like the beads of a rosary." Whether or not any left-handed blows are—in fact or (counter)fiction—"decisively dealt," here there are only multiple beginnings, multiple endings, and, in between, the fragments of multiple narratives shown jostling and crosscutting with one another. No linear "once upon a time." No "whole story." But a totality of fragments. Of sorts.[24]

> Method of this project: literary montage. I needn't say anything.
> Merely show.
> *Walter Benjamin*[25]

Benjamin's usage of the literary, or textual, montage was meant to show. Nothing more. Or less! In the most artful and compelling of his completed montages, *One-Way Street, A Berlin Chronicle,* and *Berlin Childhood around 1900,* it is only Benjamin's own voice that is montaged in the form of "thought figures," recollected vignettes, and other devices.[26] In the never-completed *Arcades Project,* which survives as a *collection of raw materials* for a number of interrelated thematic montages, the subject folders, or "convolutes," take one of two forms. In most a more or less large assortment of quotes dominates the material, with Benjamin's occasionally commenting or reflecting voice confined to the background. In the remaining instances, and most notably in "On the Theory of Knowledge, Theory of Progress" (convolute N), Benjamin's own aphorisms and commentaries predominate and the voices of others are secondary. In other words, Benjamin never fully realized a montage in which his voice intermingled with others.[27] And, whatever else the case, he never gave voice to the prostitute, the ragpicker, or any of the other marginalized Parisian figures so central to his *Arcades Project.*[28]

> The first stage in this undertaking [The Arcades Project] will be
> to carry over the principle of montage into history. That is, to
> assemble large-scale constructions out of the smallest and most
> precisely cut components.
> *Walter Benjamin*[29]

In the two interlocking montages that constitute this book, my voice persistently intermingles with others. And the marginalized repeatedly speak. . . . My voice darts in and out of the text frequently, intervening and interrupting. Coming to the foreground among other voices in order to provide background, or popping up intermittently in order to supply the telling aside, to question at length, to problematize and to reflect, to orient in a critical direction and to disorient from the preknown and preseen, to introduce a multitude of perspectives and to produce a multitude of contradictions—so as to show. Voices, including mine, speak sometimes to one another, sometimes past one another, sometimes in sympathetic vibration, sometimes in grating dissonance, sometimes illuminating one another, sometimes overshadowing one another—so as to show. Ordinary and extraordinary voices, commonplace and out-of-place Other voices, the words of (f)actually existing people and fictional-text voices, are (con)joined by mine and heard in monologue, dialogue, and polylogue—so as to show. Differently situated voices, Us/Sameness and Them/Difference voices, then/there and here/now voices, including mine, are made to articulate with one another, often resonating at several levels at once—so as to show. . . . Marginalized and mainstream voices are deployed in a film-like manner, zoomed in on and interspliced with one another so that shifts of angle and scale may occur; given close-up focus and then seen from afar so that different vantage points may be brought into tension; placed in startling juxtaposition with one another so that past and present may be seen fading in and out of one another; allowed to move rapidly between flash-backs and flash-forwards—bolting back and forth in time—so that the past and present may be (thunder)bolted together. With or without these cinematic parallels, my voice speaks through the very manner in which I have purposefully positioned and sequenced other voices, through the very manner I have attempted to show.[30] . . . Thus, through these various maneuvers, in effect, other voices become my voice and my voice becomes other voices. Never as an end in itself. But as a means to render the complex and heterogeneous intelligible and re-cognizable.

> [C]entral to Benjamin's work is the insight that texts, objects, and images have a particular existence, or "life," of their own which goes beyond, and cannot be reduced to, the intentions and purposes of those who created them. . . . [I]t is [his] contention that the meaning and significance of a text are not determined by the author at the moment of writing, but are contested and conceptualized anew as it enters subsequent contexts, as it is subject to reading and criticism through time.
>
> *Graeme Gilloch*[31]

The scattered textual elements constituting Benjamin's (re)vision of history, like any other textual assemblage, cannot be read and assigned meaning other than through the lens of personally accumulated situated knowledges, other than through the discourses one has been exposed to, other than through the partial perspectives and associational capacities one has built up in embodied practice. . . . Benjamin's extraordinary critical capacities emerged and continuously became between 1892 and 1940, principally in Berlin and Paris. As did his concerns. . . . I was born in New York City in 1936, and since leaving there after adolescence, my critical capacities—limited as they are—have continuously become at a number of locations, but principally in Berkeley and Stockholm. My spectacles are not the famous pair worn by Benjamin in book-jacket photos. And they are subject to periodic adjustment, to new prescriptions that alter vision. Here too then, inevitably, Benjamin's (re)vision of history cannot escape recontexualization and being "conceptualized anew." My effort to bring past and present racial stereotypings into constellation is not an act of total mimesis, an attempt to reproduce in a mechanical manner. Even if the effort relies heavily on quotations, even if it includes imagistic fragments and occasional aphorisms, even if it contains (would-be) illuminating asides, it does not proceed according to any Benjamin-supplied formula. It proceeds by my own multiply inspired devices and stratagems.[32] The most important of which have been already sketched. All of which will openly glide, flit, and dance in and out of the montages that follow. But whatever the devices and stratagems, my effort cannot escape the shadow of Benjamin's shade. . . . Here, looking back into the future.

—

Benjamin's speculative philosophy at its strongest moments does not seek truth in completeness, but in neglected detail and the small nuance. The speculative power of the excluded is episodic and unpredictable, and it is this frangibility, as of a rainbow, which makes it an occasion for hope, which is, after all, even if not for him and not for us, only another way of saying "future."
    Howard Caygill[33]

To recognize the instability of the divide between fantasy and reality, fiction and facts is to begin the difficult and painful task of constructing alternative futures.
    Gail Ching-Liang Low[34]

Part I

The Remembering and Forgetting of Badin: A Montage of (F)acts Fictionalized and Fictions (F)actualized

[I]f images from the past spring to legibility in the present, it is because they speak to its concerns.

Margaret Cohen, Profane Illumination: Walter Benjamin and the Paris of Surrealist Revolution

As a historian Benjamin valued textual exactness not in order to achieve a hermeneutical understanding of the past "as it actually was"—he called historicism the greatest narcotic of the time—but for the shock of historical citations ripped out of their original context with a "strong, seemingly brutal grasp," and brought into the most immediate present.

Susan Buck-Morss, "The Flaneur, the Sandwichman, and the Whore: The Politics of Loitering"

Foremontage: Representations of the Racialized Other

For stereotypes, like commonplaces, carry entire realms of association with them, associations that form a subtext within the
world of fiction. In the case of works claiming to create a world
of whole cloth, such a subtext provides basic insight into the
presuppositions of the culture in which the work arises and for
which it is created.

Sander L. Gilman[1]

Any representation can be circulated. And it is the character
of this circulation—secret or open, rapid or sluggish, violently
imposed or freely embraced, constrained by guilt and anxiety,
or experienced as pleasure—that regulates the accommodation,
assimilation, and representation of the culture of the other.

Stephen Greenblatt[2]

—

The more primitive a race is, the more its individuals resemble
one another both with respect to their outer appearance and
their thinking powers, conceptions, and customs. It would be
a difficult task to present a comprehensive picture of an entire
nation of civilized people by way of a single example; but take an
individual of the negro race, look at his facial movements, ges-
tures, and walk, and observe his laugh and speech—it is impossible to see any difference between that which is characteristic of
him and of 500 others of the same race.

*O. B., in a 1917 article on the "Zulu kaffirs" appearing in one of
Sweden's most widely read illustrated weeklies at a time when the
"civilized people" of Europe were in the midst of a "Great War,"
slaughtering one another by the millions just as they had previously*

3

massacred millions of Africans and other "primitive races" in the
course of colonial expansion—an article accompanied by the usual
assortment of stereotype-reinforcing images, by photos of a bare-
breasted young woman and a "wildly" attired witch doctor, by
drawings of spears, shields, and other instruments of "primitive"
violence[3]

Representations of the racialized Other, however "accurate" or "inaccurate" they may be, however "undistorted" or "exaggerated and oversimplified" they may be, however much they may erase or suppress or fabricate, are always social facts in themselves. Whether or not devoid of "fictional elements," always factual—realities in themselves—because consisting of actually produced texts and images, because constituting actually existing components of discourse, because yielding actual social and political effects, because actually precipitating or (re)producing material and relational consequences.[4]

Representations of the racialized Other, however "impartial" or "distorted" they may be, (f)actually take on a life of their own, entering into networks of circulation and social interaction, entering into a multitude of immediate and more dispersed transversal connections, becoming individually or collectively encountered in the situated practices of everyday life, occasionally simply fleeting by—being barely recognized or totally ignored, more frequently capturing attention—being made sense of, given meaning.

The traces of *[eighteenth- and nineteenth-century]* racial
stereotypes—what we may call a "racialized regime of
representation"—have persisted into the late twentieth century.
    Stuart Hall[5]

Representations of the racialized Other—once entered into local and wider discursive networks, once repeatedly given voice, once given redundant expression, once made subject to multiple exposure—are apt to become name-etched, word-wired, meaning-meshed. Are apt to become self-resonating, self-reverberating, self-reinforcing. Are apt to become essentialized reductions more or less indelibly stereo-typed upon the individual mind, deeply inscribed within the collective popular imagination. Open to reshaping and reworking with shifting context. Open to being acted upon, performed with concrete results, ontologically transformed from substanceless signifier to material consequence. But seldom easily erased or unlearned. Not readily blotted out overnight. Or over the passage of years and decades. Or even centuries. Their work, as yet, not fully (un)done.

That which is invented is not an illusion; it constitutes our truth.
   Nikolas Rose, drawing upon Foucault[6]

"Truth" is linked in a circular relation with systems of power
which produce and sustain it, and to effects of power which it
induces and which extend it.
   Michel Foucault[7]

Representations of the racialized Other—once fusing with dispersed appa-
ratuses of power, once anonymously serving economic or political interests,
once widespread, once entering the repertoire of the taken-for-granted,
once unreflectingly called to mind—are apt to become synonymous with
the social production of particular forms of remembering and forgetting.
Are apt to become surrounded with a dense field of associations, meanings,
and connotations; with a dense field of unproblematic discursive "truths"
and "laws of nature"[8] that are at once vision inducing and vision eliminat-
ing. Are apt to become one with "racially saturated fields of vision," with
a structuring of what "can and cannot appear within the horizon of white
[or majority] perception,"[9] with preconceptions that screen out and blind,
with ways of seeing that automatically project the imagined Universal upon
the actually present individual body, with reversals and displacements
that constitute a dialectics of not seeing. . . . "Truths" that yield illusions.
Illusions that, in turn, reconfirm, that reinforce "truths." And encourage
their further re-presentation, their re-citation and retelling in everyday
discourse. And the everyday recurrence of illusions. The repeated discovery
of the already "known" and previously "seen."[10] . . . The loose words and
slippery terms of hard and fast distinctions/Differences magically translated into distinct visions, and back into loose words and slippery terms. . . .
Visible geographies of the embodied and material blanked out by invisible
geographies of power and discourse. Actions actually not present repeatedly rendered visible. Actions actually present repeatedly rendered invisible.
Holey King! Wholly out of sight! (Ob)scene erasure!

Marginality is simultaneously an identity/consciousness and a
structure/place. . . . How [race, class, and gender] difference is
perceived and lived, however, is never ultimately "set." Deter-
minations do exist, and are historically contextualized, but they
are contingent on an almost infinite complex of possibilities.
   Bryan D. Palmer[11]

Once representations of the racialized Other have taken on a life of their own, once they have become widely disseminated through discursive networks, once they have slipped into the place-specific workings of power structures, once they have been incorporated into WE-confirming fields of vision, once the resultant dialectics of not seeing have entered into commonplace practice, those representations—whether or not largely invented—actually become a condition of the minority Other's everyday practical and political existence. The map of no(t)-hereness by which they must actually navigate. Centrally constituting their truth, something they must truly live with. The driving piston of their social relations and material conditions. The different-ial equation structuring their daily domination and exploitation. The means by which they are steered into stereotype-confirming circumstances, into vicious-circle entrapment. The cert(ain)ified stamp of their abnormality. The ma(r)ker of their exclusions, out-of-placeness, unbelonging.[12] The barbed wire of their borders. The raw materials of their subjection. And abjection. Something that they concretely experience. Something that is rarely distant from their consciousness. Something they must frequently wrestle with, work against, in contemplating their identities. In attempting to (re)define themselves in their own terms, to name themselves on their own terms, to seize their assigned categories and "turn them in another direction or give them a future they weren't supposed to have."[13] In attempting to open a new wor(l)d of possibilities, to convert a prolonged moment of danger into a moment of opportunity. In attempting to carve out some space for the free play of their collective and individual desires. In attempting to liberate a home place, a counterdefined anchoring for their id entities.

> [R]epresentations are not mere mirrors of the world. They enter directly into its fabrication.
> [I]n constructing multiple others as other, and in assenting to these constructions and impositions, we not only do this to others. *We do this to ourselves.*
> *Derek Gregory*[14]

Entrances
Beginnings
Namings

badinage *[F, fr.* badiner *to joke (fr. MF, fr.* badin, *joker, fool, fr.*
OProv, fr. badar *to gape, fr. (assumed) VL* batare) *+ MF-age]:*
light and playful repartee or wit[1]

[Among all the blacks who came to Sweden between the late
seventeenth century and the mid-nineteenth century, and] who
were often employed in court circles, there is only one, Badin,
who through Crusenstolpe's novel, through his entirely unique
relation to the royal family, . . . has come to stand out as the
"Blackamoor" before all others in the popular imagination.
    Lars Wikström, historian[2]

Adolph Ludvig Gustaf Albrecht Couschi (1747[?]–1822), called Badin. Pastel
portrait by Gustav Lundberg, 1775. National Portrait Gallery, Gripsholm's
Castle, Mariefred, Sweden

Few are those who recount the events of their life with honesty.
The reason is pride, self-interest, fear, sometimes shame, [or not
wishing to] expose friends. These five points most often prevent the
truth from being seen where it ought to be. But he who writes these
lines shall attempt not to stumble in truth's pure way and thereby
deceive the reader with his tales. The color of he who writes does
not resemble that of what he writes upon, but well resembles that of
what he has written with.

> *Badin, entering into his autobiographical statement, assuring his reader
> that all that follows is honest fact rather than deceptive self-serving fic-
> tion, staking out his position by (re)marking his blackness on the page,
> and in this process of reflexive self-textualization showing himself to be
> a modern individual—entrapped in questions of identity (written for the
> Par Bricole Order, in which he became a member during 1793)*[3]

Behave yourself, nigger!
First line addressed to Badin, now an adult, in August Strindberg's
Gustav III.[4] *The line is spoken by Baron Carl Edvard Taube, the
court chaplain.*

Who is it, in fact, that Strindberg is here fictionalizing?

Who is this here niggerized figure, this figure who recurs in Swedish novels and historical dramas from the 1840s through the 1990s?

Who is this man whose biographical details, whose capabilities and
physical attributes, whose acts and accomplishments, whose passions and
sexuality, have been repeatedly reimag(in)ed by historians and other "nonfictional" authors, as well as novelists and dramatists?

What may be ventured?

About his life and subsequent representations thereof?

About the racialized imaginations out of which they have emerged and
to which they have contributed?

About contemporary resonances?

About present-day rememberings and forgettings?

About the perpetual (con)fusion of facts and fictions, and the very concrete consequences thereof?

About the genealogy of the stereotype and the dialectics of not seeing?

[The natural science of Linnaeus] reduces the whole area of
the visible to a system of variables all of whose values can be
designated, if not by a quantity, at least by a perfectly clear and
always finite description. It is therefore possible to establish the
system of identities and the order of differences existing between
natural entities.

    Michel Foucault[5]

One could hardly imagine a more explicit attempt to "naturalize"
the myth of European superiority.

    Mary Louise Pratt, speaking of the 1758 edition of Linnaeus's
    Systema naturae[6]

In effect, if not intent, scientific racism textually arrived in Sweden in 1758
when Linnaeus published the tenth edition of his *Systema naturae,* a work
intended to demonstrate the wisdom of God as manifested in nature, to
prove that the "natural system" was one with the "divine plan of creation."[7] In the initial 1735 edition, the master Swedish taxonomist had
simply labeled humankind as *Homo sapiens* and subdivided that category
of primates into four distinctive "varieties," or races, solely on the basis
of physical attributes, of "perfectly clear" visible differences.[8] Now, "temperament" and "personality" were added to the formula of Difference, with
Europeans *(Homo Europaeus)* being described as "inventive, perceptive,
meticulous, and law abiding" and thereby implicitly superior to Africans
(Homo Afer), who were characterized as "lazy," "dishonest," "governed
by caprice." Now, "perfectly clear" visible differences—"black" or "black-
brown flesh"; "coal-black, rough curly hair; a flattened nose; swollen
lips"—were to automatically summon up an array of negatively charged
behavioral-cultural qualities; palpable bodies, or (verbal) drawings thereof,
and mental images were to coalesce in a "perfectly clear," no-question-
about-it, scientifically validated field of vision.[9] Now the subject matter of
Difference, the subject(ification) of the Different, was to become irrevoca-
bly altered—defined by new limits, confined by new outer boundaries. Now
Difference was to become epidermalized, now skin color was to become a
BOLD PRINT signifier, an ALL CAPS sign of a specific nature, a large font
emblem of in-born (ine)qualities.[10] Now, by way of applying **certain** principles, by way of classification and exact descriptive language, by way of
naming and representation, by way of a taxonomic system that was to be
trusted and believed,[11] by way of power/knowledge put into practice, "a
new field of visibility [was] being constituted in all its density."[12] Now the

previously unseen and never encountered could be confidently located on a "map of nature."[13] Now the "global imaginings," the "planetary conscious-ness" of Swedes, and Europeans more generally, could be overwritten with a new sense of "unity and order,"[14] one that naturalized and hierarchized Difference, one that defined the European as the Norm(al) and everything/ body else as aberrant, and thereby served to justify the exploitative so-cial relations of slavery and colonialism. . . . And yet, but one year later, Linnaeus allowed that the distantly born "Wild," the inferior, could achieve the qualities of Swedes, of *Homo Europaeus,* through cultivation. Just as he insisted that the most exotic of tropical plants could gradually adapt to the coldness of Sweden's climate, he suggested that someone of African (or other non-European) ancestry could be taught to thrive in Sweden. The "savage" of distant origins supposedly could be domesticated. The replant-ed body supposedly could adapt completely. Fully fit in. Blend in. No matter how Different. No matter how greatly dis-placed.

> Only the Sciences distinguish Wild people, Barbarians and Hottentots, from us; just as a thorny sour Wild apple is distin-guished from a tasty Renette only through cultivation. . . . The sciences are thus the light that will lead people who wander in darkness.
>
> *Carl Linnaeus, in a 1759 speech to the Royal Court, arguing that Sweden could develop an imperial economy within its own borders, and save considerable sums of money, through the planting of tea and other tropical crops*[15]

It is another story that decades later, in the 1780s, Linnaeus and his stu-dents were ridiculed in the press and novels, as they "had repeatedly, indeed spectacularly, failed to naturalize exotic plants."[16]

His plant-adaption "facts" were now recognized as fictions. His ra-cial categorizations, those fictions of the imagination, however, remained "facts." . . . And it is yet another story that those widely diffused and highly influential categorizations had multiple beginnings. Although they may have resulted from an intense desire to systematize, and although their specif-ics may have been the product of "hasty formulation and arbitrary judg-ments,"[17] they were not independent inventions. They were, instead, a set of classifications that in some measure emerged out of (and contributed to) continental discourses regarding the physical and psychical variation of humans—discourses that were one "with the mounting pile of information about distant lands" that accompanied European exploration and colonization, and that by the eighteenth century demanded "to be squeezed into some logical framework."[18] They were, in addition, a set of classifications that evolved out of his three-year stay in Holland,[19] out of his own tapping into the channels of "worldwide commerce" for specimen procurement,[20] out of his participation in extensive scientific networks of book and correspondence exchange that were gradually embellished by the far-flung research travels of his students.[21] Moreover, that set of categorizations quite evidently began to take shape in the aftermath of his famed 1732 journey to Lapland. A journey to the territory of Sami reindeer herders that he mythologized "into a formative encounter with an Edenic 'wild nation.'" A journey to the lands of a "happy" people that he characterized as living in harmony with nature—and as being "lazy dogs." A journey that contributed to the further colonization of what for some time had been referred to as "our West Indies."[22]

[N]ot without reason the Lapps may be termed northern
Ethiopians.
  Harald Vallerius, Uppsala professor, in his 1706 treatise, De varia
  hominum forma externa[23]

———

[I can personally] vouch that aristocrats, men and women alike,
have nasty-smelling mouths and blackened teeth.
  Carl Linnaeus, commenting in 1765 on the consequences of a high-
  sugar diet for those he had observed in his visits to the court of
  Queen Lovisa Ulrica, where Badin was an everyday presence[24]—
  commenting, in effect, on whiteness turning against itself through
  consuming a product of West Indian slavery

I saw ice and snow for the first time. Thought the snow was sugar; but
both the taste and temperature promptly convinced me of the mistake.
  Badin, regarding an event that occurred when he was approximately
  eight years old[25]

Badin's earliest recollection of Europe, dating to November 1758, was one of whiteness viewed and encountered while sailing toward Copenhagen somewhere well north of Gibraltar in the company of his then owner, Baron Christian Lebrecht von Pröck, Danish governor of Saint Croix—the West Indian island and sugar plantation colony where he was born. . . . Written at about age sixty, as part of a brief autobiographical account, was this a vivid childhood experience innocently recollected? A simple retrospective reworking of a life history? A mature philosophical metaphor? Or an (un?)intentional allegory, a symbolic distillation, a (un?)reflective generalization of ever-again black experience, born of hindsight and laden with foresight? The white as unreliable, as tasteless source of disappointment, as dispenser of cruel punishments. As deception and coldness embodied. As producer of white lies. As undeniable denier of sweetness, of that which has been forcibly left behind. As identity robber. As provider of substantial promises that sooner or later melt away, that eventually evaporate into thin air.

> His cradling time is believed by him to have begun in 1750.
>   *Badin, employing the third person to speak of his own birth date*[26]

> The most frequently occurring specification of his year of birth
> is 1747, and that seems to be correct, since in the announcement
> of his death, which occurred March 22, 1822, it was said that he
> had achieved age 75.
>   *Carl Forsstrand, historian, writing approximately one hundred*
>   *years after Badin's statement*[27]

Delivered to Copenhagen, and later Stockholm, under conditions clearly not of his own choosing, any precise birth-date information was whited out for Badin. There were no records on which he could lay his hands. There was no immediate family member or relative available to inform him. In the absence of accessible knowledge he could only speculate. Wanting any factual information, he in (f)act could only fictionalize. Dispossessed of nothing less than his parents and his beginnings, he could only retreat into the third person and construct his own story. . . . When Badin passed away in 1822 both his official death notification and the legally required inventory of his possessions *(bouppteckningen)* indicated that he had reached age seventy-five.[28] Whether that age was provided by his second wife, Magdalena Eleonora, who in a state of grief (and possible confusion) was forced to provide information normally confirmable through church registries, or whether that age was an estimate made and entered by an official who felt compelled to fill in all the blanks, it was a complete invention. Something that Badin himself did not know. All the same, by virtue of its public registration, by the (f)act of its entry into state records, it became a more or less established "fact" that he was born in 1747. A light observation, fluidly transcribed, that achieved solidity with the passage of time, being repeated in historical essays and encyclopedia entries and inscribed on the plate beneath his famous portrait that still hangs prominently at the National Portrait Gallery. . . . Right from the start then. What was totally forgotten somehow becomes remembered. Badin's life is translated into a set of narratives in which (f)acts and fictions become one another. As easily as snow melts into water. And later becomes frozen into ice.

≠ ≠ ≠

Entrances, present tense.

I didn't choose to flee to Sweden myself. I only accompanied the family and was part of the baggage. Now *[1996]*, owing to political problems, I cannot return to my former homeland. And now I have lived in Sweden fifteen years, just as much as in my first home country. Since I know I can't return in the near future I have staked everything on a life here in Sweden. I want to be treated as a Swede—not only on my ID-card. But in order for me to regard myself as Swedish and a part of Sweden, Swedes ought to regard me as Swedish. To not be accepted by the country you come to and not be embraced by the land you left is a very difficult experience. You are not allowed to feel at home anywhere. You have an identity forced upon you that you never reckoned with, an "immigrant" identity that prevents your becoming a part of Sweden. I and my friends in Rinkeby *[a segregated suburb of Stockholm]* don't want to have a semi- or in-between identity. No! We want to be able to keep our old identity, love our new identity, and be respected as we are—even if we don't look like the All Swedish Boy of certain advertisements.
Kurdo Baksi, author and editor, born in "Kurdistan"[29]

If Leonardo da Vinci had migrated to Sweden today [1995] he probably wouldn't even be able to get a cleaning job! His children would probably be regarded as "immigrant youths" and perhaps picked on at school. They might have been directed to one of the high-rise residential areas on the outskirts of a large city. The residential area would presumably be designated a "problem area." Their prospects for the future would be dismal.
Juan Fonseca, migrant from Colombia and Social Democratic member of parliament at the time of this statement[30]

[R"]acism is worse here than there. . . . In France I never experience the same feeling of inferiority as here. For you we are nobody. We share no history and you have had terribly little contact
with black people. . . . [T]he longer one lives as a black in Sweden,
the more one realizes how widespread racism is. How deep it goes.
*Papa Sow, Senegalese migrant studying in Stockholm to be
a teacher during 1996*[31]

≠ ≠ ≠

The time: indeterminate date after the summer(?) of 1760, when
Badin was given as a present to the King of Sweden, Adolph
Fredrik, by a member of the Danish Board of Commerce
The place: a room in the Royal Palace, Stockholm
QUEEN LOVISA ULRIKA *(speaks slowly while running her fingers
through the young black boy's hair)*: Vous êtes vraiment un
Farceur—un Badin. *(Removes his head from her lap.)* Sit down.
(Pauses to gaze through the thick-glassed palace window.) Is
there anything my Blackamoor wishes?
BADIN *(desiring food, but lost for words, says no by shaking his
head).*
QUEEN LOVISA ULRIKA: I shall nevertheless present Badin something. *(Still seated, she stretches for a sheet of paper on a nearby small table, bringing it to a short distance from her face.)*
This is a deed that old Captain Ekberg has sent us; it makes
us Badin's lawful owner. This is what we do with it. *(Grabs a
sharp pen and draws it so forcefully across the paper, which
still dangles from her fingers, that it is virtually ripped in two.
Allows it then to sail to the floor, before rising to walk toward
the window.)* Badin may go wherever he wants in the castle.
No door shall be closed to him, and henceforth he is free to say
whatever he wants and to do whatever he wants.[32]

That mischievous rascal.
Rude scamp.
Cheeky black boy.
Uncivilized.
Wild boy.
Baboon.
*Face-to-face appellations and behind-the-back terms applied to
Badin by members of the aristocracy during his first years at the*

court, as recounted in the first volume of M. J. Crusenstolpe's
Morianen eller Holstein-Gottorpska huset i Sverige *(The*
Blackamoor, or The House of Holstein-Gottorp in Sweden). [33]
Throughout his seemingly endless six-volume account of the royal
family's political entanglements and intrigues from 1751 to 1809,
Crusenstolpe employs notes, document references, and other
devices to insist upon the authenticity of his work, to constantly
underline his claim of historical accuracy. To thereby suggest the
veracity of these demeaning epithets.

   Especially in the first four volumes, Badin, the Blackamoor, is
a peripheral personage at the center of Swedish history—a shadow
whose freedom of movement inevitably allows him to be in the
right corridor or hidden passageway at the right moment, to be
behind the right door or curtain at the most critical (dis)junctures,
to witness or overhear what nobody else can witness or overhear,
to be in command of the highly sensitive and the delicately inti-
mate, to be the holder of vital information, the possessor of secret
knowledge. Always having been able to properly position himself,
to strategically situate himself, Badin is repeatedly called upon
to serve as the reliable informant, as the dependable bearer of
confidential tidings. Always able to be present and yet out of sight,
to melt into the dark, Badin is repeatedly summoned to stealthily
observe, to pry on the sly, to spy, and to subsequently report so that
momentous decisions may be reached, so that far-reaching actions
may be undertaken, so that plots and schemes may be realized,
so that History may be made. Badin is, in short, the glue holding
Crusenstolpe's narrative together, the ultimate (binding) source, the
means by which scattered, fragmented, and seemingly disconnected
documents are sutured together into a mammoth tale of supposed
truthful coherence. However, all of Crusenstolpe's assertions to the
contrary, his artistic liberties are innumerable and transparent from
the very outset of the first volume—Badin is placed at the court in
1751, whereas it is known with some certainty that he did not arrive
there until 1760. [34]

Historically so, said Crusenstolpe.
   Expression popularly circulating in Stockholm during the 1840s,
playing upon the author's repeated usage of "historically so" to
validate often weakly based claims. [35] *Whatever the (in)accuracy*
of Crusenstolpe's claims, his portrayal of Badin allowed previ-
ously circulating verbal images of that man to be converted into an

embellished textual form, to be mechanically reproduced for the first time, to be multiplied and made available at dispersed sites—where they could always come into resonance with other mechanically reproduced textual images that stereotyped, as well as be reconverted into verbal form in the practices of everyday life.

———

A Frenchman can live in New Guinea or in Lapland, but a negro cannot live in Tornea nor a Samoyed in Benin. It seems also as if the brain were less well organized in the two extremes. Neither the negroes nor the Lapps are as wise as the Europeans.

Jean-Jacques Rousseau, two years after Badin's arrival in Stockholm, in his influential novel, Émile, ou l'éducation[36]

In the *Discourse on the Origins of Inequality [1756]*, Rousseau summons men to hear for the first time the true history of their species. Man was born free, equal, self-sufficient, unprejudiced, and whole; now, at the end of history, he is in chains (ruled by other men or by laws he did not make), defined by relations of inequality (rich or poor, noble or commoner, master or slave), dependent, full of false opinions or superstitions, and divided between his inclinations and his duties. Nature made man a brute, but happy and good. History—and man is the only animal with a history—by the development of his faculties and the progress of his mind has made man civilized, but unhappy and immoral.

Allan Bloom, in the introduction to his translation of Émile, or On Education[37]

—

In my youth I resembled a wild animal, then it was corrected. I was such from 1762 to 1771. . . . Rousseau's *Émile* was the basis of my upbringing.

Badin, in his autobiographical statement[38]

At least in the West Indies, it is as good as impossible to place full-grown Negroes, who have been born and raised as slaves, in a position to make proper use of their freedom. On the other hand, the currently growing generation ought, by way of a suit-

able education, imbibe those ideas befitting a free people if their
inborn wildness is to be eradicated. Nevertheless, I consider the
Negro incapable of achieving a truly high or independent culture.
*Carl Adolf Carlsson, government-appointed teacher and pastor on
the Swedish Caribbean island colony of Saint Barthélemy, commenting in 1835, shortly after the emancipation of slaves in the British
West Indies*[39]

Therefore, child of nature, be proud of your origin . . .
*Line addressed to Badin in 1789, when he was close to forty years
old. Spoken in Strindberg's* Gustav III *by Thomas Thorild, poet
and essayist who, before altering his position in 1794, favored a
political program in the spirit of the French Revolution.*[40]

From very close to the beginning of his life in Stockholm, the molding of
Badin's subjectivity, the shaping of his identity(-conflicts), and his everyday
treatment at the Royal Palace were all evidently at least partially ensnared
in the factualized fictions then circulating in European academic and intellectual networks. Although granted to the king, he soon was taken over
by Queen Lovisa Ulrika—the learned and intellectually ambitious sister of
Prussia's Frederick the Great, the founder of an Academy of Letters in 1753,
a correspondent with Voltaire, a woman at ease in discussing plant and
animal life with her "Court Naturalist" and curiosity-collection curator
Linnaeus, and an avid reader of the period's leading thinkers, not least of all
Rousseau. Placed into the possession of a queen possessed with the author
of *The Discourse on the Origins of Inequality,* a queen newly enthralled
with this author's pedagogical handbook qua novel *Émile,* Badin apparently quickly became regarded not as a child of slavery, not as a child of a
plantation economy's practices, not as a child of the logics of colonialism
and mercantile capitalism that underpinned those practices and their accompanying discourses, but as "a child of nature."[41] And became educated
as such commencing in 1762.

One day he would become rich and buy Mamma free. That was
his most silent and secret hope. She thought he roughed around
and stole from the harbor warehouses. But she didn't know that
she had a Liberator in the family. Pappa was dead, of course, and
totally incompetent.
Characterization of Badin's thoughts, Saint Croix, 1756[42]

Badin's background and childhood were a mystery to himself: he remembered nothing of his years as a slave. As he himself writes: all of it "is not remembered by him with any precision."

In the Danish standard work *Vores gamle Trope-kolonier [Our Old Tropical Colonies]* the history of the hell of slavery in the West Indies is told dryly, matter-of-factly, in a rather dreary manner. So and so many tons of sugar, so and so many slaves transported from the Ivory Coast. There are other statistics, for example, the number of slave boys born on the island of Saint Croix in 1747. They are 216 in number.

Here he is, presumably. Among that figure. Nothing of that is left in him. If the word was not anachronistic as well as worn out, one could speak of repression—grown up as a slave boy, the son to enslaved parents: to not remember is perhaps the best solution.

Ola Larsmo, writing of the Badin he has fictionalized[43]

Whatever the tamings and traumas of his childhood slavery, seriously read representations demanded that he be perceived as a "noble savage."[44] Someone who is innately happy and good, who is as yet uncivilized and thereby unsullied. Someone who is uncorrupted and therefore can unharmfully play with the royal children. Someone who should remain in an unrestricted "state of nature," who should not have his movements or behavior confined in any way, who should have no door closed to him, who should be free to say whatever comes to mind, to spout "the dirtiest of cracks" and to distribute insults while gamboling about on the dinner table.[45] Someone who should be allowed to perform his pranks and execute his badinages without punishment . . . The text becomes concrete conditions. Representations become role assignment. Black mask transferred from white(-authored) page to black face. And adhering there. Unremovable and melted into mind. Life made a full-time masquerade. A perpetual performance. An endless enactment. Day in and day out, discursive namings producing their effects. Badin, in (f)act, becomes "wild." Badin, a subject of circumstance, in fact, remembers himself as "wild"—presumably, he believes, largely by way of his "mother's milk"—but only from 1762, the very year in which Rousseau's novelistic teachings are categorically applied to him.[46]

Untitled depiction of a court scene, by Jean Eric Rehn, about 1762–63.[47] Badin is given central stage in this tinted drawing, placed between Queen Lovisa Ulrika and her personal reader to the left, and the court sculptor and his work in progress to the right. However, Rehn—whose drawings often took the form of "friendly caricatures"[48]—has obscured most of Badin's body behind the sculptor and covered the upper half of his face in shadow, thereby largely reducing him to a broad look-at-me smile, to an essence that says "monkey business in constant progress." Badin is commanding attention by acting, if not acting up. Trying to make direct contact with the artist, he is "making a face" while all the others present are preoccupied, thoughtfully engaged, turned away. In accord with instructions/expectations, he is doing his best to be what he is supposed to be, to play an assigned role, to play "wild," to play both the "child of nature" and the jester he is decked out to be. . . . Is the character of Badin's spotlighted smile meant to signal why his unbridled and often impudent behavior frequently provoked irritation and dislike? Why annoyance was felt by court aristocrats who were the victims of his ungoverned, unpunished, "child-of-nature" outbursts? Had Badin's "wildness" given Rehn himself direct cause for displeasure? (There was ample opportunity for interaction, for at the time Rehn was serving as a drawing instructor to Princess Sophia Albertina, who—together with her two older brothers—spent much time in the company of Badin.)[49] Or was the smile in some measure a result of what Rehn already knew and saw by way of second- and thirdhand accounts? By way of vision-shaping quasi-factual, quasi-fictional rumors? Such as the story about the time the queen asked him to say something "polite or funny" to a royal councilor and he began: "Shall I talk about shitting?" Or the one about his attempting to bite a fat aristocrat in the stomach with the result that he broke two teeth on the nobleman's vest button. Or about the "many times" he said "kiss my ass" in response to "the slightest criticism" from his aristocratic "superiors."[50] . . . And what about Badin's short height? Is this somewhat of a deliberate exaggeration? A belittling gesture? An attempt to diminish the stature of a much resented Other, to reduce him to laughable size? An effort to underscore his inferiority—and thereby the superiority of those who were the target of his pranks and jests?[51] Or was Badin, in fact, small for someone of age twelve or thereabouts?[52] Or was he actually somewhat younger?[53] . . . And did Rehn's portrayal itself serve to reinforce the racialized field of vision already held by viewers of the drawing inside and outside the court?

––––––

Badin's "wildness," as (f)actually portrayed in the press more than a century later (1897), became fictionally amplified, thereby echoing and intensifying images of the African then broadly available in Sweden. The nature of blackness and Badin became congruent. The present became one with the past. The already (un)seen became the seen again. Mutual confirmation. Either way. No doubt about it!

> [*When first brought to Stockholm and delivered to a house at
> Clara Bergsgränd,*] the little savage romped directly into a dog-
> house beside the gate where a large poodle resided. . . . The boy
> slept securely in the doghouse until morning. . . . The dog did
> not attack his somewhat similar friend.

Badin himself told that his last feat in his home country
was to set fire to his parents' bamboo hut so that he could take
delight at the flames.

Once, while playing at Drottningholm [*a royal residence
outside of Stockholm*] Badin asked a peasant boy who came
riding by on a horse if he could climb up and sit beside him.
Frightened, the boy began riding as fast as he could, believing it
was the Devil himself who chased him. . . . The boy dropped his
hat and yelled at the top of his lungs. Badin kept stride beside
and roared with laughter. He continued for over three miles until
a gate broke his speed.

*Wendela Hebbe, an eighty-nine-year-old journalist and writer,
whose works included* True Stories for Young People, *recounting
in 1897 what had supposedly been told to her long ago by a woman
claiming to be acquainted with Badin's second wife, Magdalena
Eleonora Norell*[54]—*recounting, in the last instance, a "true story"
eerily echoing Jean-Jacques Rousseau's assertion that the Hottentots
"run quicker than one can imagine"*[55]

Here he is. The "true" Badin. Savage. Animal-like. Similar to a dog. Un-
cultured and uncivilized. Primitively, inhumanely cruel to his parents. Possessing (super)subhuman physical capacities. Capable of running as fast as
a horse for miles. Wild-man qualities. At least in his natural-state youth. . . .
"Historically so," said Hebbe. "Facts." Nothing but the "facts." Fictionalized (f)acts put into circulation via a weekly newspaper catering to a
bourgeois Stockholm audience. Facts apt to be given special attention, to
be believed without question, to (re)sink surely into the reader's mind, to
(re)lodge themselves like an anchor, because the press in general was as yet
a revered source of unchallenged credibility, because other stories carried
in this particular publication—largely dealing with the exploits of the royal
family, high-society members, prominent businessmen, and performance-
arts celebrities—were given an extra patina of veracity by the frequent use of
photographs, by seemingly unproblematic what-you-see-is-what-you-have
images. Facts that gained further credence in subsequent years when they
were repeated in "scholarly" publications without attribution to Wendela
Hebbe. . . . The claim that Badin cruelly burned down his parents' bamboo hut was restated without reservation during 1904 in a multivolumed,
authority-exuding reference work on privately held Swedish libraries by
C. M. Carlander.[56] In an attempt to solidify the truthfulness of this "fact,"
Carlander pointed to one of the underlined passages that Badin's Bible was
"full of," a lament of Jeremiah in which the prophet bemoans the absence

of his children and the unavailability of anyone to rebuild his hut.[57] This dubious "evidence" of Badin's regret, like the hut-torching tale itself, clearly stemmed from Hebbe, who had already connected the very same passage to Badin's purported childhood arson.[58] A doubly troubling circumstance, as there is no way of confirming the passage in question was actually underlined, since the whereabouts or even the existence of the Bible supposedly held by Hebbe's informant cannot be established.[59] A circumstance of no concern to Carl Forsstrand, who, in the first "serious" essay on Badin—published in 1911—further broadcast the fire-setting story and the Jeremiah-passage "evidence," using a footnote to Carlander as a source of verification.[60]

> In the childrens' story collections Hebbe published during the
> 1870s and 1880s [*including* True Stories for Young People],[61]
> folk-tale materials are blended with creations of her own fantasy.
>   *Gösta Lundström*[62]

An aside on putting aside much of what Wendela Hebbe has to say about Badin, on regarding her text about "Monsieur Coichi" not as an assemblage of unquestionable "facts," but as a social fact, as a set of images that actually (re)entered the popular imagination. And as, at once, her (f)act of fictionalization and her fictionalization of (f)acts. . . . Hebbe's preamble to the newspaper piece reads like an excerpt from her first melodramatic novel, *Arabella* (1841): "It was a raw and chilly March afternoon over fifty years ago as I walked through one of the narrowest and most unpleasant quarters of Stockholm *inom broarna*.[63] It was pouring rain and the wind howled through the darkening streets."[64] Freezing and drenched, seeking refuge from the elements, she makes her way into a courtyard and, after summoning up her courage, eventually into the apartment of a woman who is a complete stranger to her. Offered a chair that belonged to "Monsieur Coichi," she inquires about the man and is consequently regaled for hours with information about Badin. . . . Whether or not Hebbe chose to embellish or modify her informant's tellings, to inject her own imaginings, it is inevitable that distortions and inaccuracies, if not outright *f*(abr)*ic*(a)*tions,* were contained in her published retellings. For Hebbe was listening not to a direct witness of recent 1846 events, but to a woman who claimed to have gained her knowledge from Badin's second wife, dead since 1843. And that woman, in turn, would have been relating, with or without censorship and alteration, those versions of events that Badin had chosen to provide—events that for the most part were long-ago matters for Badin (his second marriage occurred in 1799, while much of what Hebbe presents refers to his childhood and youth, to the mid-1760s and earlier). In other words, Hebbe's "facts" were at very best highly dated hearsay flawed by the tricks of memory.

—

One has only to regard the format of a nineteenth-century newspaper, in which the feuilleton *[often]* occupied the bottom quarter of the front page, to see, literally, how thin was the line between political fact and literary fiction. News stories were literary constructions: feuilleton novelists used news stories as content.

Susan Buck-Morss[65]

—

One need not proceed any further than Hebbe's assertion about Badin's origins to recognize that her account was wanting precision and exactness, that it contained pure fictions attired as "facts." For she states, "I requested my hostess to tell me a little about this man who was transported from the Guinea Coast to the [Stockholm] shores of Lake Mälar"—even though Badin's journey to Stockholm undoubtedly commenced far from Africa, in Saint Croix. Was this geographical error a displacement of family knowledge, an (un?)intentional reworking of the active involvement of her husband's grandfather, Christian Hebbe, in the West Indian Company (Västindiska Kompaniet), an enterprise that had been involved both in transporting slaves from the west coast of Africa to Saint Barthélemy and in selling them from that miniscule Swedish colony to other Caribbean islands?[66] Or was she passing on a bungled version of a statement made in Badin's handwritten autobiography, passing on a misremembered or misread version of a masked political remark made by Badin in the process of constructing himself, in the process of reimagining the world's geography in order to underline the African component of his Afro-Caribbean origins and identity?—His cradling time is believed by him to have begun in 1750. In America, deep in in the land of Guinea.[67] . . . There is also the possibility that Badin's expression "deep in the land of Guinea" was actually a reference to the Royal Danish Guinea Company, the slave- and sugar-trading enterprise at the hub of Saint Croix's economy. As the Danish colonial island was in effect the land of the Guinea Company, in his dimly remembered boyhood years he may have heard the word Guinea much more often than Saint Croix. Or was Hebbe simply fabulizing, filling in gaps in her source's account, giving her story a beginning, perhaps based on her familiarity with Crusenstolpe's introduction of Badin in *Morianen*—for there nothing is said of his Caribbean origins, only of the "African blood which boiled in the black boy's veins"?[68] . . . And if the birthplace claims in Hebbe's background sentence are so wide of the mark, how much more (un)believable is the remainder of that prefacing remark, its declaration that Badin sailed from "the smoking dust of his paternal hut" as well as from the Guinea Coast? Whether or not Hebbe was herself inventing this "fact," whether or not she was merely repeating or dressing up what was (re-re)told to her, other evidence suggests the fire and smoke supposedly recalled by Badin in considerable likelihood stemmed from the searing experience of Saint Croix plantation-expansion activities.[69] . . . Hebbe's own writing reveals that her reception of the "Monsieur Coichi" tales was far from uncolored, unfiltered by predis-positions and pre-judgments, innocent of any foreknowledge about Badin. Five years prior to her seemingly extraordinary rainy-day encounter, this in many ways remarkable woman wrote a two-part story for *Aftonbladet,* "En resa till Stockholm" (A Trip to Stockholm), in which she reworked the experience of her May 1840 visit to the Swedish capital, where she arrived an abandoned wife intent upon carving out a literary future for herself.[70] There, describing a rowboat trip between two of the city's islands, she commented, "Among the passengers was a young negro, 'presumably a descendent of Mr. Badin,' but totally devoid of his nonchalant behavior."[71] "Monsieur Coichi," then, is someone she already knew of in 1841, when "En resa" was penned. Even though she had never met him. Somebody for whom she already had a clearly formed image, somebody already present within her field of (pre)vision—perhaps because of the recent appearance of the first volume of Crusentolpe's *Morianen;* perhaps because Badin was already a part of the received local history of the Gustavian era, a personage who had already entered into the collective memory shared by many of Stockholm's bourgeois and aristocratic residents. Somebody she already saw in a negative light. Somebody who was capable of nonchalant behavior—somebody who could act without feeling or concern, insensibly. And therefore in her mind fully capable of igniting his parents' dwelling? Whatever the case, somebody she had ample opportunity to become further familiar with between 1841 and 1846. Not only because the remaining volumes of *Morianen* appeared in this interval, but also because the fictionalized "factual" portrait contained therein might very well have been embellished upon by Crusenstolpe himself, who after his 1841 prison release eventually became a regular attendee at the literary and musical soirées held by Hebbe in her Stockholm apartment.[72] . . . Whether Crusenstolpe's mammoth novel (and conversation) directly or indirectly contributed to Hebbe's image(ination) of Badin, her act of producing "Monsieur Coichi" appears to have been of the same blurred genre. Facts were fictionalized. Fictions were factualized.[73] Flimsy textual threads were converted into the elements of an enduring stereotype. The local flapping of literary wings set a ripple in motion, eventually contributing to temporally distant bad weather. The author's field of vision, put into words, enabled the reader to (re)author(ize) his or her own field of vision—to confirm, strengthen, or embellish his or her own preconceptions. The dialects of not seeing were thus perpetuated at numerous dispersed sites. Not only with respect to Badin in particular. But also with respect to blacks in general.

—

According to *[the author]* the Negro stands at childhood level; lively imagination, little endurance, cheerful disposition. . . . The Negro lacks morals rather than being immoral. According to ethnographers the Negro race is intellectually lower than the Caucasian, Mongolian, Malay and *[Native]* American. In contrast to the last two, no Negro people has ever created a culture.
> *Summary of an entry in the eleventh volume (1887) of* Nordisk Familjebok, *Sweden's standard reference work at the time of Wendela Hebbe's published reconstruction of Badin—a stereotype-fortifying, European-imperialism-legitimating entry given further "scientific" currency in preceding decades by, among other things, the publication of Darwin's* Descent of Man *(1871), with its multiple references to "the less intellectual races"*[74]

There are no sleeping cars in Africa, but one can still travel rather comfortably if you understand what you're up to.
> *Caption to a cartoon published during 1898 in the same newspaper where Hebbe's Badin text appeared.*[75] *Image above the caption: An African male, with woolier-than-wooly hair and thicker-than-thick lips, stupidly supine, suspended in a hammock beneath a giraffe's neck. In one of his hands, a wooden club, a crude weapon confirming his crude primitiveness, his total unmodernness. In his other hand, a nearly empty bottle of whiskey, an emblem of his uncivilized adoption of civilization's offerings, his inability to deal with the fruits of Western culture. (The whiskey bottle provided a visual double entendre, inasmuch as it resonated with then-commonplace*

bourgeois views of the "underclass"[76] as an inferior, more "primi-
tive," and less "civilized" form of humanity,[77] inasmuch as it echoed
assertions that the underclass Swedish male—an incorrigible over-
consumer of alcohol in the bourgeois popular imag(e)ination—was
akin to the savage of another race, if not "apelike."[78])

—

Whatever their (in)validity, Hebbe's (f)acts readily became all the more believable, readily achieved an undeniable status, because they resonated with—and thereby reinforced—already circulating images of African blacks and their New World descendents. Almost all of Hebbe's readers would have early encountered such denigrating representations in the geography and history textbooks of the country's compulsory primary schools. Many would have been exposed to an authoritative reaffirmation of such negative stereotypes through the perusal of widely purchased encyclopedias. Such images would also have been encountered time and again in other printed outlets; in the daily press, illustrated weeklies, humor magazines, and travel books of the late nineteenth century that often echoed the discourses embedded in British imperialism and Continental colonialism.[79] Such inferiorizing images even would have been encountered by the devout in the Swedish missionary literature, which among other things often emphasized the cruelty exercised by Africans toward family members and the elderly[80]— thereby making the (f)act of parental-hut burning appear entirely natural. For Stockholm residents such images were given local fleshy substance, such images were embodied and thereby deeply mind-emplaced in place, during June 1895 and again in November 1897 via the public exhibition of forty-seven "Dinka Negroes" and then "100 natives from Africa's Gold Coast." Via the come-and-gawk display of the subject made (commodified-)object, of the subject made object(-lesson), of "the children of nature," of the "hardly civilized," of the spear carrying and the war dancing, of the near naked with their bone-pierced ears and noses.[81] . . . Such a multiplication of mutually reinforcing "facts" and images could not avoid being well remembered, could not avoid leaving traces that awaited resurfacing, could not avoid being reiterated and further perpetuated, could not avoid subsequently (re)entering into practice.

> *[Swedish]* ethnographical expeditions *[of the 1920s]* made efforts
> to describe the social organization of unknown tribes. Presenta-
> tions of them *[still]* normally adopted the vocabulary of the

colonialist: they were considered the lost and rediscovered children of the earth, primitive, simple, brutal, but innocent.
    Raoul Granqvist[82]

———

Badin is no longer what he was, five or six years ago. The queen
then tired of his pranks and bad habits, and relentlessly had him
disciplined for them until he became another person. And that he
remains now, only with the difference that he, as a real southerner,
is shrewder and quicker on his feet than we northerners.
    *Observation made in 1766 by Major General Carl Fredrik Pechlin
    (1720–1796), in arguing for the use of Badin as a source of infor-
    mation, in bringing the beginning phase of Badin's Swedish life to
    a close, in granting him the possibility of future accomplishment
    by identifying him not as an African, not as a black, but as "a real
    southerner"—an imprecise designation that might just as well
    apply to someone of Mediterranean or Asian origins, to someone
    possessing a rather different set of stereotyped attributes*[83]

———

FACTS were the foundation of his assertions.
    *Observation made by the editor of the 1814 edition of an ex-slave's
    autobiography, originally published in London in 1789.*[84] *Observa-
    tion made regarding an Ibo who was born in northeastern Nigeria
    about 1745; who was kidnapped at age eleven and spent over a
    decade enslaved, primarily in the British West Indies; who eventu-
    ally saved enough to purchase his freedom and settle in England;
    who became a leading personage in London's black community
    during the 1780s and "a central figure in the British abolitionist
    movement";*[85] *who, following the enormous popular success of his
    life story in 1789,*[86] *was made the target of politically motivated fic-
    tions by those prospering from the slave trade; who, more precisely,
    was accused of being "an impostor," someone who was born not in
    Africa but on the Danish island of Saint Croix—a site of rebellion.
    Observation made regarding Olaudah Equiano, a man who was
    assigned a fictive entrance into the world that would have allowed
    him to become a childhood acquaintance of Badin and thereby
    share common terrors with him; a man who, like Badin, was given
    a name by one of his owners that subjectified him for life—a name,*

Gustavus Vassa, which identified him with King Gustav I, the "he-roic" sixteenth-century founder of the modern Swedish state, and thereby indirectly entwined him with Badin, the (f)actual childhood companion of King Gustav III. Observation made regarding a man who, like Badin, was at a young age mistaken in his first perception of snow, believing not that it was sugar, but salt (a product of his native village)—discovering his mistake, like Badin, by way of taste and cold touch, and in the process discovering something that was emblematic of the countless white deceptions that in subsequent years were to be heartlessly rubbed into his slavehood wound. [87]

———

Another entrance never made.
A beginning never realized.
Only fantasized.
In 1758.
The very same year in which scientific racism entered Sweden
    via the publication of the tenth edition of *Systema naturae.*
The very same year in which Badin's life in Europe began.

[C]losely examine whether the ears, teeth, toes and nails, clitoris and nymphæ are identical with ours; observe in the smallest de-tail the manner in which they correspond and differ; and, above all, the genitalia. . . . If he who owns the Troglodyte should wish to sell her, let me know the price.

    Carl Linnaeus in a 1758 letter to Pehr Bjerchén, a student of his in London, requesting the physical examination and possible purchase of a sixteen-year-old Afro-Caribbean albino Negress apparently on display there, requesting that a Jamaican-born slave-woman be undressed and submitted to the object-ive gaze of the scientific eye, requesting a by-proxy sexual scrutinization in the extreme, request-ing that the mentally disrobed be physically displaced—entered into his possession. [88]

[She] is fairly shy and never will or can look at a person in the eyes.

    Pehr Bjerchén in a letter to Linnaeus dated June 14, 1758, describ-ing the Jamaican-born "white negro" woman and indicating that while he has not yet examined her naked he hopes to persuade her owner with "kind words and money" [89]

No selling price sufficient.
No purchase arranged.
Desires, scientific (and otherwise?), left unfulfilled.
No living-object addition made
    to Linnaeus's collection of natural history exotica.
No replacement for his "beautiful" Diana,
    for his recently lost monkey.[90]
No opportunity for eye contact on Swedish ground(s).
For this young Afro-Caribbean chattel,
    no Badin-like (re)beginning.
But continuations all the same.
Via the further writings of Linnaeus.
Via the circulation of discourse.
Via "fact" and fiction chasing one another's tales
    in relentless spiral.
Never seeing anything
    but something resembling
    that which is already
    before them.

    Linnaeus was "a man of two faces."
    Staffan Müller-Wille, quoting Sten Lindroth[91]

Wed to the terminology and logics of his mammalian taxonomy, his strong conviction that intermediate organisms existed in nature, and the social-fact fictions of his scientific and travel-writing readings, Linnaeus insisted to Bjerchén that the young female "has never come from Jamaica, but from Java or the East Indies or Africa" and that she was "positively" a troglodyte, or *Homo nocturnus*—a species of *Homo* listed in the tenth edition of *Systema naturae* as distinct from *Homo sapiens* or *Homo diurnis*. Panting with scientific curiosity (and nothing more?) about the woman's genitalia, what was at stake here was nothing less than the verification of Linnaeus's (f)act-ual fiction of a "cave-dwelling man," of a species situated between *Homo sapiens* and the apes. Drawing principally on medical and seafaring accounts from the seventeenth and eighteenth centuries (on descriptions that bewilderingly conflated Malayan and Bornean orangutans, African chimpanzees, pygmies, and "troglodytes"), on an address to the Swedish Royal Academy of Sciences made by Olof von Dalin in 1749, and on what he had heard from a traveler to the East Indies during his 1735–1738 sojourn in Holland, Linnaeus conjured up a physical and behavioral description of the troglodyte that appeared in part in *Systema naturae*, in part in *Menniskans*

Cousiner (Cousins of Man [1759]), *Anthropomorpha* (1760),[92] and other shorter writings whose contents and graphic plates gained wide distribution in England and elsewhere in Europe. In factualizing the fiction of the troglodyte's physical attributes, he heavily relied on the lecture given by Dalin, a centrally important man of letters who, without a word of attribution, in (f)act was repeating Voltaire's description of a "little albino negro" he had seen at a much-discussed exhibit in Paris during 1744. Not surprisingly then, Bjerchén's description of the young woman's skin, eyes, hair, and other bodily characteristics was in keeping with his mentor's already held image. Only the "fact" Linnaeus had acquired from his Dutch source was left unconfirmed by his student—the "fact" that the outer labia of the female troglodyte hung over the genitalia like an "apron."[93] . . . Whatever Linnaeus's intentions, his "fact"-ualization of the troglodyte resonated with other images that simultaneously anthropomorphized apes and simianized blacks, and in so doing helped fortify already existing stereotypes of the ape-like (hyper)sexuality possessed by blacks.[94] . . . Once again an author's word-converted field of vision enabled others to (re)author(ize) their own fields of vision—to confirm, strengthen, or embellish their own preconceptions. The dialects of not seeing were perpetuated, this time through networks of scientific discourse. Not only with respect to those of black African descent in general. But also with respect to Badin in particular.

—

I had followed the three-master *Friederic Adolph* which navigated . . . between the anchored ships, and watched how it lowered its foresail and was saluted as it dropped anchor at the Customs House. Its cargo included china, exotic animals, an ape that jumped about the ship's frame, and a little bow-legged blackamoor who was taken down the gangway and I later got to know by the name Badin.
  Carl Michael Bellman (1740–1795), famed poet and song author— in a fact-filled fictional autobiography—pairing Badin's arrival in Stockholm with that of an ape, leading him down the gangway into a world of simian associations that any black would have found difficulty totally escaping in Europe[95]

—

One has spoken about "Linnaeus' eye;" few can be compared with him as a visual genius. Nothing in nature escaped him, with

lightning speed he noticed everything and distinguished what
was characteristic. . . . The matter alone, the naked observation
was everything.
    Sten Lindroth[96]

What a deceptive sense sight is!
    Marcel Proust[97]

—

The Hottentots and blacks of Africa . . . have large testicles and are
inclined to venereal sin; therefore, in order to not increase family
size too much, they cut off one of the stones from young boys.
    *Carl Linnaeus, "fact"-ualizing another fiction in a 1751 course
    lecture*[98]

[Linnaeus's most] characteristic trait is the drastic simplification.
    Sten Lindroth[99]

Advances(?)
Love(making)s?
(Anti)Climaxes(?)

[V]enereal infections presumably originated through people
in the tropical countries, owing to their great sexual hotness
[hypersexuality], having done it with large apes and monkeys,
or so-called baboons.
  Johan Linder, Swedish scholar, in a 1713 treatise[1]

[Already by the seventeenth century] *sexuality was what one
expected of* [African] *savages.*

[Owing in part to claims (correctly?) attributed to Linnaeus]
by the final quarter of the eighteenth century the idea that the
Negro's penis was larger than the white man's had become something of a commonplace in European scientific circles.
  Winthrop D. Jordan[2]

[The eighteenth-century writings of] Buffon, the French naturalist, credited the black with a lascivious, apelike sexual appetite,
introducing a commonplace of early travel literature into a
pseudoscientific context.

During the rise of modernism *[in German-speaking Europe],* . . .
the black, whether male or female, came to represent the genitalia
through a series of analogies.
  Sander L. Gilman[3]

≠ ≠ ≠

Flash forward.

> I also want to take up the "positive" prejudices *[held by Swedes]*.
> A classic one is that we have "rhythm in our blood." Another is
> that we are hypersexual.
> > *Anna, a young black woman born in Ethiopia and adopted by*
> > *Swedish parents at an early age, speaking in January 2000*[4]

≠ ≠ ≠

> [O]ne of the black servant's central functions in the visual arts
> of the eighteenth and nineteenth centuries was to sexualize the
> society in which he or she was found.
> > *Sander L. Gilman*[5]

William Hogarth, *A Harlot's Progress,* plate 2, engraving, 1732. The she
monkey—aping the provocative (un)dress of Moll, the harlot—has already
done her business, has helped intensify the state of excitement set in motion by Moll's intentional upsetting of the table, has helped distract from
the sneaking exit of another more youthful lover, his belt as yet unfixed. The
young black servant, teakettle in hand, stands agape but, as ever, ready to
further heat up the situation, to cater to desire, to pour forth a hot stream.[6]
  In another engraving, *Noon* (plate 2 of *The Four Times of the Day,* 1738),
Hogarth leaves nothing to the imagination as to the supposed sexuality of

the African. Outside a London tavern, amid the jumble of activity so frequently found in Hogarth's works, a black man stands behind a young beauty, kissing her close to the ear while both his hands fondle her nearly fully exposed breasts. His sexuality is irrepressible—he cannot resist pursuing his advanced advances in broad daylight, in the street, where all can *see*. It is animal-like, out of control, uncontainable, multiply transgressive—not only with an English lass, not only in a public space, but on a Sunday (yards away a group of Huguenot refugees are exiting chapel services). And it is "dangerous"—the young woman is so touched that her face exudes blissful contentment despite the setting.[7]

[Badin] was a handsome and spirited Negro slave-boy . . .

[With his] hot Negro blood . . .

During his younger years his looks were—color not included—extraordinarily pleasing, and ever since that time rumors concerning relationships of the most sensitive kind have been in circulation. At all times and places he had free access to *all* of the royalty of both sexes.

Crusenstolpe, once again purportedly being factual, in a biographical sketch of Badin, originally published in 1854[8]

Here the reader's imagination, quite likely fueled by previously encountered images, need hardly have exerted itself. Badin was physically attractive. He, like all blacks, was hot-blooded. He had *free* access to *all* the spaces of female royalty. Clearly thereby, even their most intimate nooks and crannies. No door(hold)s barred. No entryways denied. No more need be intimated. No more need be said. An open book. A closed case. Truly a true rumor.

The Blackamoor, who for some time had experienced a rather cool, but not ungracious, treatment at the courts of both dukes *[Princes Karl and Fredrik, the brothers of Gustav III]*, now pressed his attentions on the princess *[Sophia Albertina, Gustav III's sister]*, who embraced him with remarkable good will, since he could draw a picture of her adored mother *[Queen Lovisa Ulrika]* as no one else. Gossip, however, has wished to give this intimacy a completely different color. . . . Even granting that this very widespread rumor is complete blather—like a previous one that cast a questionable light on Lovisa Ulrika's own favorable disposition toward her African protégé—the fact that it could get going and be believed in any case stamps the attitudes and behavior of the period.

Crusenstolpe, in his purportedly factual-fiction account of history, describing Badin's conduct of 1791[9]

An earlier and slyer(?) variant. Having it both ways? Condemning mean gossip, pooh-poohing the rumors, and yet deploying double entendres and word choices that do not completely discourage the reader from imagining otherwise. Badin "pressing his attentions" on Sophia Albertina. She embracing him "with remarkable good will." Body pressed against body? With fervor? Royal Black Amour as well as Court Blackamoor? "This[?] intimacy." Certainly not out of keeping with the parade of seductions and liaisons, with the ever-turning mistress merry-go-round, given prominent place in Crusenstolpe's multivolume depiction of court life. Certainly not out of keeping with Crusenstolpe's portrayal of Badin as "a zealous adorer of the beautiful sex" who is driven by his "southern [or red-hot] blood"[10] (a portrayal that emerges out of, and further contributes to, the by now long-existing stereotype of the black male [and female] as hypersexual;[11] a metonymic portrayal that allows Badin, the outstanding historical figure, to serve as stand-in for all blacks of African descent). Certainly not out of keeping with Crusenstolpe's observation regarding Badin's involvement with his first-wife-to-be: "No transaction of love can be held concealed within a court. There are always spying eyes behind the curtains that surround the royal bed, . . . under the sofa of the most sophisticated lady-in-waiting."[12] And what about that first wife? What consciously clever, or unconsciously concoc[k]ted, displacement is Crusenstolpe indulging himself with, what creative sexual license is he permitting himself, when he arranges for Badin to woo and marry, to enter into the bed of Olivia Ramström, who is initially depicted as Sophia Albertina's personal lady-in-waiting—when in fact the woman who became his first wife in 1782 was one Elisabeth Swartz, the daughter of a Stockholm wholesaling merchant, and when one Anna Sophia Ramström was actually a lady-in-waiting to Queen Sophia Magdalena, the wife of Gustav III?[13] Did Crusenstolpe's resort to the name Ramström involve a double displacement, a further (sub?)conscious under-lining of Badin's sexual appeal and potency, inasmuch as Anna Sophia Ramström was known to be the mistress of Count Adolf Fredric Munck,[14] the very same man persistently rumored to be the lover of Gustav III's queen, and thereby the actual father of Crown Prince Gustav Adolf, born in 1778?[15] And did Crusenstolpe again displace, again permit Badin to have sex with the princess by proxy, when he repeatedly gave him unhindered entrance to the most private of Sofia Albertina's chambers, thereby enabling him to deliver passionate love notes to the princess from her paramour, Hessenstein?[16] By the same token, was Crusenstolpe through various plot devices (sub?)consciously granting Badin sex by proxy with numerous other women associated with the court? As when he has him deliver a letter— "burning with love, . . . panting with ejaculatory statements"—from Prince Fredrik to his mistress of the moment, and when at the same time he allows the now-married Badin to express his delight at the opportunity to make "a closer acquaintanceship with the brown-eyed minx" who serves as that woman's chambermaid? As when the secret assignations between Prince Karl and his actress mistress are allowed to transpire on the very bed where Badin presumably normally made love to his wife? Or as when Badin is called upon to employ his "cunningness" to perpetuate the relationship between Prince Fredrik and another one of his mistresses? And are not all these intimations given substance when Crusenstolpe declares that some years after Badin's marriage it would have been "somewhat risky to take an oath on his marital fidelity"?[17]

———

And another peculiarity *[about King Gustav III]*, he couldn't procure a child with the Queen. He announced that the Queen was in the family way, but as a matter of fact it was his un-married sister who was in that condition in order to provide a son who would thus become heir to the throne. But at delivery it became apparent that the sister had given birth to a mulatto, a son to one of his negro footmen. And when that scheme failed, he let his first chamber-page by the name of Munck perform in the Queen's bed as if it was himself, which took on her.
Excerpt from October 31, 1787, diary entry of Francisco de Miranda—eventual liberation-movement leader in Spanish America—made while visiting Stockholm as part of a European tour[18] *(writing from a position of ignorance as to the particulars of Badin's unique situation, Miranda—presumably because of his time spent at other royal courts—demotes him to a footman, to a "mere lackey")*

Evidence of the gossip to which Crusenstolpe refers. Nasty talk that does not drop out of circulation. Salacious stories that refuse to fade. Titillating tales that a distinguished visitor cannot avoid exposure to. Badin and Sophia Albertina yet sexually conjoined in the imagination of the privi-leged, if not in the popular imagination as well. Nine years after the birth of Crown Prince Gustav Adolph. And thereby a decade after the "fact." Verbalized visions of Badin the sexually unstoppable—doing it with no one less than the Princess! Verbalized visions resonating with already acquired fields of vision. People knowing what they are seeing when they see Badin. Knowing an insatiable African/monkey when that is what they see. Seeing an insatiable African/monkey when that is what they know. (F)actually passing on the word. Gleefully speaking the unspeakable. Translating the unspeakable, by way of the taken-for-granted, by way of the automatically re-cognized, into the how-could-it-be-otherwise.

They are at it again. Tiresome. They never tire of it. Whispering not so sweet new things. And old things. Idle chatter. Dirty little echoes. About who is doing it with whom. Behind which door. Behind whose back. Detailed chuckling reports on seductions made and positions taken. On orgasms moaned or shrieked. On nimbleness or clumsiness of performance. Prying eye facts. Behind-the-drapes "eyewitness" accounts. Embellishments. Inventions. Hearsay. Rumors pure and otherwise. This time—even some of my Freemason brothers—once more coupling me with Sophia Albertina. My beloved playmate. My memory sharer. My mutual confidante. My early treasure. The younger sister I never had? Back there on Saint Croix. Where all is forgotten. Except that which awakes me with a jolt. That which makes me shudder in the unconsoling darkness of night . . . That my beloved Elisabeth's ears should be thus burned again. Will They never stop delighting in making Me an object of sexual gossip? In embedding Us with one another? Must They see every innocent glance or smile, every brief exchange of pleasantries, every little bit of mutual joking, every extended conversation, as fervent intercourse? As incontrovertible evidence of passionate activity under the sheets? Will our rumor always resurface when That other rumor resurfaces? Will Munck's supposed intimacies with the Queen, his fathering of a Royal Bastard, always be linked with my fathering a child by the Princess? Munck and his monstrous member always remembered by way of me? And conversely? Either way, my "sexual animality" time and again used as a weapon against poor Gustav? . . . Will THE rumor that enshadows me rumble relentlessly into the future? Unforgivingly reverberating through the years? Careening this way and that with the shifting of content? Will They never hear otherwise? Will They never see otherwise? Will it all outlive me by far? Is that all that will be remembered of me? Everything else forgotten? Nothing more? Of such a life? . . . God be with me. Liberate me from the contradictions that time and again set me adrift. Liberate me by way of Your Light. . . . Whatever I do(n't) do has already been said and done for me in advance. Denial forever futile? Safe mooring ahead? In silence?

The drift of Badin's thoughts, tottering between momentary uncertainty and a bout of depression, on yet another day of lead-laden Stockholm skies, early November 1787[19]

—

"Dirty little echoes . . . Unforgivingly reverberating through the years?" . . . Echoes first amplified by Crusenstolpe. Echoes now reaching into the popular imagination more than two centuries later. Old rumors newly resurrected. Old (f)acts newly fictionalized. New representations of the old that actually enter into circulation. That are actually read and talked about. That, whatever the authors' intentions, enter into congruence with sexualized stereotypes and their corresponding sexualized fields of vision, with mass media–propagated moral panics centering on young non-European males as sexual predators. . . . A matter to be returned to some pages later. As well as in the second part of this book ("Part II: The Unaddressable Addressed").

> [Miranda] is the first foreigner to speak of Swedish Sin. He tells of the shameful behavior allegedly occurring at the Drottning- holm summer palace that year, of the mistresses kept by Princes Karl and Fredrik Adolf, and of the then spread rumor about the king's sister, Sofia Albertina, supposedly having given birth to a son fathered by the court negro Badin.
>
> *Herman Lindqvist, in a best-seller popular history of the reign of Gustav III, first published 1997*[20]

> **I stood there mute** (after King Gustav III said, "My sister gave birth to a son fourteen days ago in [the German city of] Braunschweig"). **It would be untrue to say that I was untouched; but the occurrence was going to lead to complications regardless of my emotions.**
>
> *Badin's supposed reaction to a delicate situation in March 1783, about eight months after the death of Queen Mother Lovisa Ulrika and four months after his marriage to Elisabeth Swartz*[21]

—

Here then, for posterity, is a story about the reunion of the King and Queen and their first marital intercourse that—I testify and avow before God and my conscience—is every bit as truthful as it is strange. I would be lacking respect and reverence for my majesties if I made this story known during their lifetime, but likewise I could not rest in my grave without reproach unless, by way of this work, I cast light on all the fabricated and false rumors flying about.

> *Alfred Fredric Munck, in a spare-no-details account of how Queen Sofia Magdalena supposedly first lost her virginity and eventually became pregnant after nine years of marriage—dated March 22, 1779*[22]

In writing, at least, Adolph Fredric Munck chose to deny all those won't-go-away rumors that portrayed him as a frequent visitor to the queen's bed, that gave him easy access to that love-making site because of his relationship with the queen's lady-in-waiting.[23] Munck chose to counter those rumors that insisted he had fathered the crown prince—rumors that became all the more widely believed when, following the childbirth, the queen favored him with a ring and a personal annual pension as well as one for his mother to go along with her previous presents to him, including a heavily bejeweled watch with her portrait on its case.[24] With even Queen Mother Lovisa Ulrika having openly promoted the notion that the newly born prince was a bastard,[25] and with the rumor thereby having become even more personally troublesome, Munck chose to record a version of events that was at once remarkably intimate in detail and extremely unflattering to the royal couple. Its contents were such that, if spread by word of mouth in certain discontented aristocratic circles, it probably would have subjected the king to even greater ridicule than the "fact" of his cuckolding by Munck. For its particulars provided a gold mine of images for anyone already disposed to mocking the king: his "manly organ had such a tight foreskin that it couldn't be pulled back"; the Queen's vaginal opening was "so small that a complete conjugal union couldn't occur without smarting pain and considerable labor"; Munck verbally coaching Gustav III in advance; Munck being called to the bedside during the first night's effort and told "I haven't found any hole"; on a soon-thereafter occasion being brought into the act and finding it "necessary to move both him and the Queen with my hands"; and so on.[26]

> Is this a song the entire city is singing in the streets?
>> *Outburst ascribed to Gustav III, in fictionalized fact, upon discerning the widespreadness of the Munck rumor*[27]

As far as can be determined from his own written legacy and the gossipy memoirs and letters of court contemporaries, Badin time and again chose to keep his silence amid all the psst-psst whisperings and public singing, to not provide an alternative account of his supposed dalliance with Princess Sofia Albertina and the living consequences thereof.[28] Whether or not Badin was ever (f)actually sexually familiar with the princess, what was to be gained by denial in a climate where his "ape-like" hypersexuality was automatically announced by the color of his skin; in a court setting where sexual license was the norm, where "the married and the unmarried, men and women alike, carefreely entered into more or less loose sexual relationships"; in an environment where the exchange of sexual gossip was an everyday pastime, "where all kinds of scandalous rumors flourished"—and were readily accepted as true (f)acts?[29] With court wits at the ready to link Couschi and *couchez-vous*, did he not realize that any effort to deny would go disbelieved, would not have any chance of counteracting already entrenched (p)re-cognitions, would fall deaf on the ears of those already entranced by foreseen conclusions? Did he not understand that it was best to ride out the recurrent rumor storms as if sailing upon the calmest of seas? Even if, as in the case of the 1787 rendition noted by Miranda, he was being diminished to a political pawn, an instrument for further blackening Gustav III's reputation at a moment when the king's (ab)uses of power were making him ever more unpopular with portions of the nobility?[30] Did he not understand that outright denial might bear higher personal costs than the rumor itself? That a cooked-up story might expose him to such deep derision or widespread scornful snickering as to further jeopardize an already contradictory state of nonbelonging belonging? That a cooked-up story—if given no credence—might be turned against him, might be used to reduce him to a cartoon figure, to give a more graphic quality to his purported (s)exploits, to make them more readily retained in the popular imag(e)ination? Make them more readily etched into collective memory? Make them more readily apt to echo down through the ages?

The gossip mill's lampooning image of the royal couple's "happy union." Caricature by Carl August Ehrensvärd (1749–1805). Undated, most probably 1795–96. National Gallery, Stockholm. This still often reproduced sketch—

which may be seen as a cartooning of Munck's version of events[31]—may very well have become known to Badin, even though Ehrensvärd's most savage drawings supposedly did not circulate "beyond a small private circle."[32] Ehrensvärd was a member of the aristocracy (eventually a count) who rose to the rank of first admiral in 1784—and thereby someone who moved in the same secret society and order circles as Badin. Hence, if Badin never actually saw this scandalous depiction, this representation whereby rumor is given considerable flesh, he is quite apt to have heard a guffawing reference to it at the Freemasons Lodge or elsewhere.[33] All the more reason, then, for Badin to hold his tongue, to not (ad)venture any public denial of his fatherhood? All the more reason for avoiding any further risk of his extension becoming his image, of his becoming but an extension of his image? All the more reason for diminishing the likelihood of being further image governed? Long into the future?

[T]he glistening blackness of his face, which at first was so repugnant *[to Olivia Ramström]* . . . afterward ceased to appear repulsive. She hardly noticed it, but instead found an attractive concordance between the dark color of his flesh and his sparkling eyes whose globes shone alabaster white in the surrounding night, as did his pearly row of teeth.

[Queen Lovisa Ulrika] dismissed *[Olivia Ramström]* for the evening with the observation that the girl was too white for a blackamoor.
   Crusenstolpe's imagination at work in 1840[34]

T]he blackamoor's longing for a new white lifetime companion has long constituted a subject for court jokes.
   Crusenstolpe's imagination again at work, (f)actually placing this
   1792 observation into the mouth of Baron Gustav Mauritz Armfelt,
   a person close to Gustav III[35]

While Crusenstolpe's fictional factualization and factual fictionalization of Badin made much of his "red-hot" blood and "zealous" relationship to "the beautiful sex," while Crusenstolpe's multivolumed novel and subsequent biographical sketch employed various devices that reinforced the myth of black hypersexuality, there are indications sprinkled throughout *Morianen* that Crusenstolpe's attitude to Badin's sexuality was not without (subconscious?) complexities and reservations. Complexities and reservations that may well, among other things, have spoken of a certain confusion or ambivalence regarding the acceptability of sexual relations between a black former slave and highly positioned Swedish women. . . . Why is it that Badin's Olivia (Ramström) never becomes—as another lady-in-waiting fears—"the first mother of an entire lineage of Swedish mulattos"?[36] Why is it that the only child to which she gives birth is described as a "light-complexioned love-token, whose looks challenged every thought of southern [African] origin"?[37] Why is it strongly suggested that Badin has been cuckolded, that he has not provided his wife satisfaction in sufficient volume, that she must turn elsewhere in order to adequately fulfill her carnal desires? Is it simply because she is now described as the lady-in-waiting of the queen, rather than of Princess Sophia Albertina, and consequently in a position to become acquainted with Adolph Fredric Munck? Is it simply because "oral and written accounts" indicate that she and Munck "did not look at one another with indifferent eyes"?[38] Is it simply because Crusenstolpe knew that it was "historically so" that Munck fathered three children by his lady-in-waiting mistress, Anna Sophia Ramström? Or is it because, in allowing Olivia to give her body to Munck, Crusenstolpe is allowing her to "give back" to Badin for his (heavily hinted at) multiple infidelities? Or was Crusenstolpe innocently making something of the fact that Badin failed to father a child by either of his actual wives? (While both of Badin's marriages were childless, his autobiographical statement indicates that each of his wives experienced a miscarriage, and that the first delivered a stillborn girl during the eighth month of her pregnancy.)[39] . . . Why is it that Olivia at first finds Badin's blackness "repugnant"? Why does Badin's protector, Queen Lovisa Ulrika, tell the love-smitten Olivia that she is too white for him? Is it simply because Crusenstolpe wishes to make a self-serving political point? Is he simply attempting to illustrate "attitudes and behavior of the [Gustavian] period,"[40] attitudes about the physical appeal and hypersexuality of Africans and their descendants, attitudes supposedly not held either by Crusenstolpe himself or other Swedes of his time? And if this is the case, why does Crusenstolpe's biographical sketch note that Badin's looks were "extraordinarily pleasing" *except* for the color of his skin? . . . Why is it that Baron Armfelt, in interpreting a dream for Gustav III, is allowed to refer to the constant joking about Badin's desire for a "new white lifetime companion"? Is it simply because Badin's wife appears in that dream beside another famously voluptuous court wife? Is it to suggest that the otherwise so-willing women of the court would never make a long-term commitment to him because of the color of his skin? That they would regard such an idea as laughable? Or is it to suggest that no woman would wish to endure his ceaseless infidelities? Or is it again to play on Ramström's own infidelity? Or is Crusenstolpe simply appealing to the "attitudes" of his own time?

Meanwhile, . . . Badin's eyes had become fixed on a shepherd-
ess, surely somewhat powerfully built but exceptionally shapely
for her size and wearing a woman's mask which could be called
attractive, if ever such an expression was appropriate for such a
thing. Flower bunches were abundantly attached to her gossamer
garments and fetching straw hat. She didn't seem offended by
Badin's insistency; but turned him aside, giving a sign that she
would make her identity known sooner than near the masquerade's end. During their mutual dispute about the provision of this
favor, about which the blackamoor showed greater and greater
anxiousness, they both mingled in the great swarm of masks.
> *Crusenstolpe's account of a fervent pass made by Badin during the*
> *famed Opera House ball of March 16, 1792, at which Gustav III*
> *received the shot that led to his death*[41]

[*Both before Queen Sofia Magdalena gave birth and thereafter,*]
rumors were spread that Gustav III had homosexual tendencies.
People attempted to base these suspicions on the fact that the
king surrounded himself with a succession of young pages and
virile, fine-looking youths.
> *Oscar Nikula*[42]

[A]lmost all of the courtiers here are said to be Ped (the men are
pederasts and the women tribades).
> *Francisco de Miranda, (f)actually noting what he had heard,*
> *in a diary entry from October 23, 1787*[43]

Why is it that, in describing a pivotal event in Swedish history, Crusenstolpe
lingers to yet again illustrate Badin's sexuality at work? And then allows
Badin to discover—after the king has been felled—that the woman he hotly
pursued possessed "the ugliest male face"?[44] Is it simply to tell a parallel
tale of deceit? Or is it to make suggestions about the voracious, omnivorous
quality of Badin's sexual appetite? To make suggestions about his being
drawn to "powerfully built" bodies? To make suggestions in keeping with
his elsewhere-made hint of Badin's (hyper)bisexuality, his elsewhere-made
claim that Badin "had free access to *all* of the royalty of both sexes" at
"all times and places"? To make suggestions in keeping with the purported
homosexuality of Gustav III and those about him, with Admiral Carl
August Ehrensvärd's cartoonings of the king as a prancing-mincing fox
and a showy peacock, with his sister-in-law's claim that "his pages are *mi-
gnons*, and he even reportedly at times seeks more intimate company with
an even lower class"?[45] . . . Or is it possible that this scene is part of some

elaborate intertextual game, that here and elsewhere Crusenstolpe is playing off the contents of *Drottningens juvelsmycke* (The Queen's Diadem),
a much discussed novel, first published in 1834, by the (in)famous Carl
Jonas Love Almqvist, one of Sweden's literary giants and an acquaintance
of Crusenstolpe (as well as a friend of Wendela Hebbe)? Playing off a novel
that included the subtitle "An Account of the Events Immediately before,
during, and after the Murder of King Gustav III," and that has the Opera
House masquerade ball of March 16, 1792, at its pivot. Playing off a novel
whose narrator claims to make use of "authentic documents, hand-recorded
discussions, and letters."[46] Playing off a novel whose principal character is
also a socially marginal figure who has spent time as a child in the royal
palace and has come to know its passageways well, an androgynous young
woman of bastardly origins who is highly attractive to men when in female
guise and who sets women's hearts aflutter when in male (dis)guise. Playing
off a novel whose principal character is informed by her actress-courtesan
mother that the young prince who has just assumed the throne upon the
death of Gustav III "is *he,* who I know is the son to him, *him,* who I know
is your father"—a "fact" that not only makes her a half-sister to the new
king, but also the daughter of Adolph Fredric Munck, and thereby a half-
sister to the child borne by Badin's fictional wife.[47] Playing off a novel
whose free-spirited principal character is described as follows in a mixture
of French and Swedish by Gustav III, minutes before being shot: "This child
is of *obscure* [dark, gloomy] *race.* Her *taille* [fashion], her *façon* [manner] is
gai, but yet, *si voulez vous, sombre,* yes, *noire.*"[48] And shortly thereafter is
referred to by a French ballet choreographer as an *animal capricieux, im-
pertinent, voluptieux,* as nothing less than a *noble badine.* All the while
rehearsing her to assume the role of a black-clad "savage" who saves her
own life by performing an enchanting dance of "wild love"—a highly sexually charged role that a momentarily displeased admirer terms "a damned
hottentot pantomine."[49] Playing off a novel whose principal character goes
by several names, who regrets not having a name "which is my own . . .
like other people," who is saddened by her lack of any anchored identity,
who has no lasting name other than Azouras Lazuli Tintomara—the "savage" name attached to her by the ballet master.[50] . . . Or did Crusenstolpe's
portrayal of Badin's Opera House sexual advances, as well as his numerous other direct references and allusions to the "blackamoor's" physical
attractiveness and hypersexuality, involve some deep, elaborate reworking
of the author's own physical appeal and sexuality? (Crusenstolpe has been
described as a "radiantly handsome" man, a witty conversationalist, and a
free spender who in his youth was a "ball-room habitué" and a "favorite
of the ladies." Having often dined with him when he was a court favorite

during the early 1830s, Queen Desideria declared Crusenstolpe "Sweden's most handsome man." Whether or not Crusenstolpe frequently made use of his looks for sexual conquest is not readily determinable, but the author of his 1865 obituary noted that he was "an impassioned gourmand [who] loved all dishes just as Don Juan all women.")[51] . . . Or were all of these depictions of Badin—and their attendant complexities and reservations—multiply determined in ways that extend beyond those thus far suggested?

The abolishment of slavery and the slave trade is one of man's most noble goals and, when this goal is won, it shall become one of humanity's most noble victories.

Erik Gustaf Geijer, noted poet and historian, in a passionate parliamentary speech made on September 5, 1840, proposing a motion to abolish slavery on Saint Barthélemy, a small Caribbean island obtained from France in 1784 and sold back in 1877[52]

In certain respects the conditions of the *[almost six hundred]* slaves on Saint Barthélemy are better than those of the recently emancipated on the British *[Caribbean]* islands; yes, even better than those of free laborers in many European countries.

James H. Haasum, governor of Saint Barthélemy, in a report made in 1841 to the parliamentary committee dealing with Geijer's motion (which had been put forth in the wake of an international antislavery convention held in London)[53]

MR. WINGE: In comparison to the state of our own industrious but miserably poor countrymen, the situation and condition of these indolent slaves is considerably less wretched.

MR. SCHARTAU *[after admitting that some slaves may in certain respects be better off than some Swedish citizens]*: On the other hand it can't be denied that it is not worthy of a civilized nation to provide a shield for the trading of humans, allowing them to be bought and sold like cattle.

MR. FOENANDER *[after suggesting that many Swedish farm laborers would gladly change their place with Saint Barthélemy's slaves]*: It is quite true that the slaves lack noble freedom. But, an old proverb serves well in response to this objection: "He who has never possessed gold never cries over missing it."

Excerpts from a debate, held in January 1845, among members of the Bourgeois Estate's parliamentary delegation regarding the possible compensation of slave owners (despite Geijer's 1840 initiative, Saint Barthélemy slaves were not emancipated until 1846)[54]

Crusenstolpe wrote and published *Morianen* during a period (1840–1844) when Erik Gustaf Geijer and other leading liberal intellectuals and politicians were pressuring for an end to Sweden's limited involvement with slavery (and meeting opposition largely on the basis of the costs involved). He could hardly have been totally unaware of this sensitive matter while shaping the figure of his "blackamoor." While it is not readily discernible where Crusenstolpe stood on the emancipation issue, it is most likely that he was either somewhat ambivalent or at best weakly in favor, and that his lack of strong commitment resonated with the complexities and reservations in his portrayal of Badin's sexuality. Among Crusenstolpe's liberal credentials were his intermittent contributions (1834–1851) to *Aftonbladet,* the press flagship of Swedish liberalism, and his even longer-term association with Lars Johan Hierta, the publisher of that newspaper (and *Morianen*). As a member of parliament he proposed a bill to restrict what he termed the "barbaric" flogging of imprisoned criminals. He became a popular—even iconic—celebrity and a hero to liberals championing total freedom of the press when he was imprisoned from 1838 to 1841 for the act of penning a "treasonous" article in his own newly founded monthly periodical—an article pointing out that a certain military promotion not only had been of questionable constitutionality, but had also gone against "God's law," since *it was granted official approval by the Crown on a Sunday.*[55] All the same, he "was never a democrat at heart," even proposing in 1839 that the monarchy ought to be replaced by a regency, with the state's administration being dominated by the aristocratic estate to which he belonged. Moreover, at least one scholarly critic insists that he lacked any fast principles or convictions, that his stances were "always frothy and superficial" as he lacked "any deeper knowledge of social questions."[56] Whatever his stance, Crusenstolpe's fictional Badin was congruent with images contained in a "nonfictional" four-volume work published in Stockholm during 1841—a "detailed," "physical, historical and political" survey of the earth whose author (f)actually noted that Africans "passionately love 'dancing, tobacco, hard liquor and sex,'" while conceding that they were educable and sometimes well-behaved despite the bad habits instilled in them by slavery.[57] Once again:

[T]he fact that it could get going and be believed in any case stamps the attitudes and behavior of the period.
    M. J. Crusenstolpe[58]

Perhaps the most perplexing expression of Crusenstolpe's mixed(up?)-message portrayal of Badin's hypersexuality was his suggestion that the rumor of Badin's sexual involvement with Princess Sophia Albertina, which flourished in the late eighteenth century, would neither thrive nor find much credence in the now of 1841. Was this because his liberal acquaintances would supposedly remain silent on such a matter—were it to occur in the present—so as to avoid undermining their struggle for emancipation?[59] So as not to raise fears about the eventual sexual safety of European women on Saint Barthélemy? Or because Crusenstolpe wished to have it both ways by allowing his bourgeois readers to have it both ways? First titillating them with black and (on) white tales, repeatedly conjuring up images of Badin's particular hypersexuality, repeatedly conjuring up images that confirmed what people already "knew" of black hypersexuality, what had been sedimented in the bourgeois popular imagination since at least the mid-eighteenth century, what they could already envision because of what they had already read or talked about.[60] And then immediately assuring them that they would not entertain such salacious imag(e)inings on their own? Or did he merely wish to assert that any voluntary sexual union between a "proper" Swedish woman and a black male was now completely improper, fully out of the question—not only bordering on the bestial, not only morally unspeakable, but totally unthinkable? Because an increasingly assertive bourgeois moral apparatus would now condemn any "transgressive" female sexual enjoyment, *especially* if it came in connection with a "wild" adventure, involving someone of "savage" sexuality, someone beneath the woman's station? Because this was most certainly so for Crusenstolpe? Whatever they may have thought back then?

—

The truth is, however, that Badin always maintained a certain penchant for amorous adventures.

Wendela Hebbe's (Crusenstolpe-fed?) imagination at work in 1897 (and 1847).[61] *As a result of his connections with Lars Johan Hierta (Hebbe's paramour) and his periodic association with* Aftonbladet, Crusenstolpe, *it is to be recalled, came into contact with Hebbe after his prison release via the soirées held at her apartment.*[62] *There his "witty conversation" may well have turned on occasion to the subject of his multivolumed novel. . . . And with or without Crusenstolpe's influence in this instance, what again about that 1841* Aftonbladet *article in which Hebbe referred to "a young*

*negro" as "presumably a descendent of Mr. Badin"? Did she enter-
tain any unstated presumption about who the grandmother might
have been? Was* THE *rumor still in circulation? Still an element of
received Stockholm lore? Still part of the collective memory held
by the capital city's bourgeoisie and aristocracy? Still a juicy tale
readily associated with the Gustavian era, with that not-so-distant
period that yet preoccupied so many? And if so, still believed by
some? Despite Crusenstolpe's disclaimer? A disclaimer whose contents may have been a fictionalized (f)act, a clever act of sarcasm
that served multiple purposes? And which was given voice with full
knowledge of the readily translatable images of black hypersexuality
then available in numerous "nonfictional" works?*

The Queen *[Lovisa Ulrika]* had been against this relationship
[between Badin and his eventual first wife, Elisabeth Swartz]
which she regarded as a mésalliance.
   *Wendela Hebbe retelling what was supposedly retold to her (or what
   she chose to imagine, to state as a fact on the basis of Crusenstolpe's
   "historically so" fiction?)*[63]

He was, in his outer appearance, reportedly little and bow-legged.
   *Excerpt from a male-authored 1904 encyclopedia entry for Badin
   that in effect—unconsciously counteracting current anxieties
   regarding the sexual potency of the racialized Other?—attempts
   to dismiss his sexual attractiveness, to suggest that there were no
   amorous adventures, that perhaps unspeakable sexual contact
   did not transpire between him and various women of the court,
   that the latter were never blemished by his penetrations, that they
   would have never willingly opened themselves to the possibility of
   miscegenation*[64]

One knows, of course, that the princess *[Sophia Albertina]* was
loyal and kind-hearted *[and therefore was apt to have given Badin
financial support in his old age, as Crusenstolpe reports]*; and no
doubt she was devotedly attached to the blackamoor, who had
been her childhood playmate and once *[on the occasion of her
eleventh birthday]* even bestowed a versified homage upon her.
   *Carl Forsstrand, in a 1911 essay resulting from the first historical
   research on Badin*[65]

[A]nd with her had a child whose descendants live in Uppsala
under the name Svartsberg.

Handwritten comment appended in the margins to the above quote,
in the copy of Forsstrand's publication held at Sweden's National
Portrait Gallery (Gripsholm's Castle, in the town of Mariefred); no
name or date indicated

What was, or was not, "historically so" between Badin and Sophia Albertina? And other Swedish women in and around the court of Gustav III? And
what does it matter, if it was in any case historically so that Crusenstolpe,
in fictionally factualizing and (f)actually fictionalizing Badin to a relatively
wide bourgeois audience, was compounding the myth of the black as a creature possessed of an unbridled, animal-like know-no-(racial)bounds sexuality? If it was historically so that Crusenstolpe helped reinforce and further
perpetuate that myth in Sweden (and elsewhere) by giving it substance in
a work that was "a great success on the book market,"[66] by providing it a
Swedish setting in print for the first time, by placing it in a single body with
a singular name, by performing a metonymical dirty trick—translating an
individual into a confirmation of the Universal? If it was historically so
that the myth reinforcement and stereotype perpetuation resulting from
Crusenstolpe's characterization of Badin was not confined to the 1840s,
but also came into play at dispersed sites with each reissuing and dissemination of his six-volume work? Resonating with other images in 1880. In
1916–17. In 1928. If it was historically so that, right up through the 1990s,
subsequent Swedish authors employed Crusenstolpe as a major source for
their portrayals of Badin, for their own fictionalizations of fact that have
themselves become effect-producing social facts?

Unfortunately the natives *["Zulu-kaffirs"]* suffer from a burning
love for alcohol; many get drunk on eau-de-cologne or dena-
tured alcohol, which they steal from their master and mistress,
and when a native is drunk it is very dangerous for a white
woman to be in his proximity.

Image of the black male as sexual threat widely circulated in
Sweden via a highly popular illustrated weekly published during
1917, when various volumes of Morianen *were once again being*
republished[67]

The pastel portrait of Badin hanging at the National Portrait Gallery is remarkably striking. Captured by the hand of a highly accomplished court painter, ornately decked out—perhaps for one of Gustav III's many costumed extravaganzas—Badin appears serenely triumphant, gazing with joyful confidence directly at the viewer, smiling contentedly, as if to say: "I am a successful child of the Enlightenment. Born a slave, I have become as civilized as anybody else. I am virtually white. White plume, white ruffled

blouse, white sash of honor. I am one with the white knight. I have acquired the knowledge to play the most sophisticated of intellectual games.
Victoriously! I have become powerful. I have knocked over black on the
chessboard of life. A master chess player. A master of my situation. No
court-lackey marionette am I. Nobody pulls my strings." That he had reason to smile, that he was actually an astute chess player, that knocking over
black was not an unknown experience to him, is testified to by nobody
less than Gustav III, who, in a letter of May 1789, noted that "[Badin] has
repeatedly beaten me in our games of chess."[68] Yet to some present-day
interpreters Badin's demeanor, both winning and winsome, is also about
another kind of conquest. For them the portrait is sexually charged, as the
erect forefinger of his left hand is supposedly assuming an obscene gesture[69]
(destined for the waiting open oval formed by his right thumb and forefinger plus the white knight?).

> Now she unbuttoned her traveling cloak and he placed his hand
> over her breast. The black against the white. A soft chess move.
> *Badin in the midst of a sexual encounter in a horse-drawn carriage*
> *with Charlotte Du Rietz (born De Geer), a former "mistress"*
> *of Gustav III and purportedly the only woman "truly loved" by*
> *that king*[70]

Is this really a portrait that speaks as much about sexual conquest as about
conquering a chess opponent? Was the seventy-year-old Gustaf Lundberg—
Sweden's rococo portrait painter par excellence[71]—really acting in complici-
ty with Badin, sharing a bit of visual mischief? Was this business with the
fingers (f)actually a sexual joke, a sexual badinage coupled with seriousness
of purpose?[72] Not inconsistent with the "piquant, erotic" qualities of those
Lundberg portraits in which attractive women are costumed as Diana or
some other mythological figure? Not inconsistent with the highly charged
sexual atmosphere of the Gustavian court, with the buzz-buzz of behind-the-
back gossip and jokings that accompanied its partner-shifting promiscuities?
(Because of Lundberg's court success, and his "gallant" sociability, his studio
became "a popular meeting place for Stockholm society"—not only a site
where new affairs might be set in motion, but also a site where overlapping
social networks came into conjunction, where sizzling gossip and the ribald
jokes derived therefrom could have their circulation accelerated, where rumors regarding Badin's sexual activity could be recycled yet again.) . . . Or
is the purported sexual content of this image nothing more than the product
of a highly imaginative late twentieth-century imagination at work, the
offspring of an unconscious coupling made between long-existing "factual"

fictions about Badin and even longer existing fictionalized "facts" about the hypersexuality of black Africans and their dispersed descendents? And, could such an imagination have been (unconsciously) further fueled by knowledge that the portrait had quite apparently been a part of Sophia Albertina's art collection until her death?[73]

> [H]e is good looking. It is difficult to say whether it is his spirit or his face that make him attractive. . . . To his advantage one can note that his face has several beautifully curved lines, that his mouth is unusually well shaped for that of a blackamoor. . . . His skin looks like breakfast chocolate when it is brought into the room—and it smells, say women associated with the court, strangely enough like cardamom. . . . *[Those same]* women whisper about him; that he is a good and tender lover—but not as torrid as one generally expects a dark-skinned man to be. Perhaps expectations have become unreasonably high. Perhaps his love also speaks a language other than the one prevailing at the court; a man who doesn't slander the women with whom he has united, and never talks about the affairs others are engaged in, or for that matter his own, is a rare phenomenon in this bab-bling, arrogant setting. He seldom views himself in the mirror. Any passions he harbors are well hidden; beneath a skillfully erected openness.
> *Ylva Eggehorn*[74]

> The daughter of wholesaling merchant Svartz laughs . . . when her friends whisper in her ear that her wedding night in the fall will be both darker and hotter than everybody else's and that she ought to eat raw eggs in order to prepare herself.
> *Ylva Eggehorn*[75]

> And I shall always remember your dear, delightful hands. My skin sees you and remembers you. I wish you all the best in your marriage.
> *Charlotte Du Rietz in a letter to Badin*[76]

One of those imagining Lundberg's portrait of Badin to be highly sexu-ally charged is Ylva Eggehorn, a woman who has herself created a lengthy representation of him, who has re-membered and portrayed him in a 1996 novel—thereby helping to reinsert Badin into the popular Swedish imagi-nation at a time when blacks have a much more conspicuous presence in

Sweden than ever before; at a time when (largely unreflected) cultural racism is rampant toward blacks and non-Europeans more generally; at a time
when skin pigment, hair color, and other bodily markers are commonly
translated into highly charged cultural markers; at a time when entire
groups are racialized as a consequence of outward biological difference
being automatically (con)fused with stereotyped cultural difference. And
at a time when negative stereotyping of the Other has led to widespread
racist effects, to marginalization and exclusion, to underclassification and
de facto social apartheid, to levels of labor-market discrimination and residential segregation that are matched by few other industrial countries; at
a time when culture is repeatedly essentialized in political and mass media
discourses as well as in everyday conversation; at a time when it frequently
goes without saying that culture is immutable, that it is passed on from generation to generation regardless of setting (thereby idea-logically meaning
that the person of color or Islamic belief can never become a "real Swede,"
never become fully modern, even if born in Sweden). At a time, furthermore, when the mass media, by tirelessly spotlighting the isolated incidence
of atrocious gang rapes, periodically create moral panics, reinforcing the
popular notion that youths of color or Muslim background are hypersexual and thereby pose a threat to young white Swedish women—and
the "Swedish" nation that they symbolize.[77] Whatever Eggehorn's declared
intentions, Badin is portrayed in such a manner as to provide some relief or
reduction of cognitive dissonance, some massaging of contradictory sentiments, some opportunity for reworking guilt, for those readers who—like
a substantial portion of the population—find it more or less difficult to
reconcile their emotional, discursive, and practical responses to Difference
with central elements of their individual or national identity, with taken-
for-granted views of themselves as the most tolerant of the tolerant, with
how-could-it-be-otherwise views of their country as *the best in the world*
at social justice and equality, as *the world's moral conscience,* as the world's
most outspoken critic of racism in the United States and South Africa.[78] For
here Badin is factually fictionalized and fictionally factualized in a manner
that perpetuates and yet alters. Badin is now a much more complex person
than the figure put on the theater stage by Strindberg or placed at history's
central stage by Crusenstolpe. Badin is now a much more human being than
the person (re)presented in various biographical and historical sketches.
Still, Badin's sexuality is in the foreground. Still, well-placed women find
him physically irresistible. Still, they fall beneath this sexual knight like
so many easily captured pawns. But even if Badin the lover and lovemaker
is occasionally word-painted with a soft-porn brush, he is a tender creature rather than a sexual animal. Not a savage in bed, he is considerate

and discrete. His performances are "good," are "memorable," but not in keeping with stereotypes of the torrid. He is the negation of Charlotte Du Rietz's aristocratic husband, "who took her as if she was just like any other object in his house."[79] He is capable of reflective pining and yearning, of entering into a mutual relationship of "true love," not with Princess Sophia Albertina, but with a woman who is otherwise taboo, a woman whose closeness to the king has been fused by physical intimacy rather than sibling status and shared childhood memories. He is capable of capturing the emotions of, and gaining the respect of, a Charlotte Du Rietz who is no mere courtesan, who is not merely the only woman reputedly to have had a "passionate love affair" with Gustav III (in the fall of 1768 while still crown prince),[80] but a woman of independent mind, a student of chemistry and metallurgy, an intellectual who perhaps feels most at home in the capacious library of her father's estate.

> This novel is a historical fantasy about Adolf Badin. . . . It is for
> the most part played out in the year 1782. Exercising creative
> license, I have allowed myself some deviations from historically
> documented reality. I have not written an eighteenth-century
> novel, but a twentieth-century novel about a part of the eigh-
> teenth century.
> *Ylva Eggehorn, in an endnote to the reader*[81]

While in fiction a twentieth-century woman in eighteenth-century garb, Charlotte Du Rietz was, in fact, the daughter of the great-grandson of Louis De Geer (1587–1652), a Dutch banker who migrated to Sweden in 1627 to help maintain that country's Great Power status by developing its iron and armaments industries. De Geer, moreover, played an instrumental role in founding the Guinea Company, or Africa Company, which in 1649 established a trading post at Cape Coast, southwest of Accra, thereby pioneering Sweden's relatively peripheral role in the exploitation and enslavement of blacks. Inasmuch as the Swedish colony was already taken over by Denmark in 1658; inasmuch as the Danes soon became involved in trading slaves to sugar-cane plantation operators in various European colonies in the Caribbean, including Badin's birthplace, Saint Croix; Badin's fictional affair with De Geer's daughter allows for the closing of a circle, for the completion of one revolution, for a full swing of relations and reconciliation, for a rotation and redefinition of circumstances. In the beginning, the white Swede, in exercising his desire, in acting for the love of profits, willingly contributes to the humiliation, violation, and complete subjection of the body of the black Other. Generations later, the white Swede, in exercising her desire, in acting for the profits of love, willingly subjects her body completely to the black Other. New conjoinings. Full emotional and intellectual, as well as bodily, engagement. No humiliation or violation. Mutual pleasurings rather than personal gratification by way of pain infliction. . . . This reimag(e)ining of history, this re-membering of the past, facilitates a forgetting of the present, a displacement of existing social inequalities and injustices, a shoving aside of what one dimly or clearly knows about the existence of discrimination and segregation, a seeming resolution of painful contradictions, severe uneasiness, intense cognitive dissonance. . . . The erasure of actual current wrongs by way of the fictional redressing of deeply sedimented wrongs. A whiteout of the present by way of mental blackout. Some level of comfort, if not atonement, achieved by way of amnesia. All together then. If not now.

—

Black and/on white, past tense.

> A beautiful woman, . . . *[but I can't]* understand her fondness
> *[for Badin].*
> *Märta Helena Reenstierna, resident of a farmstead immediately outside of Stockholm, commenting in an April 1813 diary entry upon her dinner encounter with Badin's second wife, born Magdalena Eleonora Norell*[82]

≠ ≠ ≠

Black and/on white, present tense.

> Is he ever going to go home to his *[kind, country]* wondered my
> paternal grandmother. "And think if you get children, it's not,
> of course, just a matter of mixing." "Is it him?" giggled a male
> work colleague and pointed toward my husband to be. "You
> surely could have gotten something better." Prejudices against
> black men as well as white women who strike up a relationship
> are alive and thriving.
> *Anna Norrby, cultural analyst, in 1997*[83]

> I have occasionally encountered a pushy flirtiness from men who,
> owing to their high age or considerable overweight, normally
> would not dare to meet my glance. When I recently ate lunch at

a restaurant, two greasy elderly men flirted with me in an intru-
sive manner. The reason was obvious. I had once again degraded
myself. The person I ate lunch with was a black man. "If he is
good enough for you we are good enough also."

A fifty-one-year-old Stockholm woman in 1997[84]

I have heard comments in my vicinity such as: "Damn, what a
fucker, go home to where you belong, nigger whore." My friends
think that I'm exaggerating when I tell them such things.

A Stockholm secretary regarding reactions to her having a black
male companion, in 1997[85]

Re Reading
Rereadings
Reading Numbers Numerously

[T]here are NEGROE slaves dispersed all over EUROPE, of which none ever discovered any symptoms of ingenuity, tho' low people, without education, will start up amongst us [Europeans], and distinguish themselves in every profession. In JAMAICA indeed they talk of one negroe as a man of parts and learning; but 'tis likely he is admired for very slender accomplishments like a parrot, who speaks a few words plainly.

David Hume, in 1748[1]

I have made Badin a considerably finer writer and (presumably) much deeper thinker than he actually was.

Ylva Eggehorn, again in her endnote to the reader[2]

———

[I]f you, the reader, wish to find] the way to Truth and life . . . then read, and read connectively. Thus have I done with the over 800 books that I own.

Badin, in his autobiographical statement[3]

GOD was constantly at my side, as well as in my thoughts; especially during my now lonely nights [following the death of my wife]. I read perhaps more than ever before: the Bible, theology, astronomy. Two volumes were always with me: Mr. Fourmont Lécine's *Reflexions sur l'origine des Peuples Anciennes,* vols. I and II. It was especially heavy reading, and I could manage only a few or more pages a week.

But something got me to believe that a deep truth was hidden here,
expressly for me to find out.
Badin, in reflection[4]

In written (f)act, as well as in fiction, Badin is a man in search of the Truth, in search of knowledge and self-understanding, trying to situate his black Otherness, seeking his identity. By way of reading and rereading among the 1,030 works he eventually accumulated in his book collection.[5] Works that ran a wide gamut.[6] From the Bible and numerous theological writings— many presumably acquired in the 1760s when, in accord with the pedagogical demands of Rousseau's fiction, he [f]actually underwent six teenage years of moral and religious training. To Ovid. To Spinoza. To books on astronomy—an interest that emerged when he accompanied Queen Lovisa Ulrika to the court of Fredrik II in 1771.[7] To a diverse array of "universal" and territorially oriented histories. To travel accounts—including Pehr Kalm's *Journey to America (Resa till Amerika)*. To farm-household management treatises—shortly after Queen Lovisa Ulrika's death and his marriage to Elizabeth Swartz, Badin was granted three separate pieces of Crown property by Gustav III, which he operated by way of peasant tenants. Works whose fictions, by way of actual exposure to them, became the facts of his life. Works whose facts, by way of association and recombination, became the fictions of his life. Works that placed him in extensive European and more limited Swedish networks of shared reference. Works whose contents contributed to the complex constitution of his situated knowledge, whose discursive categories now and then, in ways unknowable, presumably entered into his subject (re)formation. Works that on occasion quite probably spoke rather directly to the question of his identity. Such as the French translation of a three-volume Spanish work: A General History of the Indies from 1492 until 1554. Such as Fourmont Lécine's *Reflexions sur l'origine des peuples anciennes*, which had been published in Paris in 1735.

I know who I am: Couschi.
I know my origins: I am the son of Chuso, the King of the Ethiopians,
the Lion of Judah. My end is in my beginnings.
*Badin, in a moment of self-illumination, of self-discovery, of text-
precipitated self-identification, of rooting that family name he bore with
him from Saint Croix*[8]

Badin's reading of Fourmont Lécine's *Reflexions sur l'origine des peuples anciennes* proved pivotal. Epiphany! Moment of startling revelation! Past and present brought into stunning constellation. Roots unveiled. Self-discovery achieved. Mind put to rest. Or at least that is the tale told in Ola Larsmo's moving, tightly conceived, and superbly structured novel *Maroonberget* (The Maroon [Fugitive Slaves'] Mountain)—a novel in which Badin's life and search for identity is fictionally reassembled and re-membered through bringing it into tension with the 1990s identity search of a young Stockholm resident, the son of a white Swedish woman and an Afro-American. . . . But in what sense was that literally the case? Was it (f)actually so? A MORE or less accurate fictional representation? Or are there some telling silences? Additional (f)acts of Badin's life that permit different imaginings, other constructions, alternative tales to be told? . . . Larsmo's insertion of Lécine's treatise into the hands of Badin, and Badin's consequent identity resolution, spring from a clever piece of detective work, from his close examination of the hodgepodge contents of the notebook Badin sporadically kept from the 1780s until his death in 1822. Among the seventy-four pages of scattered scribblings in that little volume is the following entry in a mixture of French and Swedish: "second vol. of *Reflexions Sur L'origine* by Mr. Fourmont Lécine Page 501 Lines 3–4." Going to the source, Larsmo encountered the following lines: "Did not Nimrod rule over Babylon? Was he not a *Couschi,* or son of *Chuso,* the King of the Ethiopians? When Abraham departed his character was Babylonian, like that of *Couschi* . . ."[9] Pursuing other leads, tracing other cryptic entries to the Bible, Larsmo is able to show that there very probably was a coupling in Badin's mind between the fingered Lécine excerpt and Old Testament passages that speak of the centuries of slavery on foreign soil to befall the seed of Abraham, that speak of eventual free-dom and property ownership, that allow one to see Couschi as the missing link between Noah and Abraham (since he is the grandson of Ham—that son of Noah who, according to then prevalent understandings of the Bible, is the forefather of all blacks).[10] . . . Couschi, biblical ancestry, slavery, landholding—strong resonances with Badin's life and learning, resonances that enable him to realize that he quite possibly is somebody with a purpose in life, not merely some*thing,* some embodied *object.* (At one point in his notebook Badin observes, **"When I sensed that I was of matter made, I wanted to know for what I was intended.")**[11] . . . A neat piece of sleuthing. A nicely packaged solution. All the pieces in place. Very tidy indeed. Even obvious, were it not for the fact that Badin himself chose to put matters otherwise, to give another version in his autobiographical statement—that document where he sought to recount his life with honesty, to **"not stumble in truth's pure way,"** to not **"deceive the reader."**[12]

> The name Couschi is my mother's father's brother's name and is the family name on my mother's father's side. My father's name is Andris, my mother's name is Narzi(?), my brother's name is Coffi. These . . . names I learned of an old man, black like myself.

It was he who told me from where I was descended. In regard to
my mother's father's brother's name, which I bear, Couschi is the
same as Nimrod. Or Couschi, he is Chuso's son, and the Forefather
of the Ethiopians. Nimrod is known, but not under the name
Couschi. Furthermore, the same old man said that the song I have
heard about a man who had a staff that became a snake belongs
to my family. And is[n't] it strange [a fateful coincidence] that I am
baptized to Gustaf; this staff, also called Gud Staf [God('s) Staff],
and Moses was married with an Ethiopian woman. So, when I name
Gustaf III's name . . .

　　Adolph Ludvig Gustaf Albrecht Couschi, or Badin, in a marginal observa-
　　tion contained in his handwritten autobiographical statement[13]

No anticipation of a **"deep truth"** lying hidden in Lécine's text? No lightning-
bolt revelation upon reading the lines on page 501? No later recollection
that **"Immediately, in the same instant, the scales fell from my eyes"**?[14] But
a happenstance confirmation of the already known? Or? . . . Plausible(?)
alternative tellings and rereadings suggested by the above.

Version one: The trauma of being ripped from his parents at an early age,
of being cruelly separated for life, without even the dimmest prospect of reunion, is never fully repressed. On the contrary, the jagged edge of that experience repeatedly resurfaces. Set into motion, cutting yet again, by involuntary memory, by the push button of a painfully inescapable association.
Each winter the first snows are a reminder of his initial encounter with that
white matter of little substance, of the sugar cane that was not, of the cold
touch and sweetless taste that said the everyday as I have known it, parents, home, the past, are all a vast ocean away. And forever unattainable,
unrecapturable. Yet, because *where he was* cannot be revisited, because the
detailed daily thereness of Saint Croix is almost completely lost—beyond
intentional retrieval, beyond being otherwise summoned up—Badin is periodically preoccupied with *who he was*. He cannot elude the ever-returning
triple-edged question: From whence the name Couschi? What does it signify? Who am I? Thus, Badin's search leads him to question other blacks, to
interrogate others who had been brought to Stockholm from the Caribbean
or Africa during the mid-eighteenth century when there was "somewhat of
a fad in the highest circles, and especially the court, to have young blacks
serve as liveried footmen or merrymakers."[15] Because Badin does not have
to go out of his way to meet these other blacks, and because some of them
may very well have come from Saint Croix owing to various economic and
political interconnections between Sweden and Denmark, he eventually

is put into contact with an older man familiar with his family who had been brought to Stockholm several decades earlier.[16] It is this fellow Afro-Caribbean, this stand-in for a lost father, who purveys the **"deep truth,"** who supplies the lightning-bolt revelation. It is he who in effect provides fore(father)knowledge. For the knowledge provided by Badin's much-thumbed Bible and copy of Lécine is merely a corroborating resonance, a verifying echo, a reassuring buttress for an already established, but tenuous, element of identity.

—

To "find one's way home" is to find one's identity. To be estranged from home is to be estranged from one's self.

Karin Johannisson, commenting on nostalgia as a "painful longing for home"[17]

—

Version two: Prior to arriving in Stockholm during 1760, roughly between the ages of eight and ten, Badin spent two years in Copenhagen, a city where the number of Afro-Caribbeans in service to the aristocracy and the monied bourgeoisie numbered in the many hundreds, largely as a consequence of the scale of Danish involvement in Saint Thomas and Saint Croix.[18] There the man mentioned in his autobiography unfolded all, spurred to do so by Badin's spontaneous whistling/humming/mouthing of the staff-into-snake song.[19] Because of his age at the time, and the constant crowding of new impressions, the man's account lingered in his mind in fuzzy and not readily recallable form. Until suddenly awakened by the reading of certain Bible passages, until the (bad-)dream fog was almost completely dissipated by Lécine's words, leaving only his mother's forename—"Narzi(?)"—enshrouded in uncertainty.

—

[T]he first impulse of the black man is to say no to those who attempt to build a definition of him. . . .

In every country of the world there are climbers, "the ones who forget who they are," and, in contrast to them, "the ones who remember where they came from."

Frantz Fanon, another Afro-Caribbean, who, like Badin, spent much of his life in Europe[20]

[T]he concentrated intensity of the slave experience is something
that marked out blacks as the first truly modern people, handling in
the nineteenth century dilemmas and difficulties which would only
become the substance of everyday life in Europe a century later.

*[In reassessing the relationship between slavery and modernity I
am concerned]* with the variations and discontinuities in modern
experience and with the decentred and inescapably plural nature
of modern subjectivity and identity.
    Paul Gilroy[21]

—

Version three: All his protests to the contrary, all his claims that he will not
"deceive the reader" to the contrary, his account of the roots-revealing old
man was in (f)act a fiction, a calculated concoction, a sly badinage prompt-
ed by a personal politics of identity. Writing at around sixty, and addressing
a very particular audience—fellow members of the Par Bricole Order, largely consisting of men of letters, military officers, and successful merchants
and manufacturers—Badin could not leave decades of lived Difference and
contradiction totally unreworked. And yet, he could not straightforwardly
speak of the scattered slights and periodic humiliations that interrupted
his everyday world of apparent acceptance, could not directly refer to that
resulting cloud of uncertainty and ambivalence that hung over his identity, could not bluntly reveal that his accumulation of dispersed negative
experiences occasionally left him weighed down by a sense of powerless-
ness, could not confess that those same emotionally scarring experiences
prevented him from ever feeling fully Swedish, could not openly admit that
unremitting reminders of his blackness left him torn between his past and
his present, torn between simultaneously being neither Afro-Caribbean nor
Swedish and being both/and. . . . If the ultimate act of power lies in assigning names and categories that stick and enter into subject formation, Badin
the trickster challenges the power relations in which he is engulfed by virtue
of inventing his ancestry informant and by virtue of invoking his family's
song. For, in doing so, he is in effect asserting that his origins and name
are a matter of African(-Caribbean) oral tradition, in effect insisting that
Couschi is not simply derived from the authority of the European(-Swedish)
text, in effect placing the African(-Caribbean) and the European(-Swedish)
on the same footing, in effect thumbing his nose at "eighteenth-century
European speculations on the absence of writing among Africans and its
significance," at arguments claiming that the absence of writing in African

languages was proof that their speakers were "innately" mentally inferior to Europeans.[22] Or, in confronting the fractured doubleness of his identity, the nagging nohereness/nothereness/nowhereness of his in-betweenness, Badin undertakes, and thereby takes over, his own signification. In naming himself, in invoking his distant kingly past, he with swift stroke decolonizes his name, names his own independence, alters the subject. Self-significance at last. At least for the moment in his own mind. Since in the name-clarifying procedure everything remains masked. Especially his lingering ambivalence and uneasiness toward native Swedes, his gnawing doubts about whether or not They are really taking him at his true worth. In any given situation. Or ever at all.

—

> *[Linnaeus]* named plants for women, farmers, and artisans, and
> once even, to the envy of his "master," for a Surinam field slave.
>   *Lisbet Koerner*[23]

≠ ≠ ≠

(Be)longings, present tense.

> I'm lucky because I have my roots in two cultures. I love my
> Sweden, but regardless of how Swedish I feel I will always be
> an immigrant in the eyes of others, even though I never left one
> country to live in another.
>   *Aysegül, a young woman born in Sweden of Turkish parents who
>   is reminded of her otherness almost every day*[24]

> My mother comes from Tanzania and my father is from England.
> I've lived here since I was four years old, and now I'm twenty. . . .
> In Sweden I'm from Africa, and in Africa I'm from Sweden, in
> England I'm from Africa. It's hard, I don't know what I am. . . .
> In Sweden I'm different, but when I come to Tanzania, where my
> mother is living now, I can't say that I have come home. There
> they say that I am Swedish, and if I say that I come from Africa
> they make fun of me. When I come to Sweden, and the passport
> control police ask where I come from, I often say "from England,"
> and then they get mad. The same thing in Tanzania. I don't belong
> at home anywhere, and I've noticed the same aggression in Africa

as I do here in Sweden. They don't accept me and they yell at me
that I'm a fucking foreigner.
  "Marlene"[25]

Those who see me of course only see the outside of me—a black
gal. But I am a Swedish black gal.
  *Nyamko Sabuni, daughter of a Congolese political refugee, speak-
  ing in 1998, at age twenty-seven, after fifteen years' residence in
  Sweden*[26]

I feel like I'm 50-50. Sweden doesn't allow me to be Swedish.
People primarily go on appearances, and it's easily seen that I'm
not completely Swedish. . . . I don't feel like I belong completely
at home anywhere.
  *Samir, son of a Moroccan migrant and a Swedish woman, speak-
  ing in 1998, at age twenty-three—"throughout his entire life he has
  been called 'every possible thing' because of his physical appearance.
  He tries not to take it personally any longer."*[27]

≠ ≠ ≠

When young not yet fully grown men are forced into military
service and lose hope of returning safe and sound to their beloved native country, they are seized by a peculiar sorrowfulness.
They become taciturn, apathetic, reclusive, brooding, sigh and
moan a great deal, and finally become completely insensitive and
indifferent to life itself. This is the sickness *nostalgia*, or *homesickness*. Nothing can help them. . . . The body withers away as
their entire ego fixes on this futile yearning. . . . I have opened
many corpses that have died from this sickness.
  *Leopold Auenbrugger, Austrian doctor writing in 1761, intensify-
  ing the notion that nostalgia is a disorder that speaks through the
  body with possible life-threatening consequences*[28]

[In 1763, in his "genera morborum,"] Linnaeus classified nostalgia under "Mental Illnesses—emotional," that is, under sicknesses
of the soul characterized by intense expressions of feeling. . . . He
translates nostalgia as "homesick" and defines it as a "longing for
one's fatherland or kinfolk."
  Karin Johannisson[29]

Jean-Jacques Rousseau saw the illness as an expression partly for
a longing for freedom, partly for a longing back to childhood—
a highly strung state of mind often called forth by music *[by a
remembered tune or song]*.
   Karin Johannisson, *referring to an entry made by Rousseau in his*
   Dictionary of Music *(1768)* [30]

Was that song Badin had heard "about a man who had a staff that became a
snake" capable of calling forth nostalgia as then understood by Linnaeus,
Rousseau, and others? Is it at all possible that Badin somehow failed to become aware of nostalgia as an affliction that left its marks upon the body?
Given the breadth of his own readings in French and Swedish, as well as the
likely variety of writings discussed by others in his presence, could he have
escaped learning something about that "illness" and its supposed symptoms? Given the networks of discourse circulation that converged at the
Royal Palace and other sites of his daily life, given that many upper-class
Stockholmers were avid readers of the French encyclopedias in which the
"disease" was described, were not the notions of nostalgia and homesickness almost certainly a part of Badin's situated knowledge? Especially since
they had become a part of the "popular medical vocabulary" in Sweden
during the latter half of the eighteenth century—and coupled with terms
such as "yearning sickness" and "mother longing"? [31] Was there any way
in which he could avoid recognizing himself as a prime candidate for a bad
case of that sickness, any way in which the term and its associated discourse
could not prey upon his mind, acting as an infectious agent? Was it not a
condition triggered by a lost sense of belonging, a condition that resonated
with his own mental dis-ease, his own sense of eternal dis-place-ment and
involuntary (un)mooredness? After all, what was the (hopefully) temporary
separation from home of the soldier compared to his own permanent removal? And had not Albrecht van Haller, a leading medical authority, described
nostalgia in an influential 1777 French encyclopedia article as "a state of
melancholia caused by a strong longing to see one's parents again and by
being forced to reside among strangers who don't love us in the manner we
have been loved by our parents"? [32] Was there not, by 1800, almost universal
agreement among European doctors "that all peoples and all social classes
were vulnerable" to nostalgia, including "Negroes serving in slavery"? [33] Is
it not likely that each recurring episode of prolonged yearning for THERE
became more intense as Badin's temporal distance from Saint Croix and his
family increased, and as his exposure to written and spoken representations
of nostalgia further accumulated? Until well on in years—having heard so

much of its possible fatal consequences—he feared it would be the cause of his own death?[34] That his dwelling on a past discontinuity—and all that he had forgotten, everything **"before the year 1758 that is not remembered by him with any precision"**[35]—would precipitate the ultimate discontinuity?[36] Something he could count on? His own day of reckoning?

———

That 2 and 2 make 5
> *Line from Aimé Césaire's epic revolutionary poem,* Notebook of a Return to the Native Land *(1939), in which the rationalism under-pinning West Indian colonial slavery is subverted*[37]

$4 = 12 = 35 = 87$
$457 - 2 = 12.$
$25 = 2 = 9 = 35 = 68 - 1.$
$5 = 41 - 2$
$15 = 41 = 82$
$31 - 2 = 35$
$20 = 22 = 31 = 47 = 69$
> *Selection of unexplained numerical sequences in Badin's notebook*[38]

He sometimes occupied himself with writing and when doing so made cabalistic calculations of his own manufacture and invention. The following item, discovered among his surviving papers, ought perhaps be ascribed to him, although the handwriting is not his.

"The name Gustav Adolphe has 13 letters. He was the 13th King of the Vasa dynasty; became king at age 13; reigned for 13 years after coming of age; was arrested on the 13th of March; 22 times 13 makes 286 years, which equals the time the Vasa dynasty has reigned in Sweden (from 1523, the year of Gustav I's coronation, until 1809, the year Gustav Adolphe the 4th was arrested). If 13 is reversed it becomes 31, which was the king's age when arrested. If 1 and 3 are added to 13 you get 17, which equals the length of his reign. He was succeeded by Karl the 13th. The 13th of July, 1782, he for the first time met and talked with his paternal grandmother, Queen Lovisa Ulrika."

> *Wendela Hebbe, relaying an account with an unusual reluctance to be unreservedly "factual,"*[39] *relaying a numerical curiosity loaded with personal meaning to Badin as it touched upon the death of*

*two of the most central figures in his life (Gustav Adolph became
king after Gustav III's death and initially met Lovisa Ulrika—
Badin's self-proclaimed "foster mother"—but three days before
she passed away)*

What is to be read into Badin's preoccupation with numbers, into his seemingly nonsensical numerical scribblings, his fantastic arithmetical jottings,
his outlandish notebook equations that sometimes became submerged beneath subsequent textual entries? Was it simply a matter of his being locked
into a dream of quickly achieved fortune, of his being hooked on playing
the Royal Lottery that had been in existence since 1771, of his noting down
numbers that might or might not work, of his falling under the spell—along
with many of his acquaintances—of a clerk named Åbom and his super-
natural "number puncturing" system for determining winning combina-
tions in advance?[40] Was it a matter of his adhering to mystical "number
puncturing" more generally, of a desire to make note of his future in advance, of his joining other Stockholm contemporaries in believing that dates
and other numbers—if properly read—could predict future events? Was it a
matter of his attempting to put "number puncturing" in reverse, of reading
both history and his own story backward, of seeing some divine order in
the world's events—as with the "cabalistic calculation" Hebbe hesitatingly
ascribes to him? Did the numbers recorded have some biblical reference,
code some textual meaning, point to something other than the book, chapter, and verse locations indicated by letters and numbers elsewhere in his
notebook? Did they, more precisely, involve a convoluted personal reworking of the Fourth Book of Moses—that number-laden Book of Numbers,
that book in which fire is deployed by God as an instrument of punishment
and employed by his worshippers as a means of sacrifice and purification,
that book in which Aaron and Miriam speak badly of Moses because he
has taken an Ethiopian wife, that book in which God displays his wrath
by turning Miriam "as white as snow" with leprosy?[41] Did those numbers
derive from Badin's belief in the **"True Faith,"** from his consequent sensing of
"Nature's Voice," from his reading of God's creational arrangement—along
lines even somewhat more complex than those detected by Linnaeus, who
wavered between five, seven, and twelve as nature's ultimate organizing
numbers?[42] Did they pertain to the operation of his farm holdings, to acreage sown and crop yields obtained? Or did they involve a bookkeeping
system, a sequence of debits and credits, financial or moral, whose logic was
known only to Badin? Or did they involve some combination of the above?
Or none of the above? . . . Whatever the case, did they simultaneously serve
some other conscious or unconscious purpose? A means for re-viewing his

past, for linking together disjunctures, for bringing the incompatible and discordant into conjuncture, for coordinating all the cruelly unpredictable shifts in his universe of meaning, for suturing together a lifetime of contradictions? A means for reworking a world of experience in which nothing was totally certain, in which one's reception and treatment was never fully predictable, in which supposed equalities were really inequalities whose magnitude of difference shifted with situation and circumstance? A means for reworking a world of experience in which instead of $4 = 4 = 4 = 4$ constantly, $4 = 12 = 35 = 87$ inconstantly? For reworking a world of experience in which the only constant is the sign l(a)ying between the numbers, the position of in-betweenness, the position of always designating something(s) else while remaining unerasably the same, the position that he perpetually occupied? A means for attempting to make sense out of that unforgiving in-betweenness?

> Numbers.
> Numbers that enter and exit my mind; that suddenly well up,
> crest, and just as rapidly recede, wash away—only to well up again.
> Elsewhere. The same. Only different.
> Numbers known and not known.
> Numbers that do and do not matter to me.
> Numbers that count.
> Num(b)erous questions that count.
>
> What is the date of my birth?
> How many generations of Couschi were then behind me?
> How old was I when taken away, separated forever?
> How many horrors did I witness before then?
> How many bloodied backs?
> How many searings of the flesh?
> How many dismembered bodies?
> How many frightful episodes beyond my recall?
> How many times did I lose sight of the sun?
> And choke on the smoke?
> How long did my parents miss me?
> How many days have I stood there, at the window,
>> inert as if a statue,
>> staring out at nothing but grayness,
>> disabled by these questions,
>> trying to remember,
>> to no avail?

How many times have I awoken with a jolt?
How many times have I found myself
   in total winter darkness
   with my hands hard-pressed to my ears?
Trying to shut out the screams?
My screams?

How many times have I fallen into doubt?
   About my acceptance?
   About what people really think of me?
   About my palpable invisibility
     and my impalpable visibilities?
   About who, what, and where I am?
How many times have friends and strangers alike—well-known
faces and faces out of nowhere—given me reason to buckle at my
mental knees, to trip over any hard-won confidence, to fall flat in
uncertainty?

How many times have I been reminded that my Difference is worn?
That it cannot be shorn?
That my skin cannot be silenced?
That my skin always speaks?
Announcing who I am?
What It is?
Given voice by way of Their preceding imaginings?

How many times have I swallowed my pride?
Ignored affronts?
And pretended?
Played the jester?
Monkeyed around?
Stuck on a smile?
Became what They saw in advance?
Felt more than a twinge in acting thusly for my enemies?

Numbers more certain:
   yesterday's coldest temperature,
   the hour last sounded by church bells,
   the current price of my favorite pipe tobacco,
   the sum of money I owe at the moment,
   the total physical area of my farm holdings,
   the net value of last year's crops,

the number of maid-servants currently and previously under
    my employ,
the number of books in my library,
the death dates of my wife Elisabeth, my foster mother
    Lovisa Ulrika, my playmate-brother Gustav III,
the amount of money Gustav promised when he offered to be
    Godfather to the child Elisabeth was carrying,
the date of her miscarriage,
the date of my marriage to Magdalena Eleonora,
the number of sleepless nights I have had this month,
the number of times I have fallen in love,
the number of days since I last made love,
the length of time I have felt God's True Love.

Numbers that I cannot remember.
Numbers that I cannot not remember.
    Ever.
Numbers that I have never known.
Numbers that are forgotten.
Numbers that I cannot forget.
    Ever.
Numbers that burn.
Memories etched.
    Ever.

Badin, sometime after 1799, in a melancholy state, an existential de-
pression, wistfully attempting to unreel his past, numbed by numbers,
contemplating a never-made notebook entry

Memory Etchings
Memory Diggings
Memories in Constellation

Memories are involuntarily summoned strips of montaged images.
Esther Leslie, characterizing Walter Benjamin's take on Proust's involuntary memory[1]

He who has once begun to open the fan of memory never comes to the end of its segments.

[Memory] is the medium of past experience, just as the earth is the medium in which dead cities lie buried. He who seeks to approach his own buried past must conduct himself like a man digging.
Walter Benjamin[2]

Futile Labor
Title of an allegorical painting by David Klöcker Ehrenstrahl dating from about 1692. Six plump, cherub-like, young white boys energetically but fruitlessly try to wash away the color of their equally plump but black companion who, according to the painter, was born in Stockholm.[3]

But why didn't the negro whiten when he resided at European courts?
Gunnar Broberg, characterizing a problem confronting some eighteenth-century subscribers to climatological determinism[4]

The negroes in the court of Adolph Fredrik here in Sweden had
to blacken themselves in order to retain their dignity.

*Jacob Fredrik Neikter, Sweden's most outspoken proponent of
climatological determinism, writing in 1797 of conditions at the
very same court at which Badin had arrived in 1760*[5]

———

[My master's] mate had a little daughter, aged about five or six
years. . . . I had often observed that when her mother washed
her face it looked very rosy; but when she washed mine it did
not look so: I therefore tried oftentimes myself if I could not by
washing make my face of the same colour as my little playmate,
Mary, but it was all in vain; and I then began to be mortified at
the difference in our complexions.

*Gustavus Vassa (Olaudah Equiano), remembering himself as a
twelve-year-old during his initial visit to England, in 1757, one
year before Badin arrived in Copenhagen*[6]

———

Because of my privileged position, my decades at the court, the
favors and protection extended to me first by Queen Lovisa Ulrika
and then King Gustav III, the incidents were perhaps not especially
great in number. But they left their marks. Their indelible traces.
Their deeply etched, unforgettable, irrepressible memories. Their
chilling thoughts readily reawakened, involuntarily, by the sight of
a site, the sound of a name, the scent of a body. They left their sticky
residue of insecurity and anxiety, of ambivalences and sensed contradictions. They weighed me down, a rock upon my spirits, when I
couldn't detour my thoughts elsewhere, or escape them with diver-
sions. They infused my soul with troubling doubts. As to the empti-
ness or genuineness of my acceptance. As to what and who I am.
And they filled me with variations of a single gnawing fear. That the
possibility of reoccurrence was lurking, waiting just around the corner. That I sometime, somewhere, any day, any place, was yet again
to face humiliation, abasement, verbal or physical abuse. Or more
indirect affronts, more subtle insults. Or even "mere" casual comments, thoughtless statements, or unfeeling remarks. That inad-
vertently revealed so much. And pained all the more . . . Behaviors
directed at me simply because of the color of my skin. Out of which

I could not extract myself. From which I could not become disassociated. However high I climbed. However much I devoured books and educated myself. However much I accomplished. However genuine my devotion to their Lutheran Church. However "truly" Swedish my actions, demeanor, or mode of expression . . . Over the years I have kept most of the consequent hurts and anxieties to myself. My fragile feelings, my deepest reactions, have been covered over. I have acted as if oblivious, unruffled. I have performed other wisely. So as not to give them any additional means. So as not to give them any satisfaction. And yet, fear of further injuries or not, as a true Christian I have learned to turn the other cheek. To forgive. And forgive and forgive. But try as I may, I can neither forgive without internal conflict[7] nor erase that ugly constellation of incidents from the night sky of my mind.

> *Badin, pensively recollecting in late middle age, in a previously unimagined document*

———

I am talking of millions of men who have been skillfully injected with fear, inferiority complexes, trepidation, servility, despair, abasement.

> *Aimé Césaire, as quoted by Frantz Fanon*[8]

"Mama, see the Negro! I'm frightened!" Frightened! Frightened. "Dirty nigger!" Or simply, "Look, a Negro!"

I came into the world imbued with the will to find meaning to things, my spirit filled with the desire to attain to the source of the world, and then I found that I was an object in the midst of other objects.

> *Frantz Fanon*[9] *re-cognizing his epidermalization, contemplating the circumstances whereby the skin of his body determines his (in)visibility, whereby he is "[f]actually cloaked in stereotypes, [tissue-thin] popular fictions and myths"*[10]

—

The sun stood low over [the waters of] Strömmen. Everything lay plunged in copper light and stillness. Somewhere a church bell rang. There weren't many people up and about, but the carpenters

and cobblestone layers stopped and dropped what they had in hand
when they saw me. Several of them were foreigners and one of them
shamelessly crossed himself. The sky was a red and wide-open,
endlessly stretching abyss.

I walked slowly, trying to assume a dignified gait, but however
I strained my trembling legs made me wobble slightly. Somebody
laughed briefly among the piles of lumber and cobblestones; I also
heard how somebody else hushed him. My first impulse was to run.

Badin, recalling one of his first excursions into the streets of Stockholm,
where he very likely—as subhuman Difference or black (D)evil incarnate—
almost always would have been gaped at with astonishment or fear;
stared at by even those who themselves were the frequent target of
staring—the beggars and ragged poor, the scabrous and undernour-
ished urchins, the crippled and invalid then so numerous in the city's
public spaces[11]

≠ ≠ ≠

Look now, then again.

As a Swedish-born blackhead[12] you reach a certain level in your
career and then it becomes difficult. There still doesn't go a
day without my feeling that people hate me for my skin color.
They stare at me everywhere. So I don't like taking the subway.
Speaking honestly, I don't like people so terribly much either.

"Dele" (Ayodele Shekoni), one of Sweden's pioneer rap artists, born
in 1966 (Swedish mother, African father), looking back in 2000[13]

≠ ≠ ≠

[One of the two] beat me in the head with a tiller in the reception
hall itself. Presumably he thought I was a purchased slave. [After
grabbing my arms they shouted:] "Get out! Get out!" . . . If my color
and my! [prejudged?] appearance in the ordinary world! gave these
two Neptune Order members the strange idea that they could beat
me in the head without self-reproach, so I ought to forgive them as
a true Christian.

Badin, in a letter to Simon Petter Bergman, the High Chancellor of the
Neptune Order. Dated "4 o'clock, Sunday morning, March 18–19, 1814,"[14]
it is the product of (yet another?) sleepless night, of a seemingly end-

*less night during which agitation and anxiety apparently (once again?)
pursued one another. A letter whose writing was made all the more
troublesome because its violent subject matter stirred difficult-to-access
memories, because it resonated with the stuff of his recurrent nightmares, with his dreamworld reliving/reworking of childhood traumas?
From which he consistently awoke with a jolt? Screaming? Unable to
return to sleep?*

By way of royal influence and court connections, Badin was able to become a part of the world of secret societies and orders so popular among
Stockholm's elites during the Gustavian era. He became an active and
reportedly enthusiastic participant in at least five major secret orders, including the Freemasons, which he joined as early as 1773, thereby sharing
membership, mystical rituals, a certain international consciousness, philanthropic projects, and festivities with the well-born, the well-monied, and the
otherwise well-positioned. He made donations to several of these fraterni-
ties, undertook much-appreciated initiatives, and rose through their various
ranks, achieving the second-highest rank in the Par Bricole order.[15] The
Freemasons—which included Gustav III, Princes Karl and Fredrik Adolph,
and the king's most powerful advisers among their number—became so central to his identity that he even incorporated their sign, a simple cross, into
his signature: Badin + Couschi. But whatever the satisfaction of recognition
and acceptance, there clearly was a ceiling to his achievements within those
organizations. And there must have been moments of order engagement—
certainly a few, perhaps numerous, or even countless—when he felt a twinge
of uneasiness, a shudder of discomfort, a rush of regret or revulsion, a surge
of anger or emotional upset. Most of which could not very well have lent
themselves to public expression, or even confidential recounting, without
further underlining his Difference, without further jeopardizing whatever
sense of security and belonging he possessed . . . For could he always have
escaped a feeling of annoyance or resentment if, regardless of his actual
mood, he was constantly required to don a smiley face, to assume the role of
a *badin*, to play the joker at Par Bricole meetings? For could he have avoided
coming to understand that at such gatherings—if not also at those of other
orders—he was principally welcome as a "merry and amusing Bacchanalian
decoration figure"?[16] For was it not so that he was humiliated in the worst
possible way, shown not a grain of respect even though well over sixty years
old, when physically assaulted and driven from the meeting premises of yet
another order he had recently joined? And was it not more than likely that
on other scattered occasions there were order "brothers" who expressed

their displeasure at his presence through a turn of the back, an avoidance of eye contact, a venomous comment slyly encased in sugar-coated words, or some other act of masked violence? Especially since, in his affronted account of the beating, Badin alludes to views held by the world at large?[17]

> *[King Gustav III]* heard my appeal *[for money]* with more calm than you would have done *[upon learning of]* an accident to a negro from the Cape of Good Hope.
>   *Johan Gabriel Oxenstierna—member of the aristocracy, poet, sometime chamberlain to Gustav III, close friend of the Munck-lampooner Carl August Ehrensvärd, and active Freemason—in a 1783 letter to a cousin, suggesting that nothing was more worthy of indifference than the misfortunes of a black man or woman*[18]

—

> Diligence and attentiveness, my dear Badin, and your fortune is made. Let me know everything that occurs at the Duke's order gatherings: everything, you understand, and promptly. Allow nothing to slip by your open eyes and ears. You value being promoted within the Freemasons, I know that, and I promise you all the ranks which depend upon my vote.
>   *Gustav III, in 1785, instructing Badin to report anything overheard or seen at order meetings regarding his brother's involvement with his opponents*[19]

In the restricted and chummy confines of the Freemason Lodge and other order meeting places, there were all manner of conversations that Badin could have accidentally overheard or bumped into, have stood at the edge of, or become actively engaged in—conversations now and then addressing matters that jolted his sense of self, that undermined any momentary sense of belonging, that left him feeling that others were totally impervious or insensitive to his presence. And that could have scarred his memory. Badly.

> The West Indian Company *[Västindiska Kompaniet]* is granted the freedom to conduct slave trading on the coast of Angola and Africa, where it is allowed, and . . . the Company may charter ships to whatever part of the world the Company finds advantageous.
>   *King Gustav III in a letter of patent issued October 31, 1786*[20]

The free importation and trading of black slaves, or so-called new negroes, from Africa is granted to all nations without payment of any fee upon unloading.

Stipulation contained in a new set of laws pertaining to Saint Barthélemy, issued by King Gustav III, March 12, 1790, as part of an effort to make the small colonized island a slave-trading center for the entire Caribbean[21]

[Carl] Arfwedsson, whom I occasionally ran into at order gatherings, was a trusted member of the West Indian Company's board of directors, well on in years, and fairly talkative late in the evening. I learned from him one evening that the price for a fully grown negro male on Saint Barthélemy was about 400 piastres, corresponding to a somewhat lesser sum in riksdaler, all according to the monthly reports sent by Messrs. Röhl and Hansen via the assuredly sporadic shipping departures available to them. And that the price was rising all the time as a consequence of the French Mess.

The sum struck me dumb with amazement. Although women and children were available for more modest sums. As he was sometimes amused by my interest in economic questions, he now emphasized that he personally didn't believe that this market had a bright future, warning me by way of advice to place my money savings elsewhere.

Badin, once again, in fictional (f)act, recalling a conversation irremovably deposited in his memory bank[22]

Might not some—or even most—of the conversations that Badin experienced as personally disruptive have involved those order-member merchants, high-level bureaucrats, and Royal Court figures—including Gustav III—who were directly or indirectly associated with the slave trade and plantations of Saint Barthélemy, the Swedish Caribbean colony acquired from France in 1784?[23] Might not Badin have become more than a little unsettled upon verbally discovering that Saint Barthélemy was an island of such little consequence (being less than twenty-five square kilometers, or about nine square miles, in area), an island of such uninspiring physical attributes (much of its surface being covered with either bare volcanic rock or thicket and thistle vegetation), an island of such limited economic potential (until then producing little more than small quantities of cotton and salt), that its most promising source of revenue was the slave trade?[24] Especially when word regarding a report made to the King's advisory council circulated shortly after acquisition, a report underlining the difficulties the French were having in supplying their West Indian colonies with a sufficient number of slaves, a report suggesting that a free port be established to function primarily as a reshipping point in the slave trade?[25] Might not Badin have felt as if the ground was (once again) being cut from beneath his feet upon being told that it was Gustav III—so long personally entwined with him—who was taking the initiative in establishing the West Indian Company, who was encouraging merchants and others known to Badin to purchase shares in that joint stock company? Might not that feeling have become intensified when there was a buzz created by the king's letter of patent, when it became no secret that slave trading would be central to the company's operations, when it slipped out that "there was no trace of any opposition toward that branch of commerce" among the King's councillors,[26] when it became evident that neither the king nor some of the men Badin occasionally encountered saw anything wrong in making a profit from selling those of his own like into miserable bondage?[27] (Might not Badin have had these revelations somewhere in mind, and not merely Gustav III's well-known physiognomic imbalance, his partially pushed-in forehead, when he noted the following almost two decades later? His head was remarkable. For anyone who saw him can say that mythology is true in its description of Janus as having had two faces.)[28] What further disillusionments might have sunk into memory when the same letter of patent revealed that Gustav III would receive 25 percent of all revenues despite owning but 10 percent of all shares? And might not Badin actually have been stunned, actually have been "struck dumb with amazement," if not completely nauseated, as a consequence of learning the high price demanded for male slaves on Saint Barthélemy, as a consequence of having it once more underlined that he might be regarded as someTHING rather than someONE, as a consequence of having it reaffirmed that he belonged to a commodified race, to an objectified population?

> The owner may place his slave in chains and whip the slave with
> a switch or rope; however without going to extreme; no punish-
> ment may exceed 29 lashes. It is forbidden to disfigure any of the
> slave's body parts or to torture the slave; in those cases where the
> slave deserves a stricter penalty than the whip, the owner shall
> instead turn over the slave to the authorities for treatment.
> *Paragraph from the slave law instituted June 30, 1787, by Per*
> *Herman Rosenstein, Governor of Saint Barthélemy*[29]

> Almost every owner had his own law for punishing Negroes.
> He has the right to handle his slaves according to his own fancy
> and conscience. It often happens that a slave runs away after

having been starved and all too harshly driven to work, after often or daily being beaten; if he can catch him, his owner then has the freedom to punish him as he fancies. In such instances the owner hangs a large, heavy chain on the slave that is locked firmly around the neck with a heavy padlock, after which he has him either held by one or more—or maybe bound to a wall or pole—and stripped of his clothes. Then he beats him on his bare body with a cane of twined leather as long as his energy permits or until his anger has passed.

Statement suggesting that Rosenstein's twenty-nine-lash limit was not always heeded—made by Bengt Anders Euphrasén, botanist, in a book released in 1795, after years of research on Saint Barthélemy[30]

[T]he negro is characterized by stupidity and any attempt to civilize this subhuman would be in conflict with Nature itself.

Observation made in 1819—three years before Badin's death—by Olof Erik Bergius, back in Sweden after serving in a judicial capacity on Saint Barthélemy[31]

While freely intermingling with the most powerful, while chatting in the most comfortable of settings, might not Badin have felt suddenly distraught and out of place upon learning that laws implemented by the royal governor of Saint Barthélemy were precise in their prescription of whippings, upon learning that laws implemented in the interests of the West Indian Company strictly forbade slaves to assemble either in public spaces or out-of-the-way locations? Might not Badin have become immediately embittered and disgusted in 1792, some months after the assassination of Gustav III, when gossip informed him that two representatives of the West Indian Company were continuing to import slaves with the sometime help of the chairman of the board of directors, despite a regency decision that it was now inappropriate for the company to conduct any slave business on its own?[32] Especially since there was now much talk of the English Parliament's efforts to abolish the slave trade? Might not Badin have been given an(other) uncomfortable start if Euphrasén's 1795 book was discussed, if the actual treatment of runaways became known to him, if he learned in detail of the lashings received by those passed on to the "authorities," of the "pistol-shot" sound given off by each snapping of the lengthy whipcord, of "the large pieces of skin and flesh that often flew from the body"?[33] (Might not a recollection of this and other discussions have mingled with his whirling emotions when, in the wee hours of an 1814 Sunday morning, he penned a protest of his beating to the high chancellor of the Neptune Order, when he strongly objected to being treated as if "a purchased slave"?) Might not Badin, in the course of order-locale social-izing, occasionally have entered into discussions about the contents of *The Report of Saint Bartholomew*—a Saint Barthélemy newspaper published 368 times between 1804 and 1819—and thereby have been painfully discomforted by various reports? By word that the physical maltreatment and torturing of blacks, including freed slaves, had reached "epidemic" proportions in the spring of 1804? By cold-prose, matter-of-fact announce-ments of shipping arrivals and their "cargo" content, of the profit motive trumping all else: the American schooner *Experiment*, with 67 slaves, after eighteen days travel from Senegal; the English ship *Kitty's Amelia*, with 210 "New Negroes," after forty-two days from Angola; the Swedish schooner *Onlyfer*, with 101 "New Negroes"; the Swedish brig *Elisabeth*, with 176 slaves, after sixty-three days from Africa; the Danish ship *Samuel*, with 200 slaves, after twenty-three days from Pongo?[34] By equally dryly writ-ten auction descriptions, such as that for one held during January 1819 in the cellar of "The Governement House," where the items for sale included "port from Madeira, wine from Malaga, champagne, old rum," and seven slaves, among them "Diannah, 2 months old?"[35] Might not Badin's sense of self have been more than a little thrown off course by any news he received of the constant expansion of Saint Barthélemy's slave population until at least 1812, of the constant increase in the number of fellow African descen-dents subject—under Swedish law—to brutal everyday treatment?[36] Might not he have been similarly buffeted by news telling of Sweden's behavior at the Congress of Vienna, of a declaration signed there favoring the abolition of the slave trade—at the very same time that slave-trafficking vessels were allowed to continue unloading at Saint Barthélemy without impediment? And might not that 1815 document signing have proved particularly up-setting, coming, as it did, in the aftermath of his Neptune Order thrash-ing?[37] Might not Badin, despite the negative wisdom accumulated from previous episodes, have drooped with dismay during 1819 upon hearing of (or directly reading) the rant of Olof Erik Bergius, upon hearing a royal appointee dismiss all Afro-Caribbeans as stupid, subhuman, and beyond civilization, upon hearing that he further characterized them as slothful, indolent, incapable of distinguishing right from wrong, exceptionally prone to lying, and unable to care for themselves? And, most mind shaking of all: thankful to be enslaved?[38] . . . Whatever his actual response in any of these situations—other than the extreme beating instance—might not Badin have felt compelled to hide his reactions, to disguise his feelings, to mask himself in actually responding? And in that masking have confirmed his perpetual (re)displacement? The ever-adrift quality of his identity? His unceasing travels to and from the State of Estrangement?

> It is forbidden for a negro to attempt to hide his identity by disguising himself. A negro or slave encountered on the street wearing a mask or otherwise disguised will be sentenced to three punishments: he shall be whipped; he shall be branded with a red-hot iron; he shall have an iron collar placed on him.
>
> *A paraphrasing of one of the paragraphs contained in Governor Rosenstein's 1787 slave law*[39]

———

On the 26th of June, at 5:45 in the afternoon, I arrived with Lieutenant Gabriel L'Esstrad, and Skipper . . . . . . as well as my wife and in-law at an inn known as the Drottningholm Palace Inn. I entered the room opposite the building's entrance. In that room was a maidservant whose attire was as follows: uncovered hair with a pigtail held up by a comb; black shoes; white stockings and a white dress with pinned up train; the apron, which had a slight tear, is dark, lemon yellow—in the evening this color is as described, but during the day it is brown with yellow leaves. This maidservant poured a beer glass into the bottle out of which it had been formerly served. At the very moment I became aware of this I said: "Don't give me any of that drink, because I know that it is customarily done in some places." She answered that she didn't do anything like that. "I well believe that," was my reply, "but I only request that I don't get any of it." Whereupon she immediately became abusive and gave me one rude and disrespectful word after the other. I beseeched her to stop being abusive. She said that not even her Mistress was capable of making her become polite toward someone like me.

Badin, in a notebook entry[40]

About to be offered someone else's bespittled beer. About to be served swill in the presence of men of rank and close family members. And then served up a tongue-lashing, whipped with wrath-filled words of insult. Completely embarrassed. Put to total shame. Verbally diminished and degraded. Not by somebody from the court. But by a barmaid! . . . How could any(Otherized)body, any "black(head)" Other, in Stockholm past or present, entirely forget such an incident, fully repress it beyond recall? When other bygone and future occurrences—even if infrequent—were apt to remind, to reinforce by way of association, to intensify the hurt? How deeply etched upon Badin's memory, how lastingly branded into the networks of his brain, were the content and tone of each and every slur spewed at him, if he registered every detail of the barmaid's attire and hair arrangement, if he vividly remembered every color nuance and imperfection of her garments? And the exact hour and minute at which it all transpired? To what extent did he again feel himself objectified, desubjectified, made inconsequential and invisible, by the dirty(-word) trick, the sl(e)ight-of-mouth trick, of transforming him from the Particular to the Universal—at once depriving him of his discreteness, his Badinness, his Couschiness, and violently reducing him to blackness, to a negatively charged always-and-everywhere-the-sameness? And in the act of jotting down the account in his notebook, did the tears well up at the thought of previous searing affronts? At the mental resurfacing of all that had been heard from his (Copenhagen and) Stockholm childhood onward? At the recalling of all those cut-to-the-bone outbursts: "You cheeky black boy." "You uncivilized thing." "You wild boy." "You baboon."?

≠ ≠ ≠

Bar(ring) abuses, present tense.

> They always have a reason. That I don't have a tie, that I'm wearing jeans, that I'm not a regular customer, that I don't have a membership card. Thirty seconds later they let in someone who doesn't have a membership card, a white guest.
>> *Statement made in 1996 by Gora Kebe, a migrant to Sweden from Senegal, a law student and newspaper deliverer who, like countless other Africans and "blackheads," had routinely been turned away from many restaurants, bars, and nightclubs in Stockholm, including some of the most well known*[41]

> It's always the same thing. You go out in high spirits and are going to party with a gang of friends. And then you get a door guard's hand in your face. You become so hopeless. You can't do anything. If you come with a Swedish friend there's no problem; but if you come with a gang of dark-skinned gals it's a lost cause. Many places in Stockholm play black music but don't allow blacks to enter.
>> *Feven, a highly successful twenty-six-year-old female rap singer who came to Sweden from Eritrea as a young war refugee*[42]

Information from the Discrimination Bureau indicates, among other things, that the number of complaints against Stockholm bars, nightclubs, and restaurants for unlawful discrimination is increasing, but up to now no case has led to formal legal action.

Discrimination at Stockholm's bars, nightclubs, and restaurants, above all against Africans, is a great problem that isn't taken seriously by the district attorney and police *[according to a report issued by the Swedish UN-Association (Svenska FN-förbundet)]*.

Dagens Nyheter, August 9, 2000

≠ ≠ ≠

The barrage of insults she—the barmaid—mercilessly unleashed. Each and every one of them stinging like a whiplash. Ripping at the flesh of my feelings, tearing at the nerve endings of my self-respect, leaving a bloody stripe upon my soul. Humiliating me like that. So publicly. In front of them . . . Days have passed since the incident. And the making of my notebook entry. That unsuccessful effort to eject it, to tear it out of myself, by removing it to paper. A totally fruitless enterprise! For still the images of that late afternoon, every visual detail, continue to invade my mind. To torment and dizzy. While the screeched words relentlessly plague my ears . . . That I was, and remain, so torn up by such a tirade. By that stringing together of conventional epithets and her own venomous inventions. Delivered so voluminously, so loudly, so mercilessly. So enormously disturbed was I, am I. That I could not record a single one of her vicious insults. Not even the mildest of them. The one about my other inescapable body marker. Atop my head. The hair half-hidden in Lundberg's portrait. "You woolly-headed monkey. You worthless grunting shit-heap. I'd rather serve proper drink to a dog." . . . A throwback to my first night in Stockholm. Although my Danish-accustomed ears were not yet really attuned to Swedish, the servant's wisecrack about my hair did not escape comprehension. Something about its resemblance to that of his master's poodle. Whose doghouse and revolting food scraps I was forced to share. A sleepless shivering night spent on damp ground beside a foul-breathed bitch. There, too, reduced to an animal. What an entrance! What a welcome!

Dare I unburden myself to Magdalena? So as to relieve the pressure of my sadness, the burden of accumulated memories that weighs me down after every disturbing incident. And if I do, will she thoughtlessly betray my confidence? Act the tattletale while off guard? In one of her garrulous moments, light-headed with alcohol, bubbling back and forth with a friend, will she let slip something that was meant only for her ears? Carelessly make an "amusing" story of my night in the doghouse? Or any of my other demeaning misfortunes? And once such a tale is retold, and retold, passed on repeatedly as just another piece of entertaining gossip, will it become all the worse? Will it become distorted and embellished? As all gossip inevitably becomes? Will I consequently become subject to further ridicule? Yet again made the target, verbally tarred, publicly embarrassed, grossly debased? Once again treated in accord with the already said and already known? Once again treated as if actually possessing the animal qualities they see in me in advance? And in so doing confirm the accuracy of their sight?

Here, too, best to remain silent? To keep it all invisible? Not to let Magdalena see? Despite her love?

Badin, brooding over his notebook omissions and the trials of not forgetting

And during the act of writing about the barmaid's verbal eruption, and the torture-filled days that followed, were there not moments when the years-ago images that raced to mind involved incidents where psychologically wounding words had been wed with physically wounding blows?

"Her Majesty wishes you to return to the Royal Palace," I said in low voice without looking at him.

I wasn't at all prepared. Count Brahe's right hand shot out and seized one of my coat lapels; then he slowly pulled me up to him. I didn't physically tense up in resistance, but tried to turn away from his alcohol-drenched breath. He noticed my displeasure and laughed. "Shut up, black messenger. The Queen's *monkey* doesn't tell an Honorable what to do." Then he struck me right across the bridge of my nose with his free, gloved right hand and dropped me to the floor.

I remained where he had placed me and observed one of his boots, where some horseshit had become wedged between the sole and the upper leather. My nose was running blood and the salt taste thickened in my throat.

Badin remembering the unwanted consequences of an unwanted message[43]

[Only after he had boldly directed his verbal badinages toward the queen herself] did Lovisa Ulrika find . . . the time ripe to punish him for his mischief. She consequently gave orders that the blackamoor should be held to respectable behavior and be corporally chastised when he forgot himself. Court attendants, long offended and made to suffer by the black tormentor, did not have to be told twice. They obeyed the orders *con amore,* far exceeding what the Queen had reckoned and wished. Badin was in his twentieth year when he was physically abused and became acquainted with the cane in a ruthless manner. The Queen's veto finally saved him from the all too long delayed method of upbringing.

    M. J. Crusenstolpe, in his biographical sketch of Badin[44]

He himself told of his first birching. He had once been present when a variety of fruits were stowed away in one of the palace cellars. He arranged things so that a small cask containing extraordinarily delicious apples was placed directly in front of an opening, through which he later cleverly could pull the enticing fruit with the help of a pole that had a nail sticking out of it. But the design was discovered, the inventor was caught in the act and punished on command of the queen *[Lovisa Ulrika]* by her valet, Ernst.

    Wendela Hebbe in another one of her long-after-the-event third-hand retellings.[45] *(In one of Hebbe's* True Stories for Young People, *"The Monkey," Luli, "a real prankster," reverses Badin's purported trickery by cleverly preventing an eagle from stealing any more food from her master.)*[46]

Prince Gustav once boxed his ear in one of the palace passages. Badin, not daring to pay the crown prince back with the same coin, turned the other ear toward him and requested da capo, since he didn't want to have "crooked vision."

    Wendela Hebbe, again recounting a (f)act[47]

———

The Negro and the higher apes were initially studied and written about at approximately the same time and thereby were joined in the European consciousness. The alleged size of the Negroes' sex organs pointed to their being especially sexually inclined; the Negress went more or less totally naked under the hot sun

and induced all kinds of lustfulness, even between the species.
It is always the male ape who *[crosses species lines and]* violates
a woman—a foreshadowing parallel to the Negro's desire for
white women. In this manner the ape was anthropomorphized
at the same time that the Negro was animalized.

> *Gunnar Broberg, contextualizing Linnaeus's writings on* Homo sa-
> piens *and* Homo nocturnes.[48] *(Figure 20 of the first English edition
> of* Systema naturae *[A Genuine and Universal Natural History by
> the Late Sir Charles Linnaeus, 1795] was captioned "The Orang-
> Outang carrying off a negro girl." It showed a highly anthropomo-
> phized ape ascending a tree with a bare-breasted young African.
> Eighteenth-century scientists, "transforming these [travel-writing]
> fables into truths," not infrequently suggested that violent imposi-
> tion was unnecessary, as "the negresses gladly went along of their
> own free will.")*[49]

"The most frightful conclusions could be drawn from this *[sup-
posed fertilization of a hen by a rabbit]*; as far as mankind is
concerned one would have reason to think that the Moors [i.e.,
the Negroes] had a rather strange origin—something that I for
my part, however, am unwilling to ascribe to them." . . .

Linnaeus's choice of the Negro to illustrate how frightful the
conclusion might be was in itself frightening. That he chose the
Negro from all the peoples of the globe revealed how widespread
the association of the Negro with the ape had become.

> *Winthrop D. Jordan, quoting from* Metamorphosis Plantarum
> *(1755)*[50]

—

"ministers of merriment (or amusement)"
("rolighetsministrar")

> *Term used at the Swedish court in the 1750s, shortly before Badin's
> arrival, in reference to pet monkeys kept there as court jesters, as
> aping creatures capable of serving both as "funny fellows" and "truth
> sayers." At least up until the time she took Badin under her wing,
> if not also thereafter, Queen Lovisa Ulrika showed considerable
> concern for these creatures, worrying about them when they coughed
> and sniffled, seeking out expert advice as to how to best dress and
> otherwise shield them during the cold of winter.*[51] *Badin, who for
> some time was encouraged to perform his badinages and bodily clown
> at will, in effect took over the role of* rolighetsministrar *number one.*

Badin. Undated ink sketch by Carl August Ehrensvärd. Badin, the "Minister of Merriment," as seen by the very same Ehrensvärd who had cartooned the "happy union" of Gustav III and Queen Sofia Magdalena. Here the lines drawn by Ehrensvärd's hand fall in line with the already "known," (re)producing an already emerged Universal and (re)enforcing it by way of the Particular. For here the lips, through which Badin's gibes, jests, and saucy remarks would have passed, are so enormously enlarged and grotesquely protruding from his face that the upper slope of his profile resembles that of a baboon. This simian similarity is underscored by the treatment of Badin's nose, which is so flattened, so deprived of substance, as to leave it with little more than a pair of nostrils. . . . How deeply devastated was Badin if he ever saw this vicious representation in which mandrill and man are melted into one? Or if he ever heard this visual (re)marking of his subhuman Difference commented upon with chuckling amusement by Ehrensvärd's Freemason friends? Or by any-body else? Likely knowing it counterproductive to openly react, likely knowing it necessary to feign indifference, likely wishing to avoid further confirmation of his nonbelonging belonging, how hard did he try to forget any such incident? Only to have the memory intensified? More deeply etched? Placed into con-stellation with other unerasable injuries?

[He] likened [Hottentots and south African Bushmen] to apes, crazy about liquor and tobacco, stinking and filthy, lazy, stupid, and hardly above the most brutish animals.

Summary of observations made by Carl Peter Thunberg, renowned student of Linnaeus, in a four-volume travel account published between 1788 and 1793—a work that Badin very well might have read or at least entered into discussion about. [52] Badin is likely to have encountered other such "scientific" views as a result of the travels, correspondence, and reading habits of academics and intellectuals associated with the Royal Court; for in general, "[Enlightenment] European naturalists tended to describe apes more sympathetically than they did Africans, highlighting the human character of apes while emphasizing the purported simian qualities of Africans."[53]

[In 1832, ten year's after Badin's death, Sweden's Linnaean Society] recommended "Satyr-Apes" as factory workers and servants to "fetch water, rotate steak spits, pound spices."
Lisbet Koerner[54]

Once again:

[The eighteenth-century writings of] Buffon, the French naturalist, credited the black with a lascivious, apelike sexual appetite, introducing a commonplace of early travel literature into a pseudo-scientific context.[55]

—

"Historically so," said Crusenstolpe. Badin was to his face called a baboon, was termed an ape, was reduced to the subhuman. Presumably repeatedly. For Crusenstolpe did not pluck the devastatingly insulting term out of the ether, as it was already a not uncommon usage at the time of his birth (1795). Many at the court may have been prone to cast the aspersion because of linkages long discursively taken for granted via the writings of Buffon and various travel authors. Whether or not Badin was frequently showered with harshly spoken simian signifiers, it is documented that on at least one occasion he was lowered to the level of the animal, being forced to play the role of a monkey in a Stockholm Royal Palace production of Le Carnaval de Venise in 1777.[56]

Badin *[was]* half-naked, wearing a red cloth about his hip tied
in a diaper knot. . . . Badin scampered and climbed about the
bridge railing, speaking ape-French.

Carl Michael Bellman, the famed poet and balladeer—he who in
fictionalized fact was accused of "babbling thick-lipped like a whole
cargo of negro slaves"—describing Badin's Carnaval de Venise *per-*
formance in his fictional autobiography (Bellman [f]actually played
opposite Badin in the Venice divertissement) [57]

If the angrily or mockingly uttered "baboon" was a walloping blow to one's
sense of self, if recurrent exposure to that and related expressions ham-
mered at one's self-respect, what lasting pain may have been visited upon
Badin when he was forced virtually to strip down, to don an abbreviated
monkey suit, to cavort on all fours, to chatter more or less incomprehensi-
bly? Was it all the more anguishing because before a large audience who,
he likely knew, could view his performance, his embodied representation,
as—in (f)act—a confirmation of the ape-like character of blacks, of their
natural aptitude for animal-like behavior, of their insatiable ape-like sexual
appetite? And if, as usually was the case, the theatrical role had been assigned to him by the king, by his childhood companion Gustav, how was
the resulting agony compounded? To what extent did the latter combination of circumstances intensify the literal and figurative assaults on his body
that variously came with each recollection of his lowering—the cold shiv-
ers, the sweaty palms, the burning ears, the nausea, the metaphoric bite?
Was Badin's ordeal of being publicly demeaned, of being made a monkey of,
any less forgettable than the experience of contemporary Swedish residents
of African or other non-European background who have had "MONKEY"
yelled at them in public spaces, who years after—with worn or pained
expression—cannot refrain from recounting in detail, who cannot see the
incident as anything but emblematic of their racialization, of their being
repeatedly subjected to discrimination and exclusion?[58]

≠ ≠ ≠

Monkey business, present tense.

One June evening *[2000]* a dozen well-educated youths are eat-
ing dinner in an apartment in Östermalm, Stockholm *[the city's*
most exclusive residential area]. One of them is a black girl who
has accompanied a friend to the party and doesn't know so many

of the others. But she is enjoying the company, Lauryn Hill is being played on the stereo, and the opening sangria drink is perfect. When the appetizer is served she discovers that she has no cutlery. She smiles politely at the host and asks him if he can get another setting and is answered: "Is it really needed? Monkeys don't eat with a knife and fork."

Fredrik Strage[59]

There's a Ghost in the House, a Ghost in the House
(Det spökar, det spökar)

> *Title of a film "comedy" made in 1943 and reshown on Swedish television on June 20, 2000. A number of animals, including a gorilla, escape from a traveling circus, some of them making their way to a large country house. Also making his way there in pursuit is a black circus hand (played by a Swede in blackface). His behavior is simple-minded, if not "primitive," and his gait and gestures are very much like those of the gorilla, who instills particular fear in the women of the house.*[60]

How do you tell an ape from a black? If you offer a banana, the ape takes it with his foot.

> *"Joke" told to a journalist by Ulf Björkman, prominent Conservative Party politician—caught by a hidden camera, the telling was shown in Sweden on a nationally broadcast program, September 10, 2002*[61]

≠ ≠ ≠

Badin was reportedly an enthusiast of the theater and appeared in several other plays and entertainments in addition to *Le Carnaval de Venise*. Although it is not possible to identify very many of his other (assigned?) roles, there were certainly some among them that were apt to precipitate associations with his sexuality or supposedly animal-like wildness. . . . In December 1770 he performed at the Royal Palace in a French troupe's production of *Arlequin Sauvage*—a work whose very title could be heard as a description of Badin himself, the court's full-time "savage" jester, the court's principal manufacturer of wild badinage. Was it this congruence that spurred one of Badin's sometime detractors to (facetiously) characterize his performance as "well carried out"?[62] . . . On another occasion, in April 1773, Badin was decked out as an "Amour," a cupid, a child(of nature)ish promoter of love, in order to recite a poem for Gustav III. Standing there holding a torch as well as a bow, what impression was he (intentionally?)

meant to create as he delivered his lines with "considerable quickness/smartness/wittiness"?[63] Whatever the director of this little divertissement had in mind, did not already-held images allow some of those present to more or less automatically see this unconventional cupid as a stimulator of enflamed love? As an agent of hot passion? As someone—like the young black servant in Hogarth's engraving—standing at the ready to heat up the situation? Did not the torch intensify what was already a sexualized scene? And did not Badin perhaps sense that full well? And in the aftermath of his monkey role four years later, did he not eventually also look back on this incident with resentment? And pained uneasiness?[64]

—

The black man has two dimensions. One with his fellows, the other with the white man. A Negro behaves differently with a white man and with another Negro. That this self-division is a direct result of colonialist subjugation is beyond question . . . No one would dream of doubting that its major artery is fed from the heart of those various theories that have tried to prove that the Negro is a stage in the slow evolution of monkey into man. . . .

Out of the blackest part of my soul, across the zebra striping of my mind, surges this desire to be suddenly white.

I wish to be acknowledged not as black but as white.

Now . . . who but a white woman can do this for me? By loving me she proves that I am worthy of white love. I am loved like a white man. I am loved like a white man.

I am a white man.

Her love takes me onto the noble road that leads to total realization.

Frantz Fanon[65]

—

[A]nd with her *[Princess Sophia Albertina]* had a child whose descendents live in Uppsala under the name Svartsberg.

Yet again, the anonymous handwritten comment appearing in the copy of Forsstrand's 1911 essay on Badin held at Sweden's National Portrait Gallery

—

The *[European]* white imagination is sure something when it comes to blacks.

> *Josephine Baker, in Paris, at a time (1920s) when she was much hyped for her "animal" sexuality and when her dance movements were described as "apelike"*[66]

———

"How would you like to be able hereafter to title yourself Royal Assessor?"

I thought it all over. Then answered: "Have you ever seen a black assessor?"

> *Badin, recalling a momentous exchange with Gustav III on July 17, 1782, the day after the death of Queen Mother Lovisa Ulrika, his long-time protector[67]—a discussion that began with the King confronting Badin with evidence that he had helped burn politically sensitive documents held by the queen mother and that ended, after reconciliation and childhood reminiscences, with Badin being awarded three separate farmsteads[68]*

Gustav III (according to another source, Lovisa Ulrika) granted him two farmsteads at Svartsjö plus the title Royal Assessor. Nevertheless Badin didn't wish to bear this title, and instead answered all those who applied it to him: "Have you ever seen a black assessor?"

> *From a 1904 "factual" portrait of Badin*[69]

Badin was given the title assessor. "I don't want to be anything, I want to be *[left?]* free" he replied when anyone spoke about appointing him to a position in government service.

> *Wendela Hebbe's passed-on version of the "facts"*[70]

Knowing all too well of his "appearance in the ordinary world," of the mental associations apt to be elicited by his mere presence, of the a = b taken-for-granteds apt to be conjured up by the mere sight of his body, would Badin actually have taken the title upon himself? Would he thereby actually have subjected himself not only to behind-the-back ridicule, but to the possibility of right-in-his-face mockery or declarations of denigrating disbelief? Remembering all too well scattered incidents precipitated by nothing more than his blackness, would he have accepted all the risks of derision and worse that came with taking on the title, with thereby suggesting either that he periodically sat as a judge's adviser at Court of Appeals proceedings, or that he was a royal official trained in the law?[71] Even if the position was well paid and demanded only occasional commitments of time, what was to be gained if more than a few of those who allowed "assessor" to roll off their tongues would be hearing something else with their eyes when addressing Badin? If, according to his memory-based understandings, it was widespread common sense that b[lack man] = a[pe-like], was not Badin making a reasonable assessment when he concluded that a[ssessor] ≠ b[lack man], when he concluded that someTHING else would meet the eye? If he ever actually posed the attributed question—"Have you ever seen a black assessor?"—would he not in effect have been attempting to reclaim his visibility, in effect have been attempting to counter a socially constructed field of vision, to undermine its ocular (p)recognitions, by speaking the unspeakable, by saying what They actually thought but wished to keep unsaid within his earshot? Would he not in effect have been attempting to short-circuit the application of Swedish proverbs that resonated with that field of vision?

> A monkey is a monkey, you see,
> whatever he tries to be.
>   *Rhyming proverb in use at the end of the eighteenth century*[72]

> The higher a monkey climbs, the more his backside is exposed.
>   *Proverb—first-known usage 1734—meant to apply "when an*
>   *unworthy person obtains a high office"*[73]

That Badin was in fact ambivalent toward his honorary title, and reluctant to employ it, is at least indirectly suggested by parish records from that area in Uppland where his farmsteads were located. There, in four different entries from the 1790s indicating temporary residential presence, he is successively referred to as "assessor Baden," "The Negro [or Black] Baddin," and "Mister Badin." While the latter two terms may well have been ascribed to Badin by the local clergyman, it is unlikely that the first could have been recorded without Badin himself volunteering the information when registering himself as required. Whatever the case, this shifting terminology once again testifies to the modern-like quality of Badin's identity(-conflicts).[74]

≠ ≠ ≠

Help (not) wanted, present tense.

I have had difficulty sleeping at night, feel stressed and have had
pains in my heart.
> *Nabil Haddad, Iraqi mechanical engineer with a Ph.D. from a
> Moscow engineering school and additional training at Sweden's
> Royal Institute of Technology, resident of one of Stockholm's seg-
> regated suburbs, speaking in April 2001, after yet another round of
> fruitless job seeking (sixty applications) and having been informed
> by local welfare authorities that he will no longer be eligible for sup-
> port unless he accepts the employment they are offering him, unless
> he accepts working as a sandwichman, or walking billboard[75]—
> unless, in effect, he completely sacrifices his dignity, allows himself
> to be reduced to a (worthless) dehumanized thing and a sign of the
> times, permits himself to become an object of public humiliation
> and ridicule, degrades himself to an in-sign(ificant) peddler of com-
> modities and mass culture rather than remaining a peddler of skilled
> knowledge,[76] and thereby acknowledges that as a socially con-
> structed Muslim Other he certainly does not qualify to bear the title
> mechanical engineer, but is most suited to bear advertisements*

It is the policy of the state-operated employment agency (Arbets-
förmedlingen) to refer immigrants to typical immigrant jobs.
> *Statement made by an employment agency bureaucrat, 2001,[77] at
> a time when labor-market shortages were leading Swedish high-
> technology corporations to seek engineers from other European
> Union countries despite the presence of numerous engineers of
> non-European and Muslim background who were either unem-
> ployed or holding low-skill jobs; at a time when the public health
> care sector was attempting to cope with a shortage of physicians by
> recruiting in Germany and other European countries where Swedish
> is not spoken, despite the presence of roughly two hundred Swedish-
> speaking doctors of non-European or Muslim background who
> were currently without work; at a time when the racially saturated
> fields of vision produced by discourses of cultural racism made it
> extremely difficult for highly qualified individuals of non-European
> or Muslim background to assume the title of engineer or doctor[78]*

Foreigners get double trouble.
For example, you apply for a job and bump into racist pigs.
> *Feven, rapping, making playful repartee, making political badinage[79]*

≠ ≠ ≠

THE NEGRO: You are here then, white wild beast! . . .
And we, the children of nature and freedom . . . I have
lived among you, I know your manners and customs;
but I loathe Europeans, in a word: you want to buy
Negroes—was it not for transporting them to America?
To force them into most horrid slavery? To make them
perpetual sacrifices for your European cruelty? To
handle them badly? To punish them without reason?
And to roast them over a low fire of unbelievable labor,
with the sole intention of providing your luxury? You
see perfectly well that I am lowering myself by talking
to you. You ought to admit these truths.

CAPTAIN: I confess it, but I haven't introduced these practices; since America was discovered all European states
have purchased Negroes to use them for cultivating
indigo and sugarcane, which had become indispensable
to them. . . .

THE NEGRO: . . . Why didn't you make a compact with
us instead of forcing nature to propagate plants in
America that grow along Senegal's shores? Why didn't
you say to us in a kindly and friendly manner: "Raise
these plants that thrive in your country, allow us to
erect mills in those places where your hospitality has
permitted us to stay, and we shall in return give you
products which our country produces"? . . . Then we
would have believed that you were humans like us, and
the blacks and whites would have made the world a
family. I repeat that color makes no difference if you
are human. But you and your like only have a human
appearance.

Excerpts from a fictional conversation between an African and a
shipwrecked captain, published in 1783 in a Stockholm newspaper
by an anonymous author, almost certainly a Swedenborgian[80]

The largest human societies may be placed into two groups,
civilized and uncivilized, and the former's obligations toward the
latter bear exactly the same relationship as the duties of parents
toward their children.

. . . the enlightened and civilized peoples ought for their own
good to unanimously work for the salvation of the wild and
uncivilized nations.

Let us then build settlements along the African coast, settlements with no other purpose than that of summoning these peoples to the enjoyment of those riches that cultivation of their own native soil shall create, and then to participation in the benefits of civilized nations. Two objectives which the Negroes are certainly able to cooperate toward gladly and eagerly. Let us then raise an altar to humanity upon the ruins of tyranny. Let us give this weak, cowardly, and ignorant people a manly and fearless upbringing. Let them sense the nobility of their origins so that, under our tutelage, they may become noble-hearted through sound consideration of their own welfare, and no longer be slaves but humans. . . . Let us infuse them with a firm resolve to hereafter no longer allow themselves to be torn from their native coasts, to shake off their bonds and thereby revenge themselves upon the blind tyrants who shackle them, so that they become more profitable to Europe as a free people.

Carl Bernhard Wadström, Swedenborgian and abolitionist, in 1789[81]

[H]ow grossly the very people of whom we are treating, have been misrepresented by those who first made merchandize of their persons, and then endeavoured, by calumny, to justify their own conduct towards them. The accounts of African governors and other slave merchants, have been but too implicitly followed by authors of no small note, who never were in Africa, and who did not suspect that the writers they quoted were interested in misleading them. Hence it is to be feared, that many well meaning persons have been led to believe that the Africans are so insensible as not to feel their ill treatment, or so wicked as not to deserve better; and have therefore, without farther examination, left them to what they think a merited fate.

Carl Bernhard Wadström, in 1794[82]

While attending ritual meetings or socializing at the Freemason's Lodge, it is quite probable that Badin now and then came into direct contact with any one of a number of Swedenborgians whose notions of freedom of religion and philanthropic inclinations—as well as their court prominence, military rank, or elite class position—gave them ready entrance to the masonic order. (In late eighteenth-century Stockholm, aristocrats in particular were inclined to become engaged in both Freemasonry and Swedenborgianism as both movements enabled them—by way of a world of unreason, of "secret" sciences reserved for the initiated—to accommodate contradiction, to "emotionally channel" and culturally rework both the growing power of bourgeois commoners within Sweden's state apparatus and the wider transformation processes being precipitated in Europe by the intellectual and political rationalisms of the Enlightenment.)[83] At the lodge, and elsewhere in the course of everyday life, Badin also may well have encountered acquaintances debating ideas currently promoted by followers of Swedenborg. While he may or may not have shown more than a passing interest in Swedenborg's writings and beliefs, while he may or may not have departed from Lutheran doctrine and shared their conviction that humans were capable of achieving contact with the divine through their own efforts, while he may or may not have shared their fascination with mesmerism and other forms of "animal magnetism" during the 1780s and 1790s, he almost surely could not have avoided reacting in some way either to their public positions on Africans, slavery, and the slave trade or to their "Plan for a Free Community upon the Coast of Africa, under the Protection of Great Britain; but Entirely Independent of all European Laws and Governments" (1789).[84] Were he actually exposed to those ideas or proposals, and some of their contradictions, he might yet again on occasion have been dragged down into an emotional whirlpool of uneasiness and self-doubt, sucked into confronting questions that would not go away, that would not leave his memory. . . . Might not Badin have been torn in his response to Swedenborg's teachings on Africans, to his insistence that they were different from other peoples, that they were more receptive to divine revelation and the Bible's true meanings because they were inhabitants of *Regnum innocentiae*—the Kingdom of Innocence—because they were open and free of guile, because they were unconstricted by (European) convention, because they were capable of experiencing the world in the same manner as children at play, because they could see things as they are, because they were as yet unblinded by worldly or selfish interests, because they could unreflectingly distinguish appearance from reality?[85] Because, in a word, they were childlike? As Badin poured over the Bible, or as he made biblically inspired entries in his notebook, might he not sometimes have found himself in conflict, wondering whether his readings were blessed with true meaning because he was by nature an African(-Caribbean), or whether the spiritual essence of their contents was obscured from him owing to decades spent in and around Stockholm, owing to his absorption of court conventions, owing to his Swedification? Might not such conflictive thoughts have become amplified and compounded following the publication of Wadström's *Observations on the Slave Trade* in Swedish? Because in discussing Wadström's book his fellow Swedenborgians may not only have dwelt on his abhorrence of slavery and his nerve-shattering depictions of the conditions under which slaves were shipped across the Atlantic, but also on his characterization of Africans? Thereby not only once again reducing Badin to an innocent child of nature, but further perplexing him by suggesting that salvation was to be delivered and enabled by "civilized" Europeans? A foreshadow of "the white man's burden" that confounded because his tutors of the 1760s, Royal Chaplain Nathanael Tenstedt and those others who had schooled him in the teachings and meaning of the Bible, and who had prepared him for his 1768 baptism, were anything but Swedenborgians? And had, on the contrary, perhaps robbed him of his "innate ability" to receive the inner meaning beneath every word, to achieve immediate insight, to see the True Light? And yet not honed his reason in such a manner as to otherwise leave him open to the Pure Truth, the Heavenly Truth?[86] . . . What mixed feelings, if any, might Badin have developed upon realizing that the very same people who despised the enslavement of Africans would have liked nothing better than to see them cultivate "their own native soil" so as to export agricultural commodities in exchange for manufactured goods, so as to "become more profitable to Europe as a free [but colonized] people"? Upon realizing that some saw slavery and the slave trade as bad because they were bad business? Upon realizing that Negroes were meant to become a cultivated people, to participate "in the benefits of civilized nations," not through self-cultivation, not through an Enlightenment education, not through science and reason, but through cultivating land (and thereby cultivating markets for Europe's emerging industrial capitalists)?[87] . . . What divided sentiments, if any, might have invaded Badin's thoughts if he discovered that an expedition dispatched to the Senegal coast in 1787 was designed to explore the possibilities of establishing a Swedenborgian settlement that would also permit the newly born West Indian Company to pursue its slave-trading interests? If he further discovered that the reconnaisance undertaking, set into operation with the approval of Gustav III, was dreamed up, organized, and led by Carl Bernhard Wadström, at the time a driving force in the spread of Swedenborg's word? If it later came to his attention that it was only in the aftermath of the expedition that Wadström—"by no means a sworn enemy of the slave-trade from the outset, as his biographers would have it"—turned against the inhuman traffic in human black bodies?[88] . . . What anchors of identity, if any, might Badin have pulled up (again) upon recognizing that the very same people who denounced the gross misrepresentation of Africans, the very same self-styled humanitarians who most vigorously spoke on the behalf of those of African origin, did not hesitate to depict them as "weak, cowardly, and ignorant," demanding of "a manly and fearless upbringing"? . . . And how might have Badin responded when told that Gustav III had outlawed any distribution of *Församlingsformen uti det Nya Jerusalem*, the Swedish version of the "Plan for a Free Community" dedicated to him and published in Copenhagen in 1790? Or when Swedenborgian gossip reached him, one year later, describing Gustav III's behavior when approached to endorse the slave-trade abolition movement based in England through action of his own? When he learned that the king in one breath waxed sympathetic, claiming "that he often reminded himself of the hard lot" of slaves on Saint Barthélemy? And in the next asserted, "he had never heard of any merchant from his country who had taken part in the slave trade"?[89] Even though he had himself signed papers granting the West Indian Company permission to transport slaves from West Africa to Saint Barthélemy and eventual sale? Was Badin overcome with simultaneous disbelief and resignation? Did he experience keen disappointment? Or a sense of betrayal? The Janus face seen again? Was there a renewed awareness of his out-of-placeness? Was his reaction—whatever its form—one that was totally unforgettable?

Tintomara! Two things are white
Innocence—Arsenic
> *Title-page epigram employed by Carl Jonas Love Almqvist in his novel,* Drottningens juvelsmycke *(The Queen's Diadem), published in 1834. Almqvist's intellectual development and religious beliefs were much influenced by the Swedenborgianism he came in contact with during his student years at Uppsala.*

ADOLFINE: The uncivilized *[wild, savage]* blacks so often
     have deep feelings.
Line spoken in Almqvist's Drottningens juvelsmycke[90]

If, as evidence directly and indirectly suggests, there was an ever-expanding array of unpleasant and disturbing incidents that were etched upon Badin's memory, deeply stowed but readily subject to involuntary surfacing. If a morning walk threaded through Stockholm's streets could summon to mind any number of past insults and unfriendly or threatening glares. And just maybe produce new ones. If even the most enjoyable of order events could yield a jolt from the past, a face or setting that reminded of something said or overheard, some unkind word or personal violation, some encounter with perturbing news from within the Royal Palace walls or from across the Atlantic. Or just maybe produce new shocks for future recall. If a potentially pleasing stop at an inn, or other drinking establishment, could trigger recollection of a terrible verbal assault. Or just maybe produce some new embarrassment. If a visit to the theater, a costume ball, or a range of other entertainments could precipitate unwanted remembrances of being forced to play the monkey (literally!), or of being openly referred to as a baboon, a monkey, an ape. Or just maybe, yet again, produce circumstances either requiring that he play the jestering *badin*, the grinning Minister of Merriment (the figurative monkey!), or placing him at the receiving end of another simian reference. If there were other sites and situations that could automatically conjure up past incidents of blows received or possibilities foreclosed. Or just maybe produce new debasements or disappointments. If each and every one of these memory etchings, and their corresponding anxieties, stemmed from Badin's blackness, and if there was no other black of similar station in whom he could confide, no other similarly privileged person of slave descent to whom he could unburden himself, with whom he could share his identity quandaries. Then maybe, just maybe, there would be times when the combination of spiritual isolation and bad memories in constellation would prove overwhelming, would plunge Badin into the nightness of depression, leaving him alone and brooding, dis-eased by multiple anxieties and uncertainties, pursued by poisoned thoughts, by the whiteness of those who constituted his everyday life. Wondering, even when surrounded with cheer. Who in the world am I? What in the world am I? Where in the world am I?

≠ ≠ ≠

Growing sad, present tense.

>At a restaurant, in the subway, at school. They can crop up anywhere. The contemptuous remarks, the more subtle insinuations, the glances. On such occasions it makes no difference that you are called Amanda, Anna or Sara *[common Swedish names]* or speak Swedish without even a hint of an accent.
>   *Comment prefacing the conversation excerpted below*[91]

>>SARA: [A]nd sometimes it can make one almost paranoid. You can never feel truly safe, all of a sudden someone says something awfully insulting. Many times they surely aren't even conscious of the significance of what they have said.
>>ANNA: At a party a girl asked me if it was OK to say nigger. Then I answered that I didn't think so. Then she

said: "I think so." It can feel really annoying to have
to argue about something like that.

AMANDA: When I was walking downtown one evening an
alcoholic old man began yelling: "Fucking blackhead,
you're taking our jobs." Naturally I was provoked and
argued a while with him. But then I decided to try to
end the discussion, so I said: "It's cold, here's some
money, go and get yourself a cup of coffee." Then
he got terribly embarrassed, which also was my aim.
But how one feels differs so much from time to time.
Sometimes one gets angry and snappish. On another
occasion you just lose your spirit and grow sad.

Excerpts from a conversation held in January 2000, between three
young black women of Ethiopian parentage who were adopted by
Swedes at an early age and brought up in Stockholm[92]

Geography Lessons
Night and Day Weather
Navigating Darkness
and Lightness

Christmas Eve night. Twelve o'clock midnight. A large halo around
the moon. Snow and stormy continuously from midnight until a
quarter to one. The moon was [now] seen dimly among the clouds,
winds from the south-southwest. . . . Two a.m. The stars were seen
dimly and fuzzily. The wind was stronger than in the preceding
hours. . . . At a quarter to four the wind was the same [as the last
hour] from the east-southeast, but more overcast. 4:00 a.m. to
5:30 [the skies] began to clear and the stars again were seen dimly
between the clouds. . . . six Christmas morning it has been stormy
and alternately clear and cloudy. Until five o'clock there were small
amounts of snow. . . . From 7:00 to 9:30 the weather was shifting
between somewhat clear and cloudy. The thermometer has been
10 degrees [C] below the freezing point. . . . All the way from 9:30 to
3:30 it was windy and snowy so that the sun was not visible. . . . The
skies were clear and bright with sparkling stars until 8:30, where-
after the entire sky began to cloud, which increased along with
winds so that at 11:00 p.m. it was still cloudy and at 12:00 it began
to be [more fully] overcast.
Badin, in a notebook entry[1]

Whether or not he had a clearly thought-out purpose, well established in
advance, at midnight, December 25, 1801, Badin pulled aside the silk window curtains of the drawing room in his Stockholm residence and peered
out into the turbulent murk, perhaps being able to discern the silhouette of

the Old Town's more prominent buildings only a few hundred yards away on the opposite side of Strömmen's waters.[2] Apparently alone, almost certainly bundled up and occasionally shivering, he sat there throughout the night and on into the next day, noting the ever-changing weather conditions that met his eye, doing so with some detail at relatively frequent intervals, sometimes no more than fifteen minutes apart. Whether or not the numbers and observations in themselves were of any significance to him from the outset, whether or not it was the act of measuring and recording itself that gave meaning to the enterprise by enabling him to identify with the "quantifying spirit" of Enlightenment science[3]—by allowing him to self-reaffirm his status as a student of astronomy[4]—Badin continued this undertaking throughout Christmas day, filling his self-lined notebook with well over four pages of dense statistics and commentary. Whether or not this observational activity had its origins in the sensitivity of his farm-based income to climatic swings in general and the disastrous summers experienced by grain cultivators during 1798–99 and 1801 in particular,[5] whether or not he was attempting to escape thoughts of his current economic predicament by fixating on the weather,[6] whether or not he was intentionally seeking to deflect another bout of "nostalgia," it is as if Badin was totally oblivious to anything but the meteorological circumstances of the moment. Badin, the avid Bible reader, the man so otherwise readily inclined to express his faith—**Blessed are those who believe**—and to speak of the Heavenly Father or of the Love and Mercifulness of God,[7] has nothing to say of the day's religious significance. He makes no reflection on the birth of Christ. He gives no indication of having taken a break to attend Julottan, the traditional early morning Christmas service—or of having made any other church visit. He writes not a word of feasting or festivity, or of any form of human contact whatsoever with his wife, his maidservant(s?),[8] his friends, and neighbors. And, after presumably catching a few hours of sleep, he was back at it again early on the morning of the 26th, documenting among other things the commencement of snow at 6:00 a.m. and the failure of the sun to be seen either at its scheduled rising (around 8:30) or at any other time during the day. Although the frequency of notation occasionally diminished, he continued to record his observations, noting in the margins "third day of Christmas," "fourth day of Christmas," and so on through January 4, when a polar high pressure system finally began to settle in and he made this final firm-handed and especially readable entry: "The sun shone from the time it went up until it went down. The wind was unsteady and swung between northerly and westerly. At 2:45 the wind was observed becoming west-southwest-¼ southwest." . . . For eleven days Badin seems to have been absorbed—to the exclusion of anything else—with recording the vicissitudes of Stockholm's weather. What, if anything, is to be made of this temporary obsession with wind direction and intensity, with temperature measurements, with the presence or absence of snowfall, with the extent of cloud cover and the visibility of the moon, the stars, the sun? Whether or not he was consciously aware of it, did this set of fixations resonate with a corresponding set of questions? Wind direction with questions of origin and destination?[9] Temperature with questions regarding the nature and consequences of coldness? Snowfall with questions concerning the appearance of whiteness? Cloud cover and visibility with questions of lightness and darkness? Whether or not he planned it as such, is it not possible, even probable, that this project of meteorological chronicling drove Badin to yet again confront and rework the issue of his sometimes drifting identity? At least intermittently in the course of that Christmas season?

> Montesquieu had hundreds of precursors, but it was his reformulation of climatic influence that made these ideas so powerful in the second half of the eighteenth and the early part of the nineteenth centuries.
>
> Du Bos asks: Why do men differ despite their descent from common parents? The divergence began with migration—it was a gradual process toward both the pole and the equator—and ten centuries were sufficient to make the descendants of the same parents as different as are the Negroes and the Swedes today. . . . Du Bos writes as if it were a matter of common knowledge that climate is more powerful than blood or origin *[in affecting genius and inclinations],* . . . [that] climate makes different people alike and keeps them alike.
>
> Montesquieu likens the people of cold countries to young and brave men, those of hot, to old and timorous men; individuals going from one climate will be subject to the influences of the new climate, as had happened, he says, to northern soldiers who fought in the War of Spanish Succession.
>
> Although Montesquieu was opposed to slavery, he saw how it could arise in countries whose climate induced so lazy and slothful a condition among the people that their masters could force them to work only by fear of punishment.
> *Clarence J. Glacken*[10]

If we travel toward the North, we meet people who have few
vices, many virtues, and a great share of frankness and sincerity.
If we draw near the South, we fancy ourselves entirely removed
from the verge of morality; here the stronger passions are pro-
ductive of all manner of crimes, each man endeavoring, let the
means be what they will, to indulge his inordinate desires.
    Montesquieu[11]

By the closing decades of the eighteenth century, ideas regarding the influence of climate on humans were "common intellectual property" in Sweden
and no portion of Montesquieu's *De l'esprit des lois* was more widely discussed than his climate doctrine.[12] Given that context, is it not very possible, or even extremely probable, that Badin, much of whose reading occurred in French, had been exposed to the writings of Montesquieu and his
predecessors, as well as to those contemporary echoes and reworkings that
confirmed the European as the human norm? Is it not even more likely that
he had at least come into contact with those widely flourishing ideas regarding racial and national differentiation and its alterability, either by way
of discussions and debates in the corridors of the Royal Palace or by way of
conversational exchanges with Swedenborgians and other of his well-
educated, up-and-coming bourgeois order brothers?[13] Or by way of familiarity with the late eighteenth-century output of Sweden's most noted
climatological determinist, Jacob Fredrik Neikter, a man who vehemently
insisted upon the influence of climate upon external and internal human
qualities, a man who explicitly argued against the notion "that Lapps and
Negroes are incapable of any form of cultivated education"?[14] Is it not very
possible that he had become enthralled with everyday weather because
Montesquieu, Neikter, and others enabled him to argue that his long-term
exposure to Stockholm's atmospheric conditions made him truly acclima-
tized; put him, the Caribbean-born chattel, on an equal footing with anyone of Swedish birth, possessing at least as much virtue and mental acu-
men?[15] Even if he believed the latter to be the case—weather or not? Even if
he believed not a word of the climatically determined degeneracy, sloth-
fulness, mental insufficiency, cultural inertia, and hot-bloodedness variously attributed to Africans and Afro-Caribbeans? Or is it instead possible
that Badin approached his weather observations with vexed and conflicted
mind, in the midst of a winter depression, not only because of his less than
healthy pocketbook, but also because he was torn between wanting to
believe Montesquieu and his antecedents (including the similarly named
Bodin),[16] and the doubts cast by what he could remember of Rousseau's
Émilean teachings? Could he fully forget Rousseau, who insisted that the

brain organization of Negroes made them less wise and adaptable to extreme climates than Frenchmen and others of temperate-zone birth?[17] And
were there not very likely other written words and words of mouth that he
could not ignore, acquired bits of knowledge that bit into his mind, that
precipitated uncertainty and uneasiness, that left him divided on the matter
of climate and (him)self?[18] . . . On those several occasions when making
observations at 2:00 a.m. or later, when unable to sleep and facing out into
wintry bleakness, when sensing solitude in the night-dead city, could Badin
have prevented his mind from anxiously wandering in time and space, from
feverishly conjuring up temporally and geographically distant memories,
from torturing himself with weather-based associations that underlined the
now-and-then precarious, tottering state of his identity? . . . As the snows
came and went, could his thoughts always have escaped that first encounter
with the phenomenon? Or evaded whirl-by images of those subsequent hap-
penings that led him to link snow with disillusionment (not sugar!), with
the inconstancy, unpredictability, and unreliability of the white? Or, consequently, eluded any contemplation of his position vis-à-vis the white? . . .
As the temperature continued to plummet, from twenty degrees below zero
(minus four degrees Fahrenheit) at 10:45 p.m., January 2, to twenty-five
degrees below zero (minus thirteen degrees Fahrenheit) at 7:00 a.m. the
following morning, could he have avoided any chilly contemplations?
Regarding whether or not he was ever meant to survive in such coldness,
ever meant to really adapt to such frigidity? Regarding whether or not the
cold air really altered the qualities of his blood, and thereby his spirit and
inclinations,[19] in such a manner as to make him like a native Swede?
Regarding—along rather different lines—the cold reception that he occasionally met, not only from the anonymous encountered on the streets, but
also without warning from those of high station? Regarding a recent instance of such body-language-announced social distancing, or the seemingly increased frequency of such icy welcomes since the 1792 assassination
of Gustav III and his diminished access to the court? . . . As the brief daylight hours of late December and early January time and again became enshrouded in clouds, and especially as the visibility of the stars and moon
repeatedly waxed and waned in the deep night hours of that period, could
thoughts concerning lightness and darkness have never rushed in and out of
his stream of consciousness? Could he have escaped any consideration of
his own darkness in a world of lightness? Could he somehow have side-
stepped any reflection upon his own ambiguous state? Upon the contradictions between his own at least surface-level acceptance in the most
respected of circles and the French and Swedish taken-for-granteds prevailing in those very same circles—linguistic taken-for-granteds that equated

darkness, or blackness, with evil, ugliness, the negative, and the flawed, and lightness, or whiteness, with virtue, truth and beauty, the positive and the pure?[20] Could he not have poetically imagined that his achieved lightness/whiteness/Swedishness was doomed to be over and over removed from Their field of vision by the darkness/blackness of his skin in much the same way that the lightness of the moon, the stars, and the sun were ever subject to being obscured, removed from sight, covered over by darkness? And if this recognition brought gloom, might he have not grown all the more dismal by his own readiness to automatically characterize gloomy thoughts as dark thoughts? And could the repeated clouding over of the sun—the yet-again drenching of the sky in grayness—have further contributed to depression by reawakening extremely vague memories of his lost childhood and parental separation? By dragging up hazy images of countless days spent in choking smoke and unbearable fire-fed heat, of sweat-drenched living-hell days, of days on Saint Croix when the sun was smoke-hidden and the temperature soared owing to the tree and undergrowth burning required for the rapid expansion of sugar-plantation acreage?[21] By summoning up otherwise suppressed images of sunlessness and extreme physical discomfort, of a smoke-shrouded landscape devoid of wholly perceivable bodies, of a world of nonvisibility and haunting absences? . . . As he exercised particular care in noting wind direction—with precision referring to a wind as coming from "the east, ½ southeast," or from "the east, ¼ southeast"—were there not moments when his mind wandered off, wondering about lands off in the direction of the wind's origin or destination? Would not the inclination and ability to perform such a mental-map scanning have emerged from his *Émile*-based tutoring, from Rousseau's "pronounced views on the need of instruction in geography at an early age,"[22] from the various travel books assembled in his library? And is it not possible that, as a consequence of such cartographic fantasizing, Badin experienced an epiphany as he made his final entry? Is it not possible that his entire weather watch consciously or subconsciously involved the awaiting of some heavenly sign, that his entire undertaking wed Enlightened empirical observation with elements of the occult then so fashionable among the aristocracy in general and his Freemason brothers in particular? Is it not possible that a project that commenced at a moment as auspicious as the very first minute of December 25 involved a conscious or subconscious search for an auspicious indicator, that his final recorded observation provided just such a revelation? An invisible lightning bolt/jolt out of the at-last-clear blue skies? A realization that the wind that was beginning to come from the "west-southwest-¼ southwest" was a wind coming from a direction that coincided with the location of Saint Croix, with the location of his Caribbean slave origins? A realization that a wind that was blowing from the direction of

There, was at one and the same time a wind blowing Here, freely; and in a single instant was unifying Stockholm and elseWheres; was by virtue of its motion being neither just There, nor just Here, but almost entirely in-between?[23] A realization that this wind was unfixed in nature, that it would move on, become re-placed, that other aeolian conditions would succeed it, but that, sure as death, it would sooner or later return again, ever the same, only different? A realization that this wind was asserting itself at just that hour, 2:45 p.m., when the skies were entering a liminal phase, starting a slow fade from the unblemished lightness of an especially bright day into the darkness of another lengthy winter night, when the transition from whiteness to blackness was once again commencing, when the one was be-ginning to blur into the other? A realization—in the light of a much-longed-for cloudless sunlit day—that at least for the next few months the days would grow longer and the nights shorter; that the daily proportion of light-ness would expand at the expense of darkness, only to begin surrendering its advantage anew next summer? And a realization, in the light of all this, that it was time to stop? Not another atmospheric condition to be regis-tered. Another milestone passed in the know-no-end passage, no-end-known voyage, from property to personhood. Once again, momentary peace of mind. Acceptance of contradictory circumstances, of internalized contrary tendencies. Some things, some relations, some meanings realized. But still en route. Still now-(t)here. Multivalent. In-between. As clear as day. Or the darkness of a starlit night.[24]

—

> The sciences are thus the light that will lead the people who wan-der in darkness.
>
> *Carl Linnaeus, in an Uppsala speech made in the presence of "their Royal Majesties," September 25, 1759*[25]

≠ ≠ ≠

Now again then: geography lessons, (un)belonging, and snow.

> Sometimes I stayed only in my room. I always took my headset, atlases, and a drawing pad. Then I built stuff in my mentally disturbed skull. I learned the maps by heart, made up my own countries, redrew the boundaries, made up wars where Morocco and Sweden always invaded their neighbors. I loved atlases.
>
> *Big Fred (Fredrik Eddari), rap-singer son to a native Swedish woman and a long-resident Moroccan, recalling his response to*

being repeatedly stared at, to being made to feel more like an "immigrant" than ever before, while visiting his maternal grandmother in northern Sweden[26]

Hässelby is our living spot
Where love is hot
Huhh!
Where nobody gives you a crooked stare
  Words from one of Big Fred's numbers, referring to the increasingly segregated Stockholm suburb where he resides, one of whose areas is popularly referred to as Arab Valley (Arabdalen)[27]

Fred always shouts the name of his suburb when he comes to a new place *[to perform]*. The farther he is from home, the more often he does it. Sometimes to create a home-like coziness, sometimes to scare the life out of people.
  Fredrik Strage[28]

Migrants get the blame for unemployment, narcotics crimes, the housing shortage—even that it's been warm and snowless on Christmas Eve.
  "Bettina," a medical student who migrated from Iran in 1984[29]

≠ ≠ ≠

Newton's *Opticks* had shown black for what it was—a deprivation.
  Winthrop D. Jordan[30]

[T]he dark areas of a Baroque painting *[could]* call on every color of the spectrum in order to create their deep shadow.
  Lise Patt—speaking of an eighteenth-century artistic practice occurring in Sweden as well as elsewhere in Europe[31]

—

Don't make me have anything to do with Liljensparre![32] I'll be ears and eyes for the King, but to spy for the chief of the police—that's ugly.
  Badin, in 1789, responding to a request from Baron Gustav Mauritz Armfelt, to a request to keep his eyes on both Pechlin—the king's "worst enemy"—and those of "the King's best friends" recently observed

in his company, to a request to operate in the shadows, in the dark—
figuratively and literally[33]

—

Complaints about bad lighting conditions were innumerable in
Stockholm at this time and Badin joined himself to the chorus of
complainers.

Lars Wikström[34]

Badin's chronicle of dark and stormy nights and days, and the identity
wrestling presumably attendant to it, occurs near the very beginning of his
notebook. A few pages from the end, he submerges himself once again in
questions of darkness and lightness. And although these questions are of
a rather different sort, they yet again suggest the possibility of some grap-
pling with his identity. . . . Writing in an unspecified year subsequent to his
1799 remarriage,[35] Badin refers to lighting conditions on Tollgate Street
(Tullportsgatan), the thoroughfare on which his father-in-law, Lars Norell,
resided. He notes there is no additional lighting between the lantern outside
of Norell's house and the end of the street (meaning, according to maps of
the time, that there was but one light source over a distance exceeding four
hundred feet).[36] This circumstance he contrasts with conditions on certain
streets of Södermalm, the portion of the city south of the Old Town, and
closes with the more sweeping observation that conditions in the northern
part of Stockholm (Norrmalm) are "unreasonable." While the dearth of
lanterns on Tollgate Street might have been extreme, Badin is protesting
more generally of the relative inadequacy of public lighting in Norrmalm,
the very same area of the city in which he resided. (A royal decree, issued in
January 1749, required that Stockholm, like "other large and well-ordered
cities in Europe," should have lighting established on all of its streets.
Landlords were to provide candlelit or oil-burning lanterns thirty paces
apart on both sides of each street, zigzagging their placement in such a
manner as to provide a light source every fifteen paces, except where plank
sidewalks presumably made stumbling in the dark less likely.)[37] Not only
did the spacing of Norrmalm's lighting frequently fail to come up to the established standard, but its quality, as throughout the city, was usually quite
poor—the volume of light emitting from most lanterns was so scant that
they were popularly referred to as "cat eyes" or "wolf eyes."[38]

—

When European civilization came into contact with the black
world, with those savage peoples, everyone agreed: Those
Negroes were the principle of evil. . . . In Europe the Negro has
one function: that of symbolizing the lower emotions, the baser
inclinations, the dark side of the soul. In the collective unconscious of homo occidentalis, the Negro—or, if one prefers, the
color black—symbolizes evil, sin, wretchedness, death, war,
famine. All birds of prey are black.
Frantz Fanon[39]

—

I truly believe that the color of their skin testifies to their evilness,
that they are destined to slavery, and consequently ought not have
any freedom.
Reimert Haagensen, a Danish visitor to Saint Croix during the 1750s,
while Badin still resided there[40]

No coal or ash dust comes into the laboratory, so now I can be
white and escape looking like a little devil.
Carl Fredrik Bergklint, Swedenborgian, commenting in 1788 on the
new modern-furnaced alchemy laboratory provided to him and his
partner by Gustav III at Drottningholm, a country palace outside
of Stockholm much frequented by Badin[41]

[*Olof Erik Bergius, who had been a justice on Saint Barthélemy*
between 1813 and 1816, described how the slaves there] differ
in appearance, character traits, and qualities depending upon
where they come from. *[However, he also wrote,]* one cannot see
the differences among them when it is dark at night.
Göran Skytte[42]

She Was as Dark as a Tropical Night
*Subhead contained in a newspaper story (*Hudiksvalls Nyheter,
July 12, 1944) referring to a pastor's family that returned to
Sweden in 1824 from Saint Barthélemy with two young slaves
in their possession

Why should Badin express his discontent with Norrmalm's lighting conditions? Was he merely echoing the dissatisfaction of those men of station he
socially encountered, of those men most likely to feel threatened by hard-

times-based economic disgruntlement, of those men most likely to serve as late-hour targets for hostile panhandling or robbery—if not physical attack? Or was there something more personal involved, something rooted in repeated personal experience? If venturing out in darkness was regarded as a risky undertaking—the royal decree of 1749 was explicitly directed against the "commission of violence during dark evenings and at night"[43]— and if the "ordinary world" of the daylit street was the venue where Badin was most commonly prejudged by the color of his skin, most subject to the piercing stares and unfriendly glares of strangers, how much more was he apt to be reminded of his Difference when suddenly encountered in the heavy silence of night, when appearing out of nowhere, when ascribed an Evil or Devilish appearance, when (pre)seen as a menacing embodiment of the Powers of Darkness? Especially if the nighttime street was more apt to be frequented by those to some degree fortified with alcohol; by those whose imaginations might gallop off upon the sight of Black Difference because they were simply happily inebriated, because a drink too many had at once washed away their inhibitions and encouraged aggressive responses, or because they were so reeling with drunkenness that they saw the world through a haze?[44] If the public streetlight was an instrument of surveillance, a technology of identification, a means by which the unknown could become known and made subject to judgment,[45] is it not possible that Badin's after-dark Norrmalm excursions were fraught with uncomfortableness, anxiety, and ambivalence? Did he not sometimes wish to navigate the seas of darkness between the tiny islands of light as quickly as possible so as to minimize the risk of physical assault, and sometimes wish to keep to the anonymity of the unlit seas, thankful for the spatial dispersion of the lantern archipelago, as it provided him with a sense of safety and freedom, allowing him to somehow find his way while minimizing exposure to identification and verbal assault? If mandatory street lighting was the expression of a would-be panoptic power, an early attempt to regulate the streets, to regulate bodies in urban space, and if, as de Certeau would have it, the route selection associated with walking in the city involves an expressive/poetic manipulation of spatial organizations "no matter how panoptic they may be,"[46] what experiential self-references, what place- and site-bound memories, were evoked by Badin as he authored his way from home to Tollgate Street or some other Norrmalm destination after the fall of night? Most pointedly, did his physical movement between small patches of light and extensive stretches of darkness metaphorically resonate in his mind with his constant passage between the whiteness of his demeanor and habits and the blackness of his skin, with the ways in which the latter could somehow outshine the former? And if so, how did he navigate his dis-ease?

How did he reroute the course of his pedestrian journey? And his identity?
Which theres and thens were avoided? Which revisited?

> In his younger years Badin was very afraid of the dark, and conse-
> quently the queen once arranged a masquerade with the intent of
> curing him of his cowardice. One evening, when he was sleeping
> alone in his room, she sent in some masked people who were
> carrying dimly lit candles. Badin then became so frightened and
> screamed so extremely loudly, and with such despair and for so
> long that they feared he would lose his senses. The king and queen,
> who had stood in the anteroom awaiting the outcome of the ven-
> ture, rushed in to him and the former took up his watch and gave it
> to the crying boy. Afterward Badin was allowed to keep the watch.
> *Wendela Hebbe (fabulizing?) in 1897*[47]

> *[During their colonial occupation of the Virgin Islands]* the
> Danes exhibited a cruelness toward their slaves that is without
> counterpart in the history of the world. . . . In 1733 the Danish
> Governor introduced a law that in detail regulated the punish-
> ment of slaves. This Danish slave law *[which remained in effect
> as late as 1791, has been described as]* the cruelest law that has
> ever been written down on paper.
> *Göran Skytte*[48]

1. The leader for a group of runaway or escaped Negroes should
   be pinched three times with a red-hot iron tongs and thereafter hung.
2. An accessory to an *[escape or revolt]* plot should lose a leg,
   or, if the owner grants a pardon, an eye, and be administered
   a beating of 150 lashes.
3. Participants in a plot who don't convey *[knowledge of it]* to a
   White person should be branded on the forehead and receive
   one hundred lashes. . . .
5. Eight days of escape should be punished with 150 lashes,
   twelve weeks' escape should result in the loss of a leg, and six-
   month escapees should forfeit their lives, or lose a leg if their
   owner grants a pardon.
6. A Negro who steals for a value of four riksdalers shall be
   branded and hung. Small thefts should be punished with
   a brand-mark on the forehead and from 100 to 150 lashes.

7. Slaves who receive stolen goods, or who are accessories, should be branded and have 150 lashes. . . .

9. A negro who lifts his hand against a White person in anger or threatens him, or who speaks disrespectfully to him shall without mercy be pinched three times with tongs and thereafter hung unless the White in question does not wish it, in which case he should lose a hand. . . .

11. A Negro who meets a White person on the road shall go to the side and stand still until the White person has passed or otherwise be punished with a whipping by the White.

12. No slave may be seen in town bearing a cudgel or knife, or fighting with another, without therefore receiving 50 lashes. . . .

14. Any Negro who can be proven to have attempted to poison someone shall be pinched three times with red-hot iron tongs and thereafter have his body broken on the wheel while still alive. . . .

16. All dancing, festivities, games, and the like shall be forbidden to Negroes without the permission and presence of their master or overseer. . . .

19. The island's prosecutor shall strictly assure that these articles are observed.

Excerpts from the 1733 law signed by governor Philip Gardelin, subsequently embellished to require the castration of male thieves[49]

If a slave misses a day's work he is tied up and whipped 100–200 or more times.

Reimert Haagensen, testifying in 1758 to what he had seen on Saint Croix during the immediately preceding years, which coincided with Badin's childhood there. Haagensen reported that the mistreatment of slaves was so extreme that—regarding death as a liberation—many committed suicide by hanging, poisoning, or drowning. However, believing them to be "evil by nature," he held not the least bit of sympathy for them.[50]

If you have tears prepare to shed them now. . . . no class in the known world [has undergone] so complete a servitude.

Philip Freneau, poet, characterizing the "the cruel and detestable slavery" practiced on Saint Croix in a letter to a friend in 1776[51]

What if Badin actually had a deeply embedded fear of the dark? What if there was at least a grain of truth to Wendela Hebbe's tale, even if at best it was based on a thirdhand account, on temporally distant hearsay?[52] What if—even allowing for some poetic embellishment on Hebbe's part—Badin's concern with inadequate street lighting was at least in part traceable to a fear that already manifested itself somewhere between the ages of ten and fifteen, if not considerably earlier? What if Badin was actually prone to being scared out of his wits in the dark, to screaming uncontrollably upon tumbling out of some recurring dream hell—without the assistance of unidentifiable figures bursting into his room in the dead of night? What if his fear of the dark was rooted in trauma(s) dating to his Saint Croix childhood? Given what is known of the brutally inhuman conditions under which Saint Croix slaves existed, is there not more than a small chance that he had on one or more occasions personally borne witness to an incredibly inhuman act, to power put into perverse practice, to the logics of capitalist colonialism in savage action? Especially as there apparently was a climate of mounting paranoia during the years preceding his departure from Saint Croix, a highly charged atmosphere among the island's greatly outnumbered whites,[53] an ever more intense fear of rebellion that readily translated itself into an escalation of punishment and physical abuse, into a merciless meting out of retribution in advance, into yet another redeclaration of Danish domination via marks upon body after body?[54] (So deep was the accumulated dread held by whites that in 1759, a few months after Badin was taken off, eighty-eight supposed insurrection "conspirators" were seized on the basis of a single confession extracted under physical duress—a confession that was immediately retracted in full by its "author" before he slit his throat.)[55] Is there not more than a small chance that repressed images of directly observed atrocities would occasionally well up in his dreams? Is there not more than a small chance that his nightmares involved an assault on the senses: that he resaw the flailed back, the running blood, the detached limb, or the tortured body writhing with unendurable pain; that he resmelled the burned flesh; that he reheard the terrifying shrieks and moans of the whipped, the branded, the dismembered, the castrated? Is there not much more than a small chance that Badin's response to being beaten with a tiller at the Neptune Order reception hall, his comment that he was being treated as if "a purchased slave,"[56] was an indicator that he himself had been present at some bestial beating(s) or lashing(s), that the smashing of the wooden boat part against his body reawoke some of the very same memories that were the stuff of his dreams, the very same dream stuff that could cause him to reawake with a start in the terrifying insecurity of his pitch-drenched room—in a space of total nowhereness and inbetweenness, in a space of all-engulfing impenetrability and silence devoid of anything to cling to?

Except thoughts of death and the absence of light, of momentary isolation and eternal separation and abandonment? . . . And what if the horribleness of the childhood trauma(s) that underpinned his fear was compounded by parental or fraternal involvement? What if, at a very young age, and before his very own eyes, it was his father or brother Coffi who had been treated to the savagery of Danish discipline, who had been ferociously flogged or sadistically subjected to red-hot pincers, who had been reduced to a mercy-begging animal cowering in the dirt, who had been punished until his body parts were bloodied or disfigured beyond recognition, who had been left in an unconscious heap? (Three of the eighty-nine held in connection with the 1759 "plot" went by the name of Coffe. Given Badin's proclivity to spell phonetically and inconsistently, like other Swedish contemporaries, Coffi and one of the three may have been identical—in which case he may have been identified previously as a "troublemaker" and accordingly made subject to whippings or worse over several years.)[57] What if, on that island where cruelty without limits was a way of life, it was his mother who had been physically abused to the extreme, who had been multiply violated in such ways that rape is an all-too-gentle word? What if, at a very young age, and before his very own eyes, it was his mother who had been victimized, who had been roughly held down by a number of sweaty arms and forced to surrender her body, who had been reduced to a gratification-yielding piece of property, who had been sexually ravaged with such unbridled vicious-ness, who had been so heinously assaulted, so grossly degraded, so terror-ized during various penetrations and her prolonged ordeal that she was left another person—hollowed out, blank of stare, and disturbed beyond recognition to such an extent that her name no longer held? Narzi? (If Coffi and the Coffe described as a mulatto were one and the same, there may have been at least one earlier occasion on which Badin's mother was forced to have sex with a desire-swollen white, one earlier occasion on which it was the white male—rather than the black male—who exhibited an un-controllable and "animal-like" sexuality, one earlier occasion when the heartless irrationalities of "just another plantation rape" were conjoined with plantation-economy rationalities that equated profit with expanded slave-labor production *and* the reproduction of slave labor.)[58] . . . And what if the trauma(s) at root was an in-the-dark event? An overseer, bursting into his parents' thatched-roof hut at three or four in the morning, barking at the top of his lungs, demanding that they all immediately proceed to a spe-cific cane field, the plantation's sugar mill, or the forested area to be cleared today, threatening a terrible whipping if their speed was not as he desired?[59] Or Badin himself grabbed in the middle of the night by the agents of Baron von Pröck, ripped from his mother's arms *by unidentified figures,* dragged in painful grip from his parents' hut while crying-crying-crying, rushed along cane-field-lined roads in complete disorientation toward von Pröck's gubernatorial mansion, an image of his held-to-the-floor father fixed in his mind and his mother's loud wails fading into the distance? Only a day or so later taken away on a Copenhagen-bound ship by von Pröck without ever having seen either of his parents again?[60] If Badin was pushed without warning over that precipice of all childhood precipices—(for)everlasting separation from mommy and daddy, irrevocable loss of love and protection; if he experienced a trauma even only vaguely like that just here described, how could he not have been saddled with a lifelong fear of the dark? And even if the details were repressed, is it not quite likely that he would regard the unlit street, or any other light-deprived location, as a place where the unexpected might occur at any moment, as a place where unidentifiable terrors lurk, as a place where the least unfamiliar sound might be heard as a harbinger of danger or disaster, as a place where the forgotten past, well-kept secrets, the death of one's childhood—if not Death himself—resided? And, in the light of all this, is it not possible that his nightlong weather watching was in part an unreflected coping strategy, a subconsciously de-vised means of escaping it all, of focusing his thoughts elsewhere than on the feared and (un)known, of avoiding that which appeared in his dreams? A means of finding his way, himself, in the dark?

> The word Europe comes from a Semitic word that simply means "darkness."
> *Sven Lindqvist*[61]

> According to the observations I have had the opportunity to make in the West Indies, the negro is hardly half human; the rest is ape and tiger. Laziness, talkativeness, the desire to dance and play, the inclination to pilfer, bestial love and *[the craving of]* sweets, and the caricaturish imitation of the follies of white at-tire, etc., betray the ape-like in his character; while the tiger-like is testified to by the numerous conspiracies that daily occur in the West Indies and whose objective has been and is to extermi-nate the whites, often by the most incredibly cruel means.

> A planter loves his slave in the same manner a Swedish peasant loves his horse; that is to say, often more than his wife.
> *Carl Adolf Carlsson, again speaking in 1835 after years as a clergy-man and teacher on Saint Barthélemy*[62]

≠ ≠ ≠

Remembering and forgetting, present tense.

Why is it so difficult to face up to Sweden's colonial past? Time and again we are confronted with less glorious historical events that, with varying success, we have attempted to repress until now. Soon it ought to be time to come to terms with Swedish slavery.

Rolf Sjöstrom, historian, commenting in 1999, at a time when it was becoming increasingly difficult for many Swedes to deny the widespread existence of labor-market discrimination, housing segregation, and de facto social apartheid—phenomena largely resulting from the contemporary operation of cultural racism and from the unreflected summoning-up of stereotypes, from the dialectics of not seeing at work[63]

Departure Tears
Exits
Endings

[A]t or after a sale, even those negroes born in the islands it is not uncommon to see taken from their wives, wives from their husbands, and children from their parents, and sent off to other islands, and wherever else their merciless lords choose; and, probably, never more, during life, see each other! Often times my heart has bled at these partings; when the friends of the departed have been at the waterside, and, with sighs and tears, have kept their eyes fixed on the vessel till it went out of sight.

Gustavus Vassa (Olaudah Equiano) recalling mid-eighteenth-century conditions in the West Indies[1]

Badin a cheval revenant de sa campagne (Badin on horseback returning from his country home). Sketchbook drawing by Johan Tobias Sergel, unspecified date during the 1790s. Badin caught in visual image one last time. Full circle. Caught by the hand of an artist who became best known as a sculptor and who initially studied drawing under the guidance of Jean Eric Rehn.[2] The very same Rehn who was the first to portray Badin. In the company of a sculptor, P. H. L'Archevêque, who also was Sergel's teacher. Representations of Badin again spun through a web of connections.[3] Last(ing)ly caught on paper by an image carver, by one who etches in stone, who concretely fixes a personal way of (not) seeing.[4] . . . Full circle. Badin once again playing his role, once again pictured as smiling. But this is not the monkeying-around smile of Rehn's drawing, not a smile capable of provoking dislike or irritation. It is a smile that appears both weary and forced, perhaps because he is weary from being forced to paste it on for "friends" and enemies alike. For what seems like the millionth time. With his body slightly slouching, his belly protruding somewhat, and a hint of the downcast in his eyes, the smile might even be read as one of (momentary?) resignation. Because he is no longer in favor at the court? Because he is again facing economic difficulties?[5] Because he has learned THE rumor is again in circulation—and believes it reset in motion by no one less than Adolph Fredric Munck, a person he now regards as an opportunistic knave preoccupied with the "blackening" of his own reputation?[6] Because, after a long day's riding, and ample time for both daydreaming and focused reflection, he is weighed down by his inability to summon up any pleasant memory of childhood? Or by an insistent longing for his not-clearly-remembered, never-to-be-seen-again parents? Or by his wife's recent miscarriage? And the children they have not had? The vicarious childhood and experience of fatherhood again ripped out of his reach? Or by his recurrent bad dreams? Or by the contradictions of his simultaneous both/andness and neither/norness? Or by his unrelenting Difference? Or by some combination thereof? Or? Whatever the case, it would seem that Badin has little to smile about materially—his attire barely bespeaks well-being, and the bag of possessions he is carrying appears meager. He may have a whip or switch in hand, but he is hardly in control of his world. . . . Did Sergel know something about Badin that inclined him to depict the man's face and body thusly, that entered into his struggle to get the hand-held pen to obey his eye? Despite an absence of more than a decade in Rome, was Sergel familiar with Badin and the trajectory of his troublesome conflicts? And with his mood shifts? (During Badin's first years at the court, Sergel was frequently present at the Royal Palace, where he worked in a studio as L'Archevêque's assistant.[7] And after succeeding L'Archevêque as the Royal Sculptor in 1779, his responsibilities may have brought him into contact with Badin more than occasionally.) Did Sergel—who was himself inclined to "melancholy" and bouts of depression, and at times suffered "nightly terror-filled dreams"[8]—know enough to somehow identify with Badin? . . . Whether or not with conscious intent, Sergel has situated Badin in a liminal space, as if enframing his perennial in-betweenness and the multiple contradictions of his everyday existence. With no ground visible beneath the horse's feet, and not even a hint of landscape or cityscape in the background, he can be seen as if suspended in air, floating forward at a languid pace, not in a hurry to get anywhere. The eternal traveler. The always en route. The ever dis-placed. The Black Ahasverus, the Wandering Ex-Slave, condemned never to return. He is at one and the same time coming back from his country home and reentering Stockholm (where Sergel would have captured him)—and yet he is heading out of the picture, making an exit. Moving away from a distant indiscernible past. A past whose traces are traceless, whose marks have been swept away. A past that is behind his back, out of sight, empty of detail, faceless, unrecallable. Moving toward a beyond-vision unknown future. A future in which he will be embedded well beyond his deathbed. A future of Universal and particular images in mutually reinforcing circulation, coursing unpredictably through shifting networks of stereotype (re)production. A here-and-now, still-unfolding future resonating with his pasts, filled with (mis)rememberings and forgettings. A future that was, and is, palpable but unspeakable.

———

Want of accuracy, which easily degenerates into untruthfulness, is in fact the main characteristic of the Oriental mind.

The European [in contrast] is a close reasoner; his statements of fact are devoid of any ambiguity.

Lord Evelyn Baring Cromer (1908)[9]

Linnaeus described himself as "not big, not small, thin, brown eyes." Contemporaries noted mainly that he was small and dark. By the late nineteenth/early twentieth century, however, conservative opinion makers imagined that this "genuine son of the Swedish people," of the "Småland yeomanry that for centuries have tilled the inherited soil," was of "genuine Swedish inheritance" and "the most healthy and pure blood." Therefore [in their eyes] he must have been blond.

Lisbet Koerner, on the racially inspired reinvention of Linnaeus's image[10]

———

[Badin] always wore extremely elegant white linen.

Badin loved . . . to hoist the flag on a pole daily, to his own amusement and commemoration. In his later years, at least, he was pious, quiet and inoffensive. Spending his time doing nothing was his principal employment. He cried easily, and when he cried large copious tears ran down on his chest. He always cried when mentioning the malicious deed involving his parents' bamboo hut.

Wendela Hebbe, (re)presenting the hut-burning "fact" and other items supposedly told to her[11]—a hut-burning "fact" that in the end actually may have been constructed by Badin, who, nearing the exit of his life, may have become increasingly despondent over having never seen his parents since childhood; who, having totally repressed the traumatic details of his separation, may have taken full guilt for the event upon his own shoulders through translating a dim memory of fire and sun-obscuring smoke into an act of personal arson; who, ignorant of the intense campaign of tree and undergrowth burning that marked his final days on Saint Croix, imagined his shipment to Denmark as a punishment for cruelty toward his parents; who, having lapsed into increasing isolation, and wanting for an explanation of over sixty years of dis-place-ment, invented his own fact-based fiction and condemned himself. Or, if Badin actually concocted the hut-burning story, it may also be read as a symbolic killing of his parents, an act of revenge for their failure to keep him. A matter of reworking emotional burns into an incineration of the past. Or, maybe again, the hut-burning "fact" was pure Hebbean fiction, and Badin never brought himself to tears with self-incrimination.

Whatever the case, Hebbe's account of "primitive behavior" was truly a social fact.

A stereotype-confirming social fact.

A field-of-vision-reinforcing social fact.

But when Archbishop Menander bestrewed the gold-embroidered velvet casket with earth, and not another sound was heard in the temple, other than the prelate's heartbreaking cry to the breathless majesty: "to earth shall you return!," he was answered by loud sobbing from a distant part of the church, where everybody's gaze was involuntarily directed. There, illuminated by the glare from the temple's thousands of white candles, they became aware of a black head bent over in a white handkerchief.

The Blackamoor wept for his benefactress.

M. J. Crusenstolpe, re-creating Queen Lovisa Ulrika's funeral[12]

That portrait again. The one I gave her with a note undersigned, "Your most humble servant." I saw it again today when I paid a visit to Sophia Albertina to receive the pension that she has bestowed upon me out of the generosity of her heart.[13] And the fondness of her memories. Our shared times together, decades ago . . . It hung there on the wall behind her. Staring me right in the face, as it always has on such occasions. An unsettling flashback mirror, a challenge to my sense of self . . . What was that all about? And what was I, am I, all about? That ridiculous costume they had me dressed up in. That feathered headdress—was it supposed to signify something elegant or something tribal, something civilized or something wild-man-like?[14] And that grin of mine. Pasted on as always; a necessity for any and all public appearances; this time explicitly requested by the artist. What else to be expected? How else was a Minister of Merriment to appear? Not to mention that circle formed by my thumb, forefinger, and the white knight. Was that really supposed to be a gesture of triumph, or had old Lundberg, that cunning pastel-crayon wielder, tricked me into forming a zero with my own body? United with a thing, made into a thing, diminished to nothingness? No wonder that erect left forefinger. My own little get-back. My own sly signifier, my wait-a-minute indicator—my effort to say: "Stop, fix your glance here, note who is really in charge of this representational chess match." But all the same, isn't the impression as a whole infantile? Am I not, at age twenty-five or more, made to look the child (of nature) decked out to be otherwise? Is not my very own image in some measure reduced to that of an already-held image of all Africans and all of their slavery-dispersed descendants?[15] And if, in the distant future, the portrait is publicly displayed, will it not perpetuate the general image? Will they not see in me what they already see in their imaginations? And will not what they see in me confirm the appropriateness of what they already imagine? Will not the fictions through which my pasteled image is filtered be rendered "factual" yet again by the very existence of that image? Especially if it is made known that the portrait was a cherished possession of Sophia Albertina? Naturally childlike, naturally irrepressibly and insatiably sexual. Universal and particular images inseparably entangled in one another. Image imprisonment. With God knows what consequences for those who come to share my otherness . . . . And, as far as they (don't) see, naturally incapable of becoming one of them. A decorative member of their most exalted orders—yes.

A "real" Swede—no. Inside, but somehow outside at the same time.
Outside, but somehow inside at the same time. Accepted, but somehow rejected at the same time. Rejected, but somehow accepted
at the same time . . . That first seen and touched snow, sensed
again. Whiteness. Deceiving appearances. Substance promised.
Fluid results . . . And in the end, near the end, what am I all about?
Placed in contradictory position, blown to and fro by the capricious
crosswinds of everyday experience, I am neither/nor. I am neither
an Afro-Caribbean. For I cannot be what I cannot sort out from my
smoke-engulfed memories, from images of the sun obscured, of
barely discernible bodies and disembodied voices yelling unintel-
ligibly in the heat and haze, and nothing more. (God have mercy,
even my mother's name escapes me!) Nor am I a Swede. For I
cannot forget that I am never hailed as such, that I am not always
treated as if equal to one. And yet, although locked in my black
Difference, I am both/and. For I am what I am named from my start,
and what I have become en route. For by virtue of my Saint Croix
surname, I am Couschi, and can thereby brace myself with the king
of the Ethiopians. And for I am also Badin, a name bestowed upon
me in Sweden when I was still no(more than a)thing, a present;
but a name whose meaning I have appropriated and redefined
for myself. Suspended between double belonging and double
homelessness, repeatedly moored and unmoored, being like the
black ink that, in making its mark, seeps into the page's whiteness but stands out as if apart, I have created my own composite
in-out-in-betweenness. My own out-in-out coherence. My own
sense of (afloat) belonging. Always being at home with my always
being away. With God's help, His Divine Light, my faith in His Love,
Power, and Mercifulness. And by way of that creative determination
I—Badin + Couschi—am at least their equal. And above the fantasy-
fed staged drama in which they have inserted me. Whatever They
may think. Of my sexual appetite and capacity or anything else.
Can't forget that. Must remember it . . . .
in the future . . . . Enough to bring tears
to one's eyes. Like so many times . . . . in
the past.

> *Badin, in an undocumented, never-put-to-notebook-paper, interior*
> *monologue from 1821 or 1822, near the end of his life*

≠ ≠ ≠

Flashforward.

One can, in fact, be both black and white.
Sixteen-year-old girl from Eritrea who came to Sweden in the
1980s at the age of six[16]

$$\neq \neq \neq$$

[Despite its shifting meanings and transmutability over the
past three centuries,] nostalgia retains an uncorroded nucleus
that can be described as longing. Nostalgia is a feeling of longing, a longing for something that has been lost. It expresses
separation. . . .
   Nostalgia, one could say, is to return inside one's own history.
   Karin Johannisson[17]

The illness is not seated in the body but in emotional memory
and has to do with very deep and painful sorrow *[or grief]*. . . .
It is characterized by an irrepressible urge to return home, but
most especially to witness those places where one spent one's
childhood. It most deeply affects the little child who is separated from its parents; maternal love is an existential need. . . .
Orphans who are separated from their parents forever almost
always die of nostalgia.
   Karin Johannisson characterizing a shift in the social construction
   of nostalgia as expressed in a pivotal French encyclopedia entry by
   Philippe Pinel, published 1821[18]

Nostalgia-Stenbroholt
Linnaeus, replacing his scientific definition of nostalgia from 1763
with a minimal one referring to the place in southern Sweden where
he spent his childhood years—written on a scrap of notepaper with
the trembling hand of an old man, probably not too long before his
death in 1778;[19] *written by a man who in his later years "oscillated*
between" vehemently expressed "self-esteem and brooding despon-
dency,"[20] *by a man who had become so difficult that Pehr Wilhelm*
Wargentin (Badin's apparent astronomy/meteorology tutor) could
write to a French authority on nostalgia: "All esteem [him]—but
hardly anyone loves him."[21]

Blessed are those possessed by homesickness, for they shall come home.

Opening lines of a multivolume novel (1794–1796) by the German mystic Henrik Jung-Stilling in which nostalgia is regarded as a future-oriented yearning for a home in heaven—a Swedish translation appeared in 1815–1817[22]

—

Just when I achieve some peace of mind, just when I am in command of myself, it again proves momentary. My demons resurface. I am re-haunted. By that moment of separation. That axing of my childhood. That cleaving departure. That swift eradication of warmth and security. That total spiritual divorce. That opening of an unrecrossable emotional gulf. That blow of lasting cruelty . . . Torn away. Displaced and dismembered. Permanently knocked off course. No recourse . . . I am replunged into a darkness of no apparent return. Cast into an unlit, bottomless pit. In free fall through a space ringing with the shrill silence of the forgotten. An abyss without signs or markings. Nothing but the unrecallable. However much I strain to discern . . . Panic reborn. Death relived. Sleepness nights to come. Nighttime awakeness and nightmares melting into one another. And days spent staring blankly out the window. Motionless. Immobilized. Fixed in (dis)place(ment). Incapable of so little as filling and lighting my pipe. Without appetite. Just yearning, futilely, for a glimpse of the never again accessible, for images of a home so far, far away and a family ever more temporally distant, for that which has no shape or name. Immune to Magdalena's attempts to soothe. Deaf to her words. Fighting back the tears . . . THERE again. Torn apart by one departure of irreversible finality and another looming on the horizon. Grieving for a lost past. That relentlessly recedes . . . Nostalgia to swing its scythe?[23] . . . Mentally enslaved, mentally flogged and branded over and over again by that which eludes my recall, by that maternal love that remains buried in my boyhood years of enslavement . . . Little remembered, other than that I have forgotten . . . The dreadful emptying horror of it all . . . Oh Glorious Almighty Lord, grant me mercy. Suspend my agony. Relieve me of my burden. Give me back my then/there. Here/now. Cast Thy Light. Allow me to see through the smoke and to discern their voices—even for the briefest of moments. Allow me to suckle at the breast of lost memories. However salty, however bitter, however sickeningly sour the milk may prove . . . Fortify me thusly for my remaining days. Give me strength thusly to further accept my displacement, to remain oblivious to being seen in advance, given meaning in advance. Give me lasting comfort thusly. BeFree me thusly. Until I pass through the gates of Heaven and come home to Thee. And everlasting reunion?

Badin, again in contemplation, but minutes after his previous interior monologue

Belongs to Adolphe Ludvig Gustaf Fredrik Albrecht Coichi Badin. He was born among slaves, migrated with them, but when the Light lit up he wished to die the death of the Free.

Beginning of an oft-quoted inscription ascribed both to Badin's personal Bible and to his copy of a book on farm-household management— perhaps a fictionalized fact, as neither of the original attributions provides any sources and no copy of either book is known to survive[24]

The First Book of Moses, forty-eighth chapter, twenty-first verse reads thusly: And Israel said to Joseph, "See, I am dying; and God shall be with you and carry you back to your fatherland."

A (f)actual biblical (mis)transcription in Badin's notebook (the word following "dying;" should be "but")[25]

—

[C]haracteristically, it is not only a man's knowledge or wisdom, but above all his real life—and this is the stuff that stories are made of—which first assumes transmissible form at the moment of his death. Just as a sequence of images is set in motion inside a man as his life comes to an end—unfolding the views of himself in which he has encountered himself without being aware of it—suddenly in his expressions and looks the unforgettable emerges, and imparts to everything that concerned him that authority which even the poorest wretch in the act of dying possesses for the living around him. This authority lies at the very origin of the story.

Walter Benjamin[26]

—

Nobody knows what kind of blood runs in my veins.

According to Hebbe, "a motto often employed" by Badin[27]

On stage . . . . . *Le Carnaval de Venise* . . . Playing the monkey . . . .
Playing the assigned role . . . Gustav . . . How could he ask me? . . . . .
Make me![28] . . . . Such a blow . . . And everyday at the Royal
Palace . . . The hurt . . . . . And out at Drottningholm . . . The
hurt . . . Expected to play the Minister of Merriment . . . To ape
around . . . . After all these years . . . . They still say it. . . .
As if talking about me . . . "Everybody knows the ape, ... but
the ape knows nobody." . . . But what do They . . . . really know
about me? . . . . Other than that . . . which They have long
"known" . . . about all black people? . . . . . And if They only knew . . .
what I truly know, ... fully understand, ... about
Them . . . and Their knowing of me. . . . . . . Ever since I arrived, . . .
have not They, ... in fact, . . . been the real fools? . . . . Now
that I fall . . . . . into . . . eternal sleep, ... when will They awake?
. . . . Monsieur Couschi . . . . Après mois? . . . . .
. . . . Après mois? . . . . Unforg . . .
Badin, mind wandering-wondering in a final fever, referring to a proverb
(Alla känna apan, men apan känner ingen) then (and still) in usage—
meaning roughly, among other things: "The fool (or jester) is soon known
for his foolery"[29]

[Badin's] cause of death is said to have been a "wasting disease."
Lars Wikström, citing a newspaper death notice and church records,
two sources that could not agree whether he died on March 18 or
March 20, 1822[30]

Nothing gums up fiction like facts.
John Updike,[31] *in his review of Peter Carey's exercise in fictional-*
izing facts and factualizing fiction, a novel about the celebrated
Australian outlaw Ned Kelly (1855–1880)[32]

Nothing gums up facts like fiction.
The author in word-order-inverted echo

Gumming it up. Making the image(s) stick. In the imagination. In the mind's
eye. In taken-for-granted fields of vision. Generation after generation. For
centuries. Pulled and stretched. This way and that. Re-placed here and
there. Elastically reshaped, redistorted, re-verb-erated. But never becoming
completely unstuck. Ever becoming always the same. Again. Over and over
again. In effect, only Different.

Gumming it up. Both ways. Fictions begumming (f)acts. (F)acts begumming fictions. Begumming one another. In countless everyday instances. Intertextually. Interdiscursively. Interrelationally. On the ground. Coming into nexus in situated practice. Traveling from place to place. And over temporal distance. From one social formation to another. . . . Imag(ination)es cross-appropriated. (Inter)reiterated. Recontextualized and brought into resonance with other here-and-now images, discourses, meanings. Connected together in unforeseen, locally particular ways. New variants. New mediations. New rationales. New nuances, inflections, and undertones. The ever-begummed stereotype somewhat altered in character. Yet ever becoming always the same. Again. Over and over again. In effect, only Different . . . Repeat performances. Reenactments, mise-en-(ob)scène, with sl(e)ightly modified prescriptings. Re-turn(ing) (dis)engagements. One FACTitious F(abr)IC(a)TION after another in (not so) revolutionary full circle. Negative re-views (re)produced.

Gumming it up. Linnaeus, working with his situated knowledge, tapping into his ever-widening correspondence network, tapping into commerce-facilitated networks of discourse circulation, tapping into textual fictions that had already assumed factual status, brought a host of images into conjuncture. And innocently pieced them together with that most power-full and adhesive of glues—the author-ative category. He produced a classification of humankind, thereby giving "scientific" substance to the already "known." And through publication, through dissemination into networks stretching well beyond Sweden, pivotally contributed to the sustained Different-iation of the enslaved and the colonized, to the legitimation of emergent racializing discourses in England, the German states, and elsewhere. His labels and descriptions were actually encountered in specific situated practices, were actually received and discussed in particular places, were over and over (f)actually remembered, remembered, remembered in various reworked forms. While the flimsy bases of his categorizations were ignored, while the insubstantial quality of his fictional (f)acts was over and over forgotten, forgotten, forgotten.

———

A propensity to undue and excessive animal passion of the
sexual variety, amativeness is most readily apparent by the way
this decadent energy over a lifetime voids a space larger than
normal on either side of the skull (to the retardation of all other

cerebral growth) between the mastoids, immediately betwixt the
ear and the base of the occipital bone.

> *Excerpt from a (1829?) review of Sir Cosmo Wheeler's fictionally
> factualized* Crania Tasmaniae, *a Linnaeus-inspired treatise of sci-
> entific racism based on the analysis of thirty-six "Negroid skulls"
> from Tasmania, the most pivotal of which—referred to here—
> actually belonged to a white penal-colony official. "Reproduced"
> in a novel by Richard Flanagan, another brilliantly gummed-up
> Australian work dealing with questions of "truth," or (f)actuality,
> and the horrific cruelties of British imperialism*[33]

Having reached that point I proceeded to that truth which isn't
established but very well might have been. It is that version of
reality which is unverifiable, but which we intuitively picture
for ourselves when we come so far that we cannot find any more
facts. It certainly may be seriously wrong. But sometimes it also
may be the case that the invented is both more real and truer.
I decided to make things up.

> *Monica Braw, in a highly gummed-up novel focusing on Carl Peter
> Thunberg, that famed disciple of Linnaeus who further reinforced
> the image of African blacks as hardly different from apes; a novel
> in which the author's wedding of "fact" and "fiction" is made an
> explicit part of the narrative*[34]

—

Getting gummed up. Stuck in(to) a position not of his own choosing.
Fi¢xtionalized, (f)actually fixed into position, involuntarily glued in place.
Badin's life in late eighteenth- and early nineteenth-century Sweden—like
the Otherized in other times and places—was marked by fictions become
the lived (f)acts of everyday life. Not only through his being savaged, treated
as a "wild" thing, raised and educated as "a child of nature" in accord with
the model in Rousseau's *Émile*. But also through his being seen as hypersexual—as the embodiment of those tales that simianized blacks and their
sexual activity, those long-circulating tales of no single ultimate origin that
became all the more credible in European scientific and educated circles once
resurfacing in the form of observations and claims attributed to Linnaeus.

—

At once, in flash of lightning, I saw the little black jester who
King Gustav kept at the palace in Stockholm. . . . It was said that

he was both wise and fair-minded. But it made no difference to
the popular conception of him. He could never show himself on
the streets of Stockholm, but was restricted to a life behind golden
walls. It made no difference how he [actually] was—he was
still perceived as the little, black, apelike, monstrous plaything
with whom idle court members could amuse themselves. I saw
You before me, a female Badin, riding in my carriage through
Uppsala, stared and gaped at by students, both of us and our
child exposed to ridicule, or at best constant curiosity.

> *Carl Peter Thunberg, fraught with mixed emotions, reacting to the
> discovery that his Japanese servant-mistress has become pregnant;
> and, in the process of denying any possibility of bringing her back
> to Sweden, simultaneously denying/forgetting/repressing his own
> previous characterization of African blacks and speaking of Badin
> as if he was dead. (From a 1776 entry in a diary whose no-longer-
> existing original has been retranslated generation after generation,
> in keeping with current Japanese usage, by male descendants of
> Thunberg and his True Love—as "reproduced" in Braw's gummed-
> up work.[35] Later in the diary Thunberg confesses a fear of "only
> seeing that one already understands or knows.")[36]*

—

Helping to gum it up for others. Not so much for the small number of other
blacks then residing in Stockholm in the keep of the aristocracy and the
Royal Court. As for Others dwelling elsewhens and elsewheres. Because in
the very process of his day-in and day-out begumming, for in repeatedly
being viewed through the socially constructed lens of the Universal, Badin
the particular became a confirmation of that very same Universal. Because
he became living proof of the already-held image. Because he became a topic
of conservation and gossip, a set of images in himself, which became wired
into the memories of many—sometimes crowded away and pushed beneath
the surface, but always laying/lying there, capable of shooting up unexpectedly years or decades later. Because he became at once a received element of
Stockholm's cultural lore, or collective memory, and yet another means by
which the Universal could live on. Because his (f)actually gummed-up life
eventually served as a model for future conflations of (f)act and fiction; because (f)act-containing novels as well as fiction-containing newspaper, periodical, and "scholarly" articles became social facts in themselves—actually
read and talked about, by actual people, in actual circumstances. Because
over the years there was little difference between such supposedly "fictional"
and "factual" representations with respect to the construction of Difference,

with respect to their propping up other representations that did not involve Badin, with respect to their reinforcing other images of the Black met up with in school textbooks and elsewhere, with respect to their role in the perpetual recycling and reworking of the stereotype of black hypersexuality, with respect to their reaffirming already-held fields of vision, with respect to their facilitating the dialectics of not seeing. Even when without intention, just so much monkey business! Virtually all of it!

—

> This is the pivotal paradox of fictional literature. A scythe cease-lessly passes across human experience; everyday thousands of insights into what it means to be human disappear; simultane-ously so much remains that sometimes one can wonder if any-thing ever disappears. Or is all the knowledge we believe we have about previous generations no more than an echo from within our own? You can never know.
>
> *Ola Larsmo, under the headline "Everybody Has His Own Tale," reviewing a novel by Kerstin Ekman whose focal point is the summer of 1916—a point in time when the six volumes of Crusenstolpe's* Morianen *were once again being republished*[37]

—

Gummed-up works . . . Crusenstolpe's enormous novel partially gummed up with (f)actual documents. And, in less easily specified ways, with popular imagination imaginings and ongoing debates of the early 1840s. Hebbe's fiFcAtCiToUnAaLl (re)tellings of Monsieur Coichi + Badin quite apparently partially gummed up with Crusenstolpe's *Morianen* (and perhaps his soirée recountings of [f]acts as well) . . . The reception of Hebbe's 1897 version coming into intersection with—and becoming mutually begummed with—other then-available textual representations, including missionary publica-tions that underscored the cruelty of Africans toward family members. That reception becoming further begummed with images resulting from both the commodified exhibition of one hundred Gold Coast blacks and an unspeak-able Stockholm wax museum display as yet unmentioned here. Hebbe's 1897 version also subsequently gumming up the "nonfictional" publications of Carl Forsstrand and C. M. Carlander, supplying them with the hut-burning tale and other "factual" information that they failed to attribute to her. Providing them a smoke screen, namelessly lending authority to the further factualization of Badin fictions, allowing those particular fictions to yet again speak to the Universal, to reenter into a genealogy of the stereotype that antedates Linnaeus, that is without beginning or end, that is still in motion, still propagated in discursive networks, still moving through webs of unanticipated connection, still traveling and entering into new (not so) sympathetic vibrations of meaning, still (re)produced and reworked in practice, still wittingly and unwittingly put into racializing practice, still concretely experienced by the racialized in the situated lived (f)acts of everyday life. At countless dispersed sites.

≠ ≠ ≠

> To be an "immigrant" means that you're not allowed to be
> Swedish, that you don't belong, that you don't have the same
> opportunities as the rest of the population because of your ethnic
> belonging. As long as society chooses to treat us as, and call us,
> immigrants we are and will remain immigrants. We come from
> all corners of the world, many of us are born here in Sweden,
> many have one Swedish parent, some are adopted, some have two
> Swedish parents, some don't even know who their parents are. . . .
> To be an "immigrant" doesn't mean that you belong to any par-
> ticular ethnic group, but instead means that we aren't anything.
> We aren't real Swedes. If we were to fill in an ethnic belonging
> question in the USA we wouldn't check "European," or "Black,"
> or "Hispanic," but we would all check that garbage pail "Other."
> *Dogge (Douglas Leon, member of The Latin Kings, a hip-hop
> group from Stockholm's segregated suburbs) and Michael Alonzo
> (member of another segregated-suburb band, Stockholms Negrer,
> translatable, depending on context or tone of voice, either as
> Stockholm's Negroes or Stockholm's Niggers)* [38]

≠ ≠ ≠

More gummed-up works . . . The 1996 Badin-centered novels of Ylva Egge-horn and Ola Larsmo intentionally and unintentionally gummed up with readings of the already gummed-up works mentioned above, intention-ally and unintentionally gummed up with Badin's own (f)actually written words and with numerous other items that have touched upon Badin by fictionalizing his (f)actual life and factualizing his fictional life. Eggehorn's fiction unintentionally gumming itself up with the (f)acts of displacement and denial via which so many contemporary majority-population Swedes forget the present and rework their own cultural racism, via which they turn a blind eye to the concrete—labor-market discrimination and segregation—consequences of their own stereotyping practices, via which they help produce conditions confirming what they already see in people of non-European or Muslim background, via which they once again perpetuate the dialectics of not seeing. Larsmo's fiction deliberately gumming itself up with the (f)actualities of modern identity issues, with the identity dilemmas faced day in and day out by those who are out of place because Differentiated and Otherized, by those who are perceived through a preconstructed field of vision, by those who are at once "seen" and made invisible, by those whose sense of self consequently often hovers between neither/nor and both/and, by those who are victimized by the dialectics of not seeing. And the fictions of both Eggehorn and Larsmo quickly losing their singularity, disappearing but living on, becoming (con)fused with countless other representational social facts. Collectively begumming past fictionalized facts and factualized fictions into the future. The same. Once again. Only Different.

—

The past is not dead. It is not even past.
William Faulkner (via Peter Carey, fact-fiction gummer)[39]

—

And what about the counter(f)actings shown in this text? The (f)act-based counterfictions shown in this text? The prPeAsSeTnt (re)fusings shown in this text? The constellation of then-theres and now-heres shown in this text? . . . How, upon dissemination and reception, can they possibly counterbegum? Partially unstick? Disturb and disrupt? Interfere with and jostle? Unsettle and upset? Undermine and dislodge? The genealogy of the stereotype? The dialectics of not seeing? Swedish (mis)rememberings and forgettings? Loudly speaking discursive silences? Taken-for-granteds widespread well beyond Sweden? Even in the slightest? If at all?

——

[A]ny historical narrative is a particular bundle of silences.
   [Historical] narratives are made of silences, not all of which are deliberate or even perceptible as such within the time of their production.
   Michel-Rolph Trouillot, Haitian born historian-anthropologist[40]

—

In 1825, three years after Badin's death, a long-licensed pharmacy relocated and opened its doors at Drottninggatan (Queen Street) 23, in central Stockholm.[41] Hung over its entrance was an elaborately lettered sign reading, "Kongl. Hof och Amiralitets Apoteket Morianen," or The Blackamoor Pharmacy, Purveyors to the Royal Court and the Admirality. With its depiction of a nearly naked "blackamoor" carrying a bow and wearing a golden crown, the sign must have readily captured attention.[42] . . . For those who belonged to the aristocracy, for those who were otherwise familiar with the court of Gustav III or Lovisa Ulrika, for those who were members of the Freemasons or any of a number of other secret orders, and probably for many of the elderly among the public at large, the newly situated Apoteket Morianen and its sign must have been readily associated with Badin. For while the pharmacy's 155-year-old name obviously was not a device to memorialize Badin concretely, he was then almost certainly the first or only "blackamoor" to come to mind under any circumstance. . . . And since most other Stockholm pharmacies were named after real or fictional animals, did the chain of association always stop with Badin?[43] Was not that "monkey business" connection, that synapse of hypersexuality, at least sometimes triggered? Especially since a wordplay-based tradition of popular humor may well have allowed *Apoteket* to be heard as *Ap-oteket* (The Monkey-, or Ape-*otek*)?[44] . . . As part of a massive renewal project, Drottninggatan 23 was demolished during 1972. Apoteket Morianen consequently no longer exists. Its former site is disremembered. It has become a forgotten space. Its history has been erased. De-signed. Made traceless. Unspeakable.

—

[E]ven as we must fully comprehend the pastness of the past, there is no just way in which the past can be quarantined from the present.
    Edward W. Said[45]

Every current of fashion or of worldview derives its force from what is forgotten.

Just as Proust begins the story of his life with an awakening, so must every presentation of history begin with awakening; in fact, it should treat of nothing else.
    Walter Benjamin[46]

Epilogue

The magic lantern was operated by the Queen Mother's negro
Badin. [The] operator boasted loudly of his skillfulness.

*Hedvig Elisabeth Charlotta, Gustav III's sister-in-law (then Duchess
of Södermanland, later queen of Sweden [1809–1818]), commenting upon one of several court divertissements and amusements
arranged during February 1776 in order to celebrate the "happy
union" of Gustav III and Queen Sofia Magdalena, to rejoice over
their much-delayed commencement of sexual relations[1]—a diary
entry made at a time when rumors regarding Badin and Princess
Sofia Albertina apparently were already in circulation and but
months after Gustav Lundberg had completed his pastel portrait
of Badin*

I remember that evening so well. It was unforgettable. I was in a
most triumphal mood. I could not contain myself. I was boisterous,
as I then still could be. On that occasion it was I who was in complete command. In power. For the moment, at least, I was oblivious
to all their nasty whisperings and all the signs of disapproval with
which I had recently been met. . . . I had been given instructions and
trained and experimented much of the day. And now I was dizzied
by my competence. By my ability to manipulate the cumbersome
apparatus, to make magic with the *laterna magica*. And I let Them
know it. . . . For once it was I who projected the images. Who fully
determined what they saw. When they were in total darkness and
I was indiscernible, but for my voiced remarks. When the black sil-
houettes were cast upon the white wall. Or upon Them . . . For once
it was I who authored the fictions. Who created the illusions. Who
illuminated the "truth." Who defined the "facts." Who made Them
see what was not there in substance. Who sometimes maneuvered

the device and its mirrors so that the head of a hideous animal or
gruesome monster was superimposed upon one of Their heads[2] . . .
For once it was I who made vision a source of extreme discomfort.
Who made baboons of them. Who made Them feel my pain. Who
made Them the eye-dart target of hoots and laughter . . . It was the
world turned upside down. An opportunity I was never to be given
again. Except in my imagination, when deep in prolonged despair.
Standing at my window, taking measure of the weather and my life,
in the middle of a sleepless winter's night, I have not infrequently
thought the thoughts I then thought. Oh Lord!
Badin, in another late-in-life reminiscence

Who can wake the dead? Benjamin believed that the equivalent of a Copernican revolution in thinking must occur. Fiction
would replace history, or become history. The past, "what
has been," had previously been accepted as the starting point;
history stumbled toward the dimly lit present through the corridors of time. Now the process must be reversed; "the true
method," said Benjamin, "was to imagine the characters of the
past in our space, not us in theirs. We do not transpose ourselves
into them: They step into our life." One does not proceed by
seeking empathy with the past: *Einfühlung.* This was historicism of the old mentality. Instead he argued for what he called
Vergegenwärtigung: "making things present."
*Jay Parini, in a fictionalizing of (f)acts, in a novel about the end of
Walter Benjamin's life*[3]

Here there was to appear a full-page photo of contemporary Swedes gazing at Lundberg's portrait of Badin. That, however, proved impossible as at the time (2003) Badin's portrait was undergoing restoration.

Part II

The Unaddressable Addressed: A Montage of Racisms on Exhibit

[T]he muffled fiction of history is "a place of rest, certainty, reconciliation, a place of tranquilized sleep."
Michel Foucault, The Archeology of Knowledge *(as reframed by M. Christine Boyer, "Cities for Sale: Merchandising History at South Street Seaport")*

The nineteenth century—to borrow the Surrealists' terms—is the set of noises that invades our dream, and which we interpret on awakening.

Every present day is determined by the images which are synchronic with it: each "now" is the now of a particular recognizability. . . . It is not that what is past casts its light on what is present, or what is present its light on what is past; rather image is that wherein what has been comes together in a flash with the now to form a constellation.
Walter Benjamin, The Arcades Project

Foremontage:
Unspeakable Spaces

For Benjamin, each building, each space in the city, has its own
half-forgotten tale to tell.
Graeme Gilloch[1]

Allow me to shift focus, to shift the spotlight from Badin and the begumming
of (f)acts and fictions. Allow me to move on from the racially stereotyped
to the sites at which racial stereotyping is on public (re)display, to those
spaces where racism is an object lesson, to those spaces where it is baldly
(re)exhibited for instructive purposes, to those spaces where it is visually
(re)presented and amplified or embellished. Allow me to do so while continuing to attempt to (re)fuse the prPeAsSeTnt, to bring pivotal—but readily
overlooked—(dis)junctures of the past and present into tension with one
another, into constellation. And thereby produce flashes of lightning. Allow
me to do so while also continuing to keep an eye and an ear on both the genealogy of the stereotype and the dialectics of not seeing. And allow me to
begin approaching the spaces in question, to sneak up on them critically, by
transgressing multiply, by speaking of the unspeakable in multiple ways.

Every space of daily life, every site at which women and men bodily en-
gage in everyday practice, every meaning-filled location of the quotidian, is
riddled with the unspeakable. Every local and wider geography of human
activity has its counterpart geographies of the unspeakable. Every conjunction of situated practice, circulating discourses, and power relations is one
with the (re)production of the unspeakable. The unspeakable is, in short, a
constant presence. A constant presence that in one way or another bespeaks
an absence, a silence, an invisibility.

Riddling every space of daily life? But bespeaking absence? No riddles
here!

The unspeakable as that which goes without saying, as the taken-for-
granted. As that which just makes (common) sense, which demands no comment. As that which is seemingly self-evident, which requires no discussion.

As that which is most thoroughly socially constructed, that which appears so incapable of being otherwise, so (second-)natural, so obviously meaning-filled that it would be meaningless to give it expression. As that which is automatically remembered in place, recalled without reflection, put into action without recourse to words. As a matter of habit(us), as a habit-of-thought repertoire—always built up in practice on the ground, always triggered by specific sign(al)s in specific social settings, in specific spatial contexts.

The unspeakable as the individually or collectively forgotten, as that which is unutterable because unrecallable for one reason or another. As that bundle of situated experiences whose occurrence has been packed away, shut down under lid and lock, repressed because so deeply disturbing, so unbelievably unpleasant, so terribly traumatic. As all those details of locally lived-out life that are so fleeting, so fragmented, so momentarily observed, so briefly perceived, so numerous, so without apparent connection, as to leave no lasting impression, no possible means of expression. As all those past (geographical) histories that have been pushed beyond the horizon of collective memory because erased, made opaque, covered up, culturally reworked, radically reinvented, socially reconstructed and remythologized, given a new (would-be) hegemonic version, or otherwise removed from encounterable discourse.

The unspeakable as the taboo-laden, as the forbidden word, as that which absolutely may not be said. Under any circumstances! In any situation! Or at least not within the earshot of those in power. As that which ought to be totally unmentionable, universally unnameable, fully silent. As that which is verbally completely out of line, out of place, off the map. As power *speaking* by way of the gag and the muzzle, by way of the openly wielded stick and the glove-hidden brass-knuckled fist, by way of the tied tongue, the locked lip, and the stilled statement, by way of subjecting individuals to (self-)discipline, (self-)control, (self-)censorhip.

The unspeakable as that for which there are literally no words. As those feelings and sensations, those desires and moods, which, although evoked by concrete circumstances, are inexplicable, inexpressible, inarticulatable, unconvertible to language, beyond words. As those here and now moments of intense joy, of stupendous sorrow or stunning shock, which cannot be put into words, which leave one at a loss for words, which are impossible to voice.

The unspeakable as the "indescribably objectionable or hateful,"[2] as the "inexpressibly bad."[3] As that sited phenomenon that is so terribly attributed, so far beyond the norms of the acceptable, so gruesome or grotesque, so disgusting or distasteful, so repulsive or revolting, as to leave one speechless. In a word (or two), as the simply horrendous.

Unspeakable spaces, then, as enmeshed in geographies of the taken-for-granted, the forgotten, the taboo-laden, the literally unsayable, the absolutely appalling. Spaces and geographies not necessarily existing on their own, but sometimes—as will become painfully evident here—also in localized conjunction with one another, in joint constellation. Spaces and geographies of consequence produced by way of specific situated practices, by way of variously scaled power relations and intersecting discursive networks.

On Exhibit: Hartkopf's Unspeakable Space, or Past Moment as Forenow

Museums are important venues in which a society can identify itself and present itself publicly. Museums solidify culture, endow
it with a tangibility, in a way few other things do. . . . Museums
have always featured *displays of power*.
    Steven C. Dubin[1]

When I go to a museum, I am aware of a production of knowledge more blatant than Foucault's panopticon could survey.
    Susan A. Crane[2]

*[Subsequent to its eighteenth-century invention, the museum
evolved]* as a factory for the production of modern subjects.
    Museums thus *[became]* part of a network of eclectic modern
institutions designed explicitly to illuminate and demonstrate
important "truths" about individuals, peoples, nations, gen-
ders, classes, and races—in short, about precisely those things
that museums are simultaneously complicit in *fabricating and
factualizing*.
    Donald Preziosi[3]

Dream houses of the collective: arcades, winter gardens, panora-
mas, factories, wax museums, casinos, railroad stations.
    The waxwork figure as mannequin of history.
    No immortalizing so unsettling as that of the ephemera and
the fashionable forms preserved for us in the wax museum. And
whoever has once seen her must, like André Breton, lose his

heart to the female figure in the Musée Grévin who adjusts her
garter in the corner of a loge.

Walter Benjamin, on the wax cabinet, or museum, as commodified
erotic space[4]

———

Allow me, on the pages that follow, to continue transgressing multiply,
to speak of a specific unspeakable space in multiple ways. To catch in the
act a particular(ly) unspeakable space, a peculiar place in (un)becoming
process, a singular site at once remarkably alluring and repellent, a space
at which racial stereotyping was (re)exhibited nakedly. More precisely,
Hartkopf's Wax Cabinet and Anatomical Museum, a wax museum tempo-
rarily located in Stockholm between 1895 and 1898 on a major downtown
thoroughfare. Here was a space—like the very modernizing city in which
it was located—that was characterized by fragmented juxtapositions, by
disjointed and constantly shifting scenes, by the presence of the multivalent
and the polysemous, by the convergence of items and influences from near
and far, by overlapping fields of power, by a diversity of multiply scaled
(hi)stories, relations, and discourses come into conjuncture, by anything
and everything converted into the commodity form. Here was a space
whose ancestry could be traced to Renaissance-era *cabinets des curieux*
and *Wunderkammern,* with their wild assortments of the rare and unusual,
their exotic flora and stuffed fauna of distant origin, their mummies and
relics of the past, their "giant's teeth," "shells that produce ducks," and
"stones endowed with magical powers," their objects meant to "provoke astonishment," their collections that were accessible only to the aristocracy.[5]
Here was a space descended from the waxworks first opened in London
by Madame Tussaud during 1802, from those waxworks that eventually inspired imitations in numerous nineteenth-century European urban
centers, from those waxworks whose continually altered displays came to
include not only a dimly illuminated Chamber of Horrors, but "every kind
of person that engaged the popular imagination: familiar biblical and literary characters, heroes and villains of history, characters from folklore and
legend, even, by a kind of intramural rivalry, famous freaks such as one
could see in the flesh in nearby rooms."[6] Here was a space that could also
be traced to those "lowbrow, almost pornographic, itinerant wax anatomy
collections which [either] traveled the fair circuit" in France and England,
among other countries, or moved from city to city;[7] a space whose changing
contents had, in fact, been in previous circulation, having appeared briefly
in Paris's Passage de l'Opera during 1865, and subsequently in the Swedish

towns of Vänersborg, Växjö, and Västerås, as well as various other places.[8] Here—not least of all—was a space that housed a spectacle, a spectacle that in some measure had been placed there to take advantage of the crowds to be drawn to the most spectacular of late nineteenth-century Stockholm spectacles, the Art and Industrial Exhibition of 1897.[9] Here was a space containing a spectacle that was an entrepreneurial speculation, a venture to accumulate capital in the capital of Swedish capital, a small echo of the just-named 1897 international exposition that—by way of object lessons and (would-be) hegemonic discourse—simultaneously promoted national identity reinforcement and the papering over of class conflicts while underscoring the accelerated commodification of Stockholm's everyday life.[10] Here was a space that was many, often contradictory, things at once. A space in which reality was commodified by way of reproductions, by way of the "authentic replica,"[11] by way of the waxen-dead come to life. A space that was designed to yield profits by amusing its visitors, by distracting its working-class and (lower-?)middle-class clientele from the anxieties and hardships of everyday urban existence. And yet, a space at least pretending to educate its customers. A space whose "fact"-filled displays and personifications of truth often resonated with those of nonprofit public museums—those "machines for progress" where the exhibition of artifacts was an exercise in governmentality, an order(ing) of things "aimed at reshaping general norms of social behaviour," a state-sponsored "showing and telling" project "calculated to embody and communicate specific cultural meanings and values."[12] And yet, a space that was at least as much voyeuristic peep show and freak show as venue for subject formation, at least as much about titillation and heterosexual male arousal as about edification and the production of self-regulated, self-monitored conduct. Here was a space that made finger-pointing distinctions between "good" and "evil" through juxtaposing mannequin effigies of Florence Nightingale, Otto von Bismarck, Pope Pius IX, the "Yngsjö murderess" Anna Månsdotter, and other (in)famous celebrities. And, by virtue of doing so, also bore some resemblance to the Swedish Panoptikon (Svenska Panoptikon), a "living museum," a self-consciously more elegant and "culturally ambitious" operation that positioned itself as more "respectable," "cultivated," and "elevated" than other commodified wax displays. (A self-consciously "bourgeois entertainment," located but a few blocks away beside the fashionable Royal Gardens [Kungsträdgården], the Panoptikon was a site where the paying visitor was confronted with "painstakingly staged tableau scenes" often arranged in narrative sequence, with extraordinary hyperreal re-creations of "Stanley in Africa, . . . famous Swedish singers and actors in [the foyer of] Stockholm's Royal Dramatic Theater, or . . . a discussion in [the] ship's cabin [of] Nordenskjöld's polar expedition."[13]) And yet, here was a space that was supercharged with the erotic and the sexual by way of a diaphanously (un)dressed "Venus after the bath" in beckoning recline, the allurements of "[Sultan] Abdul Hamid's favorite slave-woman," and the suggestiveness of a chastity-belt display—a space that was by virtue of these and other soon-to-be-introduced items far removed from the realm of middle-class propriety normal(izing)ly marketed at the Panoptikon.[14]

—

Education was the fetish of exhibitions, especially the kind which sought to edify the masses.
Paul Greenhalgh[15]

Albinos from Madagascar, the foot of a Chinese child, the hairy lady and the skeleton man. The strange, the odd—the scandalous. The appetite for the deviant during the late nineteenth century was boundless.
Gunnar Broberg[16]

—

Imagine, now, that space of distractions and attractions. Imagine that space of extraordinary phenomena remarkably jumbled, indiscriminately mingled. Imagine that space of oh-so-life-like effigies of the politically, criminally, and otherwise distinguished in no-rhyme-or-reason proximity to each other. Imagine that space of would-be anatomical and hygienic lessons, their fleshier than flesh waxen bodies super-real down to the last pubic hair, in improbable promiscuity with the completely unrelated. Imagine that space of uncanny facsimiles of "the Japanese with two heads," "the pregnant dwarf," and other examples of the freakishly formed and grotesque—oddly juxtapositioned oddities whose very oddness could serve as a confirmation of the observer's normality, as a reassurance to even the economically pressed and class-bound that, in the absence of bodily malformation, one's everyday existence was relatively secure.[17] Imagine, now, *if you possibly can,* amid this stunning array of the seductive and the repulsive, amid this assemblage of the arresting and the awe-inspiring, amid this hodgepodge of the pleasurable and the fascinatingly unpleasant, a stop-you-in-your-tracks glass-topped display case containing a horizontally laid-out door-sized wooden panel. And, fully stretched out and nailed to its constituent planks, *the skin of a black African "native."* And within that same case, a smaller case. Housing an object a few inches in length. Beside it, a card labeled with impeccably neat penmanship: *A Negro penis*. In the former case, no claims to mere verisimilitude, no insistence upon an equivalent simulacrum, no resort to auraless mechanical reproduction. But assertion of the real "native" thing. In the latter case, pure detachment. Nothing more or less. Imagine that! Unspeakably unspeakable![18]

—

[I]n order to gain knowledge from museums, viewers, whether they are aware of it or not, both reify the objects they examine, treating them as decontextualized commodities, and identify with them, allowing them to generate memories, associations, fantasies.

[T]hey have experiences as a result of interacting with the museum environment, which gives them novelty, pleasure, and possibly pain.
   Ludmilla Jordanova[19]

Vision and its effects are always inseparable from the possibilities of an observing subject who is both the historical product and the site of certain practices, techniques, institutions, and procedures of subjectification. . . .

[A]n observer is . . . one who sees within a prescribed set of possibilities, one who is embedded in a system of conventions and limitations.
   Jonathan Crary[20]

—

What was or was not going on at this unspeakable space? What kinds of observational conventions and stereotypes were brought into play, what socially constructed images were evoked, what templates of knowledge became salient, what discursively established and seemingly unproblematic truths awaited verification, what practice-based preconceptions were immediately summoned to the surface, what taken-for-granteds came unreflectingly to mind, what went without saying, when the nailed-down hide and the dismembered member came into sight, when those simply horrendous subject-remnant objects entered the visitor's field of vision? When confronted by the flayed African and the severed sex organ, what was the range of responses, the spectrum of emotions, the forms of re-cognition, the chain of associations, the composition of experiential connection? What, on exposure, was remembered and thereby simultaneously forgotten because repressed or socially erased? What, upon startled reaction, could one allow oneself to say to those standing at one's elbow or encountered afterward? What, if anything, among the (shock-following?) rush of sentiments was completely beyond words, entirely inexpressible? What, not least of all, had made the elicited possible? What situated practices, power relations, and discursive networks had come into conjunction at this very spot?

—

> The sociohistorical conjuncture that facilitates development of
> a [racialized] discourse generally consists in the confluence of
> material and conceptual conditions over a period of time from
> which arises the definition of the discursive object and articula-
> tion of the field of discourse.
>   *David Theo Goldberg*[21]

> Darwin's rebuttal of theories of polygenesis entailed that differ-
> ent means be found for establishing and representing the frac-
> tured unity of the human species. By and large, this was achieved
> by the representation of "primitive peoples" as instances of
> arrested development, as examples of an earlier stage of species
> development which Western civilizations had long surpassed.
>   *Tony Bennett*[22]

—

> [The Bushmen of Africa] are barely above animal standing and
> are among the world's most uncivilized inhabitants. . . . Their
> language, which sounds like the jabbering of animals, seems
> extremely limited.
>   *K. Kastman and T. Brunius, in a Swedish geography textbook*[23] *of*
>   *the mid-1860s that was "widely distributed and checked by govern-*
>   *ment authorities"*[24]

> Since long back in time Negroes have lived in the hottest regions
> of Africa. They are distinguished by their dark brown or black-
> ish skin, wooly hair, sparse beard growth and protruding thick

lips. Although the Negroes generally dwell in settlements, they stand at a very low level of culture.

E. Carlson, J. J. Dalström, and C. Lidman, in a primary school geography book that was first published in 1887 and remained in use until 1948, generally regarded as one of Sweden's first "modern" textbooks[25]

Questions not easily answered. For there was no universal observer. No homogeneous Swede, no unitary working- or middle-class subject, no genderless subject, with an undifferentiated set of readings and reactions. All the same, at least one key common denominator provides a ground for educated speculation. . . . During the mid- and late nineteenth century, the geography and history textbooks of Stockholm's compulsory primary schools were sprinkled with references to the supposed physical, cultural, and behavioral attributes of black Africans, with descriptions of their supposed animal-like and uncivilized qualities, with not-to-be-denied indications of their moral and mental "inferiority." These representations of the supposedly primitive and savage were in considerable measure derived from contemporary German and English sources;[26] that is, from the international circulation of discourses that legitimated the colonization of Africa and the extermination of countless Africans,[27] from discourses now buttressed by Darwin-inspired notions of arrested development and a "missing link" as well as the skull-measuring "science" of physical anthropologists—from discourses whose factualized fictions were coming around full circle to the extent they had initially gained scientific authority through the tenth edition of *Systema Naturae* and other mid-eighteenth-century writings of Linnaeus.[28] Unless a perpetual truant, no child attending Swedish schools could escape repeated exposure to these verbal and pictorial images, could escape being drilled in an alphabet of interrelated ideas that systematically shaped the African as negative object, could escape the redundancy necessary to impression inscription and memory etching. Thus, many Stockholm residents or tourists who came upon the nailed-down hide might very well have spontaneously reacted with thoughts that were in resonance with racist imagery they had packed down into mental storage during their early years, might very well have been momentarily surprised but by no means perplexed by the sight, might very well have thought of the human remains as subhuman remains, might very well have almost instantly regarded the display of an African male's skin as perhaps little more unnatural than the display of an African lion's or zebra's hide—African wild things, one and all; nature's culture-lacking creatures, one and all. Such a spontaneous reaction would have been all the more likely among those wax-cabinet visitors who were devoted readers of Stockholm's daily press and various illustrated magazines, of publications whose veracity and authority were as yet seldom questioned.[29] For there, too, distantly origined stories and pictures occasionally appeared that could reinforce what one had been exposed to in school, that could underscore that black Africans were without doubt far less evolved than Swedes (and other Western Europeans), and that, in so doing, could reaffirm the more general rhetoric of Swedish progress and civilizational superiority so loudly broadcast at the Stockholm Exhibition of 1897.[30] (Some viewers must also have been especially prone to a wild response because of their encounter with either books on travel and exploration or missionary writings of the 1880s and 1890s that also reinforced images acquired in childhood,[31] that reassuringly transformed "the dark places [and peoples] of the [African] 'unknown' into the white space of the 'known,'"[32] that not infrequently spoke of Africans in terms of "the cruelest barbarianism."[33] Whatever the case, to the extent that widely available representations linked black Africans with wild "nature" and Swedes with civilized "culture" they were enmeshed with late nineteenth-century discourses of gender and class difference that employed a nature versus culture binary in order to hierarchize and thereby legitimize practices of discrimination, domination, and exploitation.[34])

———

There is never a pure access to a single object; vision is always multiple, adjacent to and overlapping with other objects, desires, and vectors. Even the congealed world of the museum cannot transcend a world where everything is in circulation.

Part of the cultural logic of capitalism *[already becoming evident at the end of the nineteenth century]* demands that we accept as *natural* switching our attention rapidly from one thing to another. Capital, as accelerated exchange and circulation, necessarily produced this kind of human perceptual adaptability and became a regime of reciprocal attentiveness and distraction.
   Jonathan Crary[35]

—

Indeed, such *["primitive"]* peoples were typically represented as the still-living examples of the earliest stage in human development, the point of transition between nature and culture, between ape and man, the missing link necessary to account for the transition between animal and human history.

> *Tony Bennett*[36]

From the mid-nineteenth century onward, the skull of the male ape provided the standard against which Africans would be measured and, as such, provided the means through which African inferiority would be established *[through which genocidal aggression could be justified]*.

> *Zine Magubane*[37]

[N]iggers *[resemble]* big monkeys dressed up for a game.

> *E. A. Freeman, English historian (named Regius Professor of Modern History at Oxford in 1884), while on a U.S. lecture tour, 1881–1882*[38]

—

The Negroes constitute but a single race. . . . The flatness of their skulls gives the Hottentot's head an apelike touch.[39]

> *Franz Otto, in a Swedish school reader circulating in the late 1880s*[40]

No. 14: *The Ape as Photographer,* showing his foul mood because the ape to be photographed refuses to sit still.

No. 16: *An Ape as Magician,* with two musicians, performing several amazing transformations on the table, "a la Bosco."

No. 19: *Four Grimacing Apes,* representing a Painter, a Lady, a Shoemaker, and a Maître de.

> *Excerpts from a catalog for a wax cabinet, with mechanically operated figures, doing business in the city of Sundsvall, 1877*[41]

Whatever their preexisting repertoire of relevant taken-for-granteds, whatever their already-held stereotypes and associational predilections, whatever their observational (pre)dispositions, whatever connections were being made to published texts, visiting gazers and gawkers were not spontaneously reacting in an immediate vacuum, but in the context of a field of possible visual resonances, of here and now representational intersections. In all likelihood, whatever was being seen was not being seen out of mere habit(us). Whatever meanings men and women attached to the stretched-out and detached African life-remnants were apt to have been influenced or reinforced by other objects encountered within the confines of Hartkopf's Wax Cabinet.[42] . . . In a setting where replicas of the real were commodified, where real-life distractions were marketed, where ticket payers could presume themselves to be purchasing access to (reproduced) authenticity, what responses might have emerged as a consequence of other African representations in juxtaposition, in echoing tension with each other? . . . What responses might have been formed if the starkly displayed hide and penis were mentally conjoined with the relatively innocent vision that greeted one's eye upon peeping through a hole into a "panorama of Hottentot daily life," the central piece of which was a lightly clad, spear-carrying, shield-wielding male in full dance? Did this suggest that the skinned African, when alive, might have been much like the dancer, been near naked and wild in everyday life, been prone to "primitive" frenzied movement? Not much above the animal, after all![43] Did the spear, thrust upward, suggest anything of the dancer's sexuality, produce some forbidden or fearful fantasy, or even lead to a direct and unmitigated association with the disconnected penis itself? . . . What fleeting thoughts might have appeared if some connection was made between the encased hide and penis and a scene depicting two fully dressed apes playing cards outside a thatched hut in a lush tropical garden? Did the unmistakably human attire and capacity for (pretending at) civilized play bring more than a smile, bring mental monkey business, bring yet another affirming suggestion that the human-like ape and the "ape-like" African were occupants of the same blurred zone, were of virtually the same evolutionary stage? Of virtually the same (un)intelligence? Equally unequal to US!? . . .

———

[T]he most powerful stereotypes in nineteenth-century Western Europe and the United States were those that associated images of race, sexuality, and the all-pervasive idea of pathology.

When a specimen was to be preserved for an anatomical museum, more often than not the specimen was seen as a pathological summary of the entire individual *[and as the "essence" of his or her entire race]*.

Miscegenation was a fear (and a word) from the late nineteenth-century vocabulary of sexuality.
    Sander L. Gilman[44]

———

What additional thoughts might have raced to mind if the observing man or woman coupled the African hide and penis with a display given prominence in Hartkopf's newspaper advertisements, with a true-to-life depiction of a "Gorilla carrying off a young white girl,"[45] with a graphic reproduction elaborated upon as follows in the wax cabinet's own catalog?[46]

> The Gorilla *(Gorilla Trygladytes, Gorilla Engina)*, discovered in 1847 at the Gabon River in Africa by a missionary named Savage, is an ape—called the "Forest Man"—belonging to the same family as the chimpanzee. . . .
>
> The Gorilla is feared for his ill-temperedness and extraordinary strength, which is so great that in a fight he can easily defeat a leopard, a tiger and a lion at the same time. . . .
>
> The ivory hunter fears the Gorilla more than any other animal, since it will attack people without provocation, crushing them with its mighty arms and tearing them to bits with its terrible teeth, which are so sharp that they can chew a rifle-barrel to pieces. . . .
>
> Some years ago news that was as frightening as it was remarkable reached Europe from the Transvaal Republic in South Africa. The daughter of a plantation owner, accompanied by several female servants, went to a nearby river to bathe. Nearly undressed and ready to step into the water, they heard a crashing sound and in the next moment an unusually large ape, a Gorilla, came out of the forest. Paralyzed with horror, the girl was unable to attempt to rescue herself by instantly fleeing. The chambermaids, with their typical Negro-race cowardice, had immediately taken to flight, while the Gorilla, captivated by the young, beautiful eighteen-year-old girl, threw himself in the water and swam to the bathing place. Realizing her desperate situation, the girl now attempted to escape, but didn't manage more than about fifty steps before the Gorilla caught up and grabbed her, and then with a dreadful roar dragged her into the woods. Informed of the calamity by the fleeing negresses, who had seen what happened from a distance, some natives soon arrived at the scene, armed with bows and arrows, in pursuit of the Gorilla, whose haunt they determined through the girl's heart-breaking cries of distress. Soon they saw how it caressed the girl in typical ape fashion. Once within bow-shooting distance, they began the battle, but the Gorilla didn't

release his victim, instead defending himself against his attackers, throwing stones against them, hitting three men with such violent force that they fell to the ground severely wounded. The natives, however, failed to kill the Gorilla before the girl's father brought it down to the earth with a well-aimed rifle shot. The girl had meanwhile been crushed to death by the ape's powerful arms. *The group we see here represents the moment when the Gorilla holds its victim in its right hand while using the left to defend itself against its attackers.*[47]

Would the catalog's identification of the gorilla as "Forest Man"—as tropical forest man, as man of the jungle—have encouraged some cognitive commingling of that fearsome creature's attraction to young European women and the unspeakable desires of the skinned African?[48] Would some (con)fusing of the racial and the racy have readily occurred? Would exposure to the story in progress have precipitated some imaginatively feverish conflation of the sexually driven primate's propensity for primitive violence and the sexually driven primitive's propensity for primate violence? Would the entire drama-drenched tableau, given a heavy overtone of scientific veracity by the resort to Latin names, have proved both erotic and threatening—the nearly undressed young beauty! the animal caresses! the shrieks for help! Would it have proved both blood rushing and anxiety producing in such a manner that unspeakable thoughts of the nearby sexual appendage could not be kept at bay, in such a manner that impermissible objects of desire could not be locked out of consciousness, in such a manner that repressed sexual fantasies could not be prevented from surfacing,[49] in such a manner that image(ining)s of Their racial essence and how They make love could not be surpressed?[50] Or would the sliced-off and limp character of that proximate penis, the fact that it was obviously not in a state of erection, have proved anxiety relieving, an antidote to psychic tremblings over one's own male sexuality, a sign that the subhuman African male was really not a threat to white women, that he was little able to miscegenate or propagate degeneration[51]—that he had been conquered, colonized, disciplined and brought under control, nailed down and rendered impotent? That he, the wild ignoble savage, the bestial subject, an ape man rather than a Swedish (super)man, was not as fit for survival, was deserving of sub-ordination, of the ultimate domination, of threat-ending emasculation?[52]

———

In our age of restless cultural development, when the arts and sciences have attained such heights, there is also no shortage of anatomical artworks depicting the mechanisms of the human body.

What in academic lecture halls may only be seen by initiated doctors and anatomists is exhibited here for one and all in a manner that is at once easily comprehensible, instructive and not the least bit frightening. . . . These artistic anatomical preparations are among the most interesting means for an educated and thinking person to occupy himself, since knowledge of our internal organs ought to bring not only scientific edification, but also the practical advantage of teaching us how to protect those organs from harmful influences.

From the 1894 catalog of a wax museum where the Gorilla tableau was then being shown[53]

Bourgeois society was built like a fortress, the walls of which defended the purity within from the dirt and pollution outside.

Male sexuality was . . . a constant threat until it was safely steered into the marital haven.

Jonas Frykman and Orvar Löfgren[54]

Sexual intercourse without love was repulsive, a crime above all crimes.

Israel Holmgren, describing his mother's Oscarian (Victorian) attitude[55]

—

The wax models of recumbent women [were] highly sexualized by virtue of their conspicuously feminine features; long hair, smooth skin, passive pose and so on. Equally, they indicate female reproductive capacities through the presence of the foetus.

[T]he viewer was intended to respond to the *[desubjectified, object-]* model as to a female body that delighted the sight and invited sexual thoughts.

Ludmilla Jordanova[56]

—

If many of the reactions provoked by the improbable display of the African skin and penis were influenced in part by immediate representational juxtapositions, if the strolling observer's responses were often in some associational tension with other objects exhibited at Hartkopf's Wax Cabinet, then items lacking any African reference may also have become involved. . . . Every now and then, did the propinquity of the all-but-nude "Venus after the bath," smiling upward in seductive repose, independently trigger heterosexual male thoughts that were at once dizzying and dangerous, at once arousing and angst-ridden—a flash-by image of the viewer himself illicitly conjoined with the white woman stretched out below, a fraction-of-a-second image of that desirous woman and the stretched-out African carnally coupled in similar fashion? Did the presence of the near-pornographic Venus occasionally prove even more intensely disturbing, even more excruciatingly destabilizing, even more stimulating *and* menacing because simultaneously brought into mental constellation with the Gorilla as well as the African? Or, here too, did the unrigid, unswollen, and bodily divorced state of the black sex organ provide some calming release, some anxiety reduction, some reassurance that neither white female virtue nor personal sexual capacity were at stake? . . . And what about all those white male genitalia totally exposed in painstaking detail, those meant-to-educate display cases underscoring that Hartkopf's was also an Anatomical Museum? . . . Was the sexual imagination of many an observer kept in check, prevented from galloping off into the realm of the taboo-laden, contained within the corral of bourgeois morality, by a depiction of Napoleon III undergoing a kidney-stone operation, by the counter-arousal sight of a metal drill extending through the full length of the emperor's penis? What more than a simple shudder was produced by the position of the surgeon's hands, by the clear indication that the drill was being rotated, by the sight of its tip blindly boring/exploring in the stone's vicinity? (Napoleon III's midsection above the groin was shown in cross-section.) Did the frisson resulting from the royal one in royal pain prove chilling in more than one way? . . . Was any dampening of runaway thoughts, any deflation of daydreamed desire, even more pronounced in the additional-admission, males-only, curtained-off area featuring three men's bodies tortured by syphilis?[57] Did the object lessons therein contained, the grossly discolored and disfigured genitalia—so grotesquely ulcerated, so utterly ugly, so disgusting beyond words—successfully convey their messages regarding the wages of (bourgeois-defined) sin, regarding the very real, corpo-real penalties of "whoring" and unfettered extramarital sexual indulgence?[58] To the extent that the connections made between errant thoughts, errant deeds, and aberrant/abhorrent consequences frequently led to self-censorship, to thoughts of: "Out errant thought, out!"? "Out African, out (de)coupled penis, out Venus, out Gorilla and girl?"[59] Or did the moral sermon made visible frequently fail to deaden desire? Was there often no blotting out at all? Because the other items in the room—completely nude and well-formed women in various stages of pregnancy or delivery—only served to further fire up the heterosexual male observer's fevered fantasies, to further intensify his eroticized turmoil, to compound the salacious scenes and uneasy virility concerns already birthed by his racialized and sexualized imagination?[60]

———

Over the course of the nineteenth century, an observer increasingly had to function within disjunct and defamiliarized urban spaces, the perceptual and temporal dislocations of railroad travel, telegraphy, industrial production, and flows of typographic and visual information.
Jonathan Crary[61]

All peoples . . . have enormous spheres of unpublicized speech, nonexistent from the point of view of literary written language.
Mikhail Bakhtin[62]

—

Of course, whatever emotional responses erupted at the stunning sight of the African's peeled and tanned flesh, whatever the preconceptions and taken-for-granted truths that instantly surfaced upon viewing the parted penis, the reactions of most wax-cabinet customers very probably were not only affected by images first implanted via elementary-school textbooks and later reinforced by occasional local newspaper or magazine accounts of distant origin. Nor were they apt to be solely influenced by juxtapositions of the moment. Whatever the thoughts and experiences of the observer, they must also have been entangled with the details of his or her everyday life, they must have resonated with meanings embedded in the situated practices, informal verbal discourses, and power relations that constituted his or her daily urban existence.[63] . . . What "commonsense" stereotypes did the observer bring to Hartkopf's as a consequence of workplace chitchat, of dinner-table discussion, of barroom banter, of words exchanged in the street with friends or acquaintances? How many readings were mapped out in advance by the gasp-filled or teeheehee-ridden accounts of earlier visitors, by the fanciful embellishments of second- or thirdhand narrations, by the raunchy whisperings of gleeful rumor spreaders? . . . How many filtered what they saw through messages received in midst of the quotidian via personal networks stretching far beyond Stockholm? . . . How many thought they knew what they were seeing because they "knew"—or had at least actually "seen"—a living male African on the streets, one of at most a handful who were to be found in the dock areas of central Stockholm where, having jumped ship, they hung about looking for stevedoring work? (In the caption to a cartoon of the period, a black with prodigiously thick lips is first described as "standing about looking after pickup work while simultaneously basking in the glorious spring sun," and then depicted in ironic manner as subhumanly ignorant, as Simple Simian.[64] For the figure addressing him exclaims: "Hey listen you, get into the shade, ha, otherwise you'll get sunburned, ha!!"[65]) . . . How many, lacking even ephemeral exposure to blacks,[66] all the same thought they knew what they were seeing because they "knew" what Africans were really like by way of the tales or popular representations conveyed to them by emigrants returning from the United States, by way of letters received from relatives or friends still residing there,[67] by way of the things said by the few privileged who had been to London, Paris, Berlin, or Vienna, where they had seen Ashantis, Senegalese, Zulus, Ndebeles, or other "real Africans" on display in simulated villages or dance performances that were a part of mass-audience-attracting exhibitions? . . . How many thought they knew what they were seeing because they themselves actually had either lived in America or been to an African exhibition in one of Europe's major capital cities—to one of those live exhibitions whose racial and more or less overt sexual messages often "gained credibility through their association with the 'science' of anthropology"?[68] . . . How many thought they knew what they were seeing because reading current German-, French-, or English-language publications was a sometime part of their daily routine, because articles and pictures that at once negatively stereotyped Africans and legitimated colonialism were a part of their reading diet? . . . How many made sense of what they were seeing because, by way of an evening's entertainment, they had been previously (re)exposed to racist imagery of African blacks, to visual "evidence" of their lack of civilization, by way of stereographic views or a magic lantern slide-show lecture?

Strömparterren Sunday March 31 and Thereafter

Weekdays from 10 AM to 11 PM, Sundays 9–11 AM, 1–6, 7–11 PM

Performances by the Great African Negro Warrior Road Show

14 persons under the command of Prince Quentin Nimla, oldest son of the king of Nanabrau on the west coast of Africa.

The negro warriors render a completely true-to-life picture of their life, manners and customs, savage war dances, and fighting and battle scenes in their distant, exotic home.

It is extremely interesting and instructive for everybody to see and learn about these uncivilized African inhabitants.

Advertisement published in Stockholms-Tidningen, *April 2, 1895, accompanied by a photograph of fourteen "primitively" dressed African males, many of them fierce-faced and wielding a spear or a shield*[69]

The Dinka Negroes *[from Sudan]* constitute the event of the week in Stockholm. . . . There can't be a word for tailor in their language, for they wear little clothing other than bracelets and ivory bones through their nose and ears.
From an article in Hvad Nytt från Stockholm, *June 22, 1895, reporting on the twenty-seven men, eleven women, and four children who were "on exhibit" at the Tivoli amusement park between June 21 and July 22*

Prince among Uncivilized Savages
Headline in Dagens Nyheter, *November 19, 1897, referring to a visit paid by Prince Bernadotte to a village of about one hundred Gold Coast "Ashanti savages" exhibited for over four weeks at Stockholm's Hall of Industry*

The profile of the African "primitive" or "savage" . . . in his nudity and with his "wild dancing," formed part of a European metaphor for uninhibited sexuality.
Jan Nederveen Pieterse[70]

Were there not a good many among the substantial number of people who visited Hartkopf's Wax Cabinet and Anatomical Museum during its three-year run who must have been especially prone to wild interpretations of the African body remains that met their eyes because they had already seen the "savagery" of African males on live display, as consumption spectacle, elsewhere in Stockholm—rather than abroad? . . . Because they had directly witnessed "savage war dances" and "battle" enactments on a variety-show stage during the spring of 1895? . . . Because they had previously strolled among the forty-seven "Dinka Negroes" publicly exhibited a couple of months later? Because they had previously viewed THOSE nearly naked! Sudanese with their bone-pierced head parts, tending to their elephants and goats, displaying their "ethnographic objects," carrying out "wild ballets like those other African children of nature are accustomed to perform," presenting their "war" songs and dances, enacting their "war games," and executing an array of exotic ceremonies?[71] . . . Because in November of 1897 they had been among the throngs attracted to the Hall of Industry in order to see "100 natives from Africa's Gold Coast," in order to "truly" behold flesh-and-blood examples of "the hardly civilized," in order to be exposed to black subjects in the form of commodified object lessons? Because they had previously been drawn to a spectacular site, to a "village" occupied by "savages," to "a long row of huts" whose interiors were "primitively equipped," to a simulated settlement where women publicly nursed their babies with "the unashamed naturalism of wild people" while men kept at their "primitive" craft activities with the help of alcohol? Because they had previously paid their way into a place where the ears were periodically assaulted by "an infernal din brought about by drums and pounding sticks" and where the eyes readily became fixed on dancers who rhythmically twisted their torsos in the most unimaginable and provocative ways? Because they had previously seen African males in person who (they already knew?) were "bad smelling," who (they already knew?) were inclined to "grin widely" in a "childlike" manner, who (they already knew?) were so "naturally cruel" as to not be beyond "working over" their wives with "a thick leather strap"? Because they had previously come into visual contact with "children of the tropics" who were so "wild" that it was out of the question to allow them to venture alone onto the nearby streets of the city's prosperous Östermalm area? (Adult "villagers" were only permitted to leave the premises in groups of two if they were accompanied by a guard who was to prevent them from either acquiring alcohol in excess of their daily ration or socializing with "Stockholm's youths.")[72] . . . If the Dinka and Ashanti exhibitions proved to be economically successful "amusements," if the latter attracted "an enormous stream of visitors daily," if it drew "about 10,000" people on a single Sunday and 50,000 during its first twelve days (at a time when Stockholm's population was somewhat short of 300,000), if a journalist quipped, "thank God the negro epidemic is over," after its twenty-nine-day stay was coming to an end, was not the probability actually fairly high that many of Hartkopf's subsequent customers brought concretely "confirmed" images of African (hyper)sexuality to the glass-encased skin and penis?[73] And thereby were all the more inclined to the wildest of sexual associations? Especially heterosexual males who had already viewed the Gold Coast village in a state that was charged with sexual anticipation, knowing in advance that the much-publicized "beautiful Nah-Baduh" was among its residents? Knowing full well that they might see she of the "antelope eyes," she whose limited garments were thin and quite revealing (like those of the other exhibited young females), she who had romantically intoxicated the Austrian writer Peter Alterberg during the village's 1896 Vienna display? (Right from the exhibition's opening the Stockholm press made much of Alterberg's having been "terribly in love" with Nah-Budah, and the guidebooks hawked to attendees by Ashanti children underlined that relationship.[74] Alterberg's infatuation led him quickly to pen a volume of sketches, *Ashantee,* that may be read as indicative of reactions among many of those confronted by the unspeakable at Hartkopf's. For it was a work whose subtext readily links blacks with "pure" sexuality, whose "subtext betrays a habit of mind that the author shares with the guilty public of reflexively fantasizing about human genitals when he 'sees' the black."[75])

———

Stockholm is an excellent place for darkies to be in. In the hearts of how many beautiful women do the strings so blissfully played upon by the Fisk Jubilee negroes still vibrate?
　　A journalist contextualizing the "Gold Coast village" exhibition then in progress[76]

Beside Mr. Louis is Mr. Payne, the second tenor, but certainly the group's number-one attraction when it comes to women.
　　From a caption to a Stockholm newspaper photo of the Fisk Jubilee Singers published in February 1895[77]

The Jubilation Fishers are back again. And there is sorrow among
the fops and joy among the girls.

*June 1985 comment made in a Stockholm humor magazine regard-
ing the return engagement of the Fisk Jubilee Singers (fisk is the
Swedish word for "fish")*[78]

Lately our daily newspapers have been filled with negro stories. . . .
A dark-skinned youth who, so to speak, has been in every man's
(and woman's) mouth is one of the Jubilation Fishers, Mr. Payne.
An obscure Copenhagen paper has spewed out that the wife of
a Swedish lawyer with a good eye for fish went crazy over the
pretty boy and traveled with him to the Danish capital. And her
husband, seized by raging jealousy *[in Swedish, literally black
illness, figuratively black passion]* raced after at the legal limit in
order to restore justice. And, in the end, the entire matter is the
blackest lie.

*A pun-filled version of a story that spread during November 1895
from Danish and southern Swedish newspapers to the press throughout Scandinavia—a story that lost all veracity when it became
evident that Payne and the Fisk Jubilee Singers had been in Finland
during the supposed events*[79]

Were there not yet others visually arrested at Hartkopf's whose immediate
associations were at least partly triggered by knowledge of another "troupe"
of blacks that had recently visited Stockholm? Were there not those whose
imaginations were partly fired by what they "knew" of the Fisk Jubilee
Singers? By what they "knew" about that group of four male and three
female black American singers who gave thirty-five "thunderously" ap-
plauded sell-out performances during the winter of 1895 and returned for
several more concerts later in the spring? By what they "knew" of that group
that "everybody" was talking about, that "made conquests within all levels
of society" and readily "roused attention on our streets" by way of their
physical difference, by way of their skin color and smile-exposed teeth "that
glittered like white pearl bands"? By what they "knew" of that group whose
members achieved celebrity status in a matter of days and whose accomplishments stood in contrast to the lot of "plantation negroes" who but a few
decades ago had been "handled worse than animals"? By what they "knew"
of that group that was repeatedly praised for the "captivating" quality of its
singing, the singular character of its repertoire, and its middle-class respectability (because of the jobs the men held and the formal attire worn by all

seven)—and yet was described as an ensemble of "straightforward children of nature," whose songs contained something "naive, almost childlike which is much in keeping with the basic character of the negro race." And not least of all, by what they "knew" of the popularity of that group among women, about the particular appeal of the handsome "Mr. Payne," about the blushing sensations that sensation could precipitate, about the suggestively titled sheet music advertised by way of his name—*Blue-Eyed Bessie; Madeline, Fly Here Oh Dove of Mine!; Dreams, If Only You Were Mine*—and about THE scandal, about his (fictional) "elopement" with the wife of a Stockholm lawyer and its dramatic conclusion in a Copenhagen hotel?[80] . . . Were there not at least a few whose Hartkopf reactions were sexually inflamed in part because they continued to believe the published rumor, even after it was invalidated, even after the stereotype of the black male as (hyper)sexual threat was contradicted? Or because they already believed, if not the lawyer's wife, certainly some other beauty must have been ravaged in his arms? Because they still thought, if not her, certainly one or more others among all those "pretty things" who filled the performance sites beyond capacity, who went back time and again, who thrilled to his voice, who would chat of nothing else? Lightning-like lateral connections made, couplings made, and an already-held field of vision confirmed before the case? That Forest Man, that Gorilla and his animal-like caresses of the nearly naked eighteen-year-old girl? Serves him right!

———

The comic press reflects the predominant discourses of an era more openly and directly than other sources. Opinions that could not be articulated by other means could be expressed in the comic press, since it was "just for fun." Humor reveals a great deal about society. "Tell me what makes you laugh and I will tell who you are." Jokes help to establish and maintain boundaries between groups. They draw the line between Us and Them. . . . the comic press was a momentous moulder of public opinion.
Lars M. Andersson writing on the anti-Semitic representation of Jews in Swedish humor magazines between 1910 and 1940 and on the importance of those representations to the construction of modern Sweden's cultural identity[81]

———

One of four cartoons accompanying the text of "The Poor Hottentot—A Rhyming Legend for More Mature Youth"—published under the rubric "Exotic Songs" in *Söndags-Nisse,* a Stockholm humor magazine, on February 17, 1895, during the first string of concerts offered by the Fisk Jubilee Singers. It ridicules the hyperfecundity/sexuality of blacks and suggests that despite their adoption of such "civilized" elements of attire as the corset and the vest, and despite their reading of books, they remain primitive savages.

›På negrerna›.

FADREN: Ser du, Gösta, di där å människoätare. Hvem tror du di skulle
äta opp först, om di komme åt, dej eller mej?
GÖSTA: Dej förstås, pappa, för dej skulle di inte behöfva plocka först.

Cartoon published in *Strix*, another Stockholm humor magazine, on November 18, 1897, during the appearance of the "Gold Coast village." Titled "At the Negroes" (also readable as "At the Niggers"), its caption reads as follows:

FATHER: You see, Gösta, over there are cannibals. If they could get at us, who do you think they would eat up first, you or me?
GÖSTA: You, of course, Pappa, because they wouldn't have to pluck you before starting.

— New Infallible Spot-Removal Product —

———— Surpasses Pears' Soap ————

~~ *Makes a Negro White in Half an Hour* ~~

Certified by Doctor Waldenström

Mock advertisement published in a Stockholm humor magazine between the 1895 visits of the Fisk Jubilee Singers.[82] *The advertisement plays off an iconic poster used to promote Pears' soap (a famed British product also marketed in Sweden), a poster whose upper panel shows a black youngster in the process of immersing himself in a tub to be washed by his Pears'-wielding British playmate, and whose lower panel shows an after-the-bath scene with the black tot's body now fully "whitened" except for his face, which "remains stubbornly black." (The "white" child has thereby acted as an "agent of history," bringing his counterpart "to the brink of civilization" and progress, transforming the colonized subject in his entirety except for that part of the body then viewed as "the seat of rational individuality and self-consciousness.")*[83]

Between 1895 and 1898 weekly humor magazines based mostly in Stockholm published numerous cartoons and other "comical" (mis)representations depicting blacks.[84] The simultaneous peddling of jokes and meanings occurring in these publications is especially revealing, not only because the comic press was "an integral part of public life," not only because it commanded a large working-class and bourgeois audience, but also since its contents often took the form of "anecdotes, sketches," and other materials submitted by members of its predominantly male readership.[85] Humor-magazine drawings and their accompanying texts were, in effect, articulations of the otherwise unspeakable, declarations of the already "known" (and feared) safely uttered and reworked in public, instructive, comic-relief reminders as to the True Nature of Difference, as to what one was really seeing and hearing when exposed to the staged performances of the Dinkas, the Ashantis, and the Fisk Jubilee Singers. . . . Several of the cartoons reminded readers that—whatever their appearances—blacks were at once threatening and laughably inferior, that they were so "bestial" as to be capable of cannibalism, that they were "niggers" capable of boiling those who attempted to civilize them, that they were so subhuman and limited in moral capacity as to consume (white) women. (In one cartoon a female head protrudes out of a huge still-boiling kettle, while one enormous-lipped African chomps on a detached stocking-clad leg, a second chews away at a severed arm, and a third is gripped with pain and yelling, "Mamma, mamma, I've swallowed a hairpin.")[86] . . . The childlike character and mental inferiority of blacks was underscored by a cartoon—"Stockholmers Drawn in the Manner Naturally Employed by a Dinka Negro"—whose crude stick figures left no doubt that They possessed little more than infantile skills, that They were all too simple to understand (the masculine Swedish) Us as We really are, that They were of another (subhuman) race, incapable of adult reason and thereby incapable of governing themselves.[87] And that Exotic Song, "The Poor Hottentott," verbally and pictorially depicted an obviously unintelligent and infantile African male being easily duped into the purchase of a lottery ticket by a huge-nosed Jew.[88] (To some this additional anti-Semitic element, this pairing of negatively charged images, may well have done double work by also touching off the sexual imagination. For, as Gilman notes, Jews "were black according to nineteenth-century [European] racial science," having been supposedly "'hybridized' with blacks in Alexandrian exile." They were, more to the point, "black because they [were] different, because their sexuality [was] different, because their sexual pathology [was] written on their skin," because they were syphilitic in nature, because they threatened to seduce "the pure and the innocent."[89] Such double work was encouraged by one of the song's illustrations, which gave the Jew's nose a clearly phallic shape, and by the text itself, which referred to the Jew as a "dark [or black] oddball."[90] Moreover, a late nineteenth-century epithet, *jud[e]apa*, or Jew ape, played on the supposed resemblance between the Satan monkey [South American *Chiropotes satanas*] and a heavily bearded Jew.[91]) . . . The supposedly simian qualities of blacks were joked about through—among other devices—a set of "Ape-ian Folk songs" derived from the work of a "famous ape-language scholar."[92] Not coincidentally(?), this animalizing (and sexualizing) gesture, this suggestion of uncontrollable urges, appeared but a very short time after the final departure of the Fisk Jubilee Singers, who had included various "folk songs" in their repertoire. . . . Time and again these and other similar representations provided readers with physiognomic "proof" of their own (Swedish) superiority, reassured readers that external corporeal difference—always the preposterously large lips, the bulging eyes, the out-of-control "woolly" hair, AND the black skin—was synonymous with inferior internal difference, with deviance, abnormality, and the absence of civilized morals, with the very antithesis of Swedishness. Time and again these stereotyping representations contributed to the construction of a collective We-ness, to the reassuring form(ul)ation of an imagined Swedish community in an era of bewildering economic and social transformation, to a distraction from the anxieties that accompanied tumultuous modernization, from the class tensions that were becoming ever more pronounced in the wake of accelerated industrialization and urbanization.[93] Time and again these comic reworkings of difference and anxiety thereby resonated with the national identity project so vigorously pursued at the Stockholm (Art and Industrial) Exhibition of 1897,[94] an event that came to an end exactly four weeks before the Gold Coast "village" was put on display in its still-standing Hall of Industry.[95] Time and again such representations insisted that the Pears' poster advertisement was all wrong. And instead "proved" the correctness of David Klöcker Ehrenstrahl's two-hundred-year-old *Futile Labor* painting, instead showed that African blacks were hopelessly savage and thereby incapable of ever becoming truly "white" or Swede-like in their behavior, instead drummed in the message: "Once an African, always an African."[96] You better believe it! . . . Did not the time and again exposure to such humor-magazine images enter into the conventions of observation unreflectively brought into play by many of those males who became transfixed by what was nailed to the planks at Hartkopf's and detachedly exhibited beside it? Did not these latest installments in the perpetuation of the stereotype often further facilitate the making of certain readings? Did they not often bounce around with other already-held images and enter into the febrile chain of associations that followed initial astonishment? Did they not frequently enhance the likelihood of a wild interpretation, of a rampant sexual fantasy? Did they not help ensure that not much was left to guessing? About what IT meant? Especially when cartoons and jokes that infantilized the adult black male—and thereby symbolically "castrated" him—also entered into the observer's on-the-spot jumble of salient images?[97]

—

The truth is, however, that Badin always maintained a certain penchant for amorous adventures.
    Wendela Hebbe, in 1897[98]

Yet again. The TRUTH . . . Yet again the Universal Truth confirmed by way of the Particular . . . Long dead, but still entrapped in a fictionally factualized image of hypersexuality, Badin popped up unexpectedly, as if through a trapdoor, and reentered the popular imagination, joining a crowded assemblage of other mutually reinforcing images.[99] Long-imprinted textbook stereotypes, Prince Quentin Nimla's road-show warriors, the Dinkas and Ashantis, humor-magazine cartoons, popular-press "facts," missionary myths, stories heard, jokes told, repeatedly encountered rumors, the handsome Mr. Payne, AND Badin. The whole lot of them! And more? All together! Coming into constellation with one another, instantaneously (re)informing one another, without conscious reflection, producing a momentary lightning flash of insight, a shock of recognition, and an ensuing chain reaction of sexual fantasy, flitter-fluttering past out of control until slammed to a stop by an anxiety-laden sense of discomfort—for how many of those brought to a speechless halt at Hartkopf's unspeakable space?[100] Or the newly resurrected image of Badin on its own automatically foreclosing any possibility of an "innocent" response? Providing on its own the Final Word, the ultimate field-of-vision (pre)script(ion), immediately telling at least a few of the dumbstruck exactly what was stretched out before their eyes? Providing on its own the connective spark that bonfired their sexual imaginations?[101]

———

There is no document of civilization which is not at the same time a document of barbarism.

    Walter Benjamin[102]

—

[T]hroughout the last quarter of the nineteenth century a large number of manuals on the method of teaching with objects were published and distributed to normal schools in Europe and abroad.

    William J. Glover[103]

—

[The international exposition is] an educational institution where the exhibitors are teachers, the exhibited objects are teaching materials, and the visitors are pupils.

    S. A. Andrée, in a book reissued for visitors to the Stockholm Exhibition of 1897[104]

The preserved black man's skin and encased sex organ exhibited at Hartkopf's Wax Cabinet between 1895 and 1898 did not merely spontaneously mobilize a certain range of observational conventions, did not merely trigger an array of confused and contradictory feelings or an assortment of sexual fantasies and anxieties that were grounded in an already existing and variously constructed popular racist imagination, that were based upon stereotypes already held. Whatever went on at that multiply unspeakable space upon exposure to those two objects was not confined to the instant of reaction, to then and there thoughts and sensations. For those objects—especially if brought into constellation with the Gorilla tableau, the card-playing apes, and the dancing Hottentot—constituted object lessons in themselves. Things that could dramatically instruct by way of the visual and therefore become deeply inculcated, well remembered.[105] Things that could flesh out already possessed images. Things that could provide physical proof of taken-for-granted truths. Things that could lend substance to previously acquired templates of knowledge. Things that could give stereotype-buttressing evidence. Things that could visually exemplify an accepted vision. Things that could serve as intensifying agents. Things that begged to be talked about and thereby reaffirmed. Things that were likely to have a lasting affective effect because, in fortifying and seemingly verifying a stereotype, they presumably lent stability to a stubbornly unstable urban world, to a world that was volatile and disturbingly beyond personal control, to a world of constant change and severe social tensions, to a world where anxieties, uncertainties, and alienation were daily encountered in new and old forms.[106] Things whose presence did not merely speak of a racialized imagination already in place, but also could further emplace by way of further (mis)education. Things that contributed to the further construction of a popular imagination that racialized and essentialized the Other. Things that were part of a late nineteenth-century forenow. Things (mis)leading to discontinuous and dispersed future consequences. Things that became part of an (un)becoming popular imagination that, although periodically dormant in subsequent decades, has time and again oozed to the surface during the twentieth century, has time and again been discursively reactivated, has time and again been put into situated practice, has time and again been reworked, modified, and embellished in Stockholm and elsewhere in Sweden, not least of all during the late 1980s and 1990s.

On Exhibit: Unspeakable Spaces of 1999, or Forenow and Present in Constellation

Wasn't History—this amalgam of stories and sighs, lumps and hunches—always threatening to reinvade the present and to become the future?

> *Jay Parini, entering into the thoughts of Walter Benjamin as he descended the Pyrenees into Port Bou, Spain, where he would commit suicide that night (September 25, 1940)*[1]

—

[T]he stereotype, *[which was the major strategy of colonial discourse]*, is a form of knowledge and identification that vacillates between what is always "in place," already known, and something that must be anxiously repeated—as if the essential duplicity of the Asiatic or the bestial sexual licence of the African that needs no proof, can never really, in discourse, be proved.

> *Homi K. Bhabha*[2]

[D]isplay not only shows and speaks, it also *does.*

> *Barbara Kirshenblatt-Gimblett*[3]

Exhibit 1: The National Historical Museum's Unspeakable Space

[A] young man *[of Ghanian birth]* completes his day's work as a care-giver at a residential facility for the elderly. On the way home, in a Stockholm subway-car, a man stares at him wide-eyed with aggression. A few stations later he of the hostile look

detrains and the object of his gaze heaves a sigh of relief. Only
to be jolted, shiveringly startled, by the sound of fists pounding
on the window beside him. And a voice screaming: "MONKEY!
MONKEY! MONKEY!"
Account of a 1996 incident[4]

DON'T LET YOUR DAUGHTER BECOME A NIGGER'S TOY
*Message widely dropped into the mailboxes of residents of Söder-
malm, a district within central-city Stockholm, during 1994*[5]

Allow me once again to transgress multiply, to speak of an unspeakable
space in multiple ways. Allow me to move the clock forward a century,
to the just-yesterday present, and to focus on another exhibitionary site,
one where the forenow/thenthere remains enfolded, one where the past
continues to echo and is yet unheard, because publicly stifled, not openly
discussed, left unaddressed.

An Itinerant Wax Cabinet is today just as much an exhibition
about human vision[s] as a journey in time. Contemporary
people need to have some perspective on their existence, to look
backward and understand why things have become what they
have become. Many explanations are here given to thought patterns and human behavior, even of our own times.
Inga Lundström, curator for An Itinerant Wax Cabinet[6]

The museum is in itself a symbol for reality. It not only stores objects and phenomena but also values that go back to the societal
conditions that prevailed at the moment of collection. . . .
When norms and social viewpoints are not explicitly defined, but presented as . . . self-evident, then it is a matter of
indoctrination. . . .
Museums are hardly attentive to the tensions lying in particular objects.
*Inga Lundström and Marja-Leena Pilvesmaa, in a government-
issued report, "Knowledge as Force—An Action Program for How
Museums Can Work to Counteract Hostility toward Foreigners
and Racism"*[7]

During the period March 17 to December 31, 1999, the National Historical
Museum (Statens historiska museum) housed an exhibit in Stockholm, *An
Itinerant Wax Cabinet (Ett Resande Vaxkabinett)*. Imagine, now, the very

same mélange of wax figures and objects as exhibited in Stockholm at the end of the nineteenth century, the very same mishmash assortment of the famous and the freakish, the very same repulsive-attractive collection of exotic, erotic, sensational, and "educational" displays. All of it there except for the Gorilla tableau.[8] Imagine now, *if you possibly can,* the presence of *the skin of a black African "native"*—once again stretched out and nailed down, figuratively and literally fixed in place; the presence of *a Negro penis*—once again faultlessly hand-labeled and set aside in a separate small case, as one would with something precious (the family jewels?) or something dangerous (extra-potent poison?); *and* the absence of any well-publicized calling into question, the absence of any widely broadcast statements of critical concern or ethical dismay, the absence of any controversy or debate in those mass media outlets where the arts and other elements of *Kultur* are reviewed and extensively discussed. Not a single word. Nothing but thundering discursive silence. Imagine that! The unspeakable unspoken of! Throughout the almost ten-month duration of the exhibit. And during the years thereafter.

> If efforts against racism and hostility toward foreigners are to have a long-term effect, then it is the real reasons that must be uncovered and worked upon, reasons that lie on a structural level. It is necessary to get at the more widespread forms of hostility toward foreigners. It is the task of museums to widen the perspective of people and add nuance to their historical images.
>
> [T]o believe that one can treat a subject neutrally is treacherous. Such neutrality always rests upon the long-existing, upon dominant thought.
>
> It is obvious that the attitudes and values that exhibitions give expression to, whether spoken or unspoken, are far more important than previously realized. . . . The contents of an exhibition are dependent upon the exhibitor as an individual. It is particularly important that the exhibitor is capable of articulating her view of life and has the ability to make it visible within the exhibit.
>
> *Inga Lundström and Marja-Leena Pilvesmaa*[9]

Even the exhibition's catalog itself allocated not a word to the African skin or the detached black member. The curator—who only three years earlier had officially pronounced that museums were to be at the vanguard of antiracism, who trumpeted the need for explicit commentary, for openly addressing structural issues, for shunning any pretense to neutrality—in practice chose virtual speechlessness. In commenting upon late nineteenth-century wax cabinets more generally, she did note that "strange races and exotic peoples" were a given attraction, that the displays offered the visitor "no reason to reevaluate his prejudices," that scientists of the time devoted much effort to proving that other peoples were of "lower standing," that the "savage" was typically shown in "crazed dance or warlike poses."[10] But why did she avoid the particulars of this instance while elsewhere providing specifics? Why did she say not a word, say not a word? Did she deem the amputated appendage and long-dead skin an exception to her own entreaties? Were the unspeakable contents of the display case thought to speak for themselves? Was this lesson thought so obvious that the teacher need not resort to a (penis-)pointer? Or did she (subconsciously?) realize that things had perhaps been taken too far, that some ethical transgression had been committed, that actual presence—even if it were to be described with historical nuance—did everything but counter racism, that the African's unmentionables were best left unmentioned? Or were her textual (in)actions quite simply in keeping with other identity-sustaining discourses, with other strategies of silence?

———

The story of Sarah Baartman is the story of the African people.
It is the story of the loss of our ancient freedom. . . . it is the story
of our reduction to the state of objects who could be owned, used
and discarded by others. . . . It was not the lonely African woman
in Europe who had been deprived of her identity and native
country who was a barbarian, but those who treated her with
barbarian brutality.

> Thabo Mbeki, president of South Africa, speaking in controlled
> anger to a crowd of thousands on August 9, 2002, at the burial of
> the returned remains of Sarah Baartman[11]—she who was labeled
> "The Hottentot Venus" and fetishized, she who was encaged and
> reduced to a commodified sexual freak; she whose naked body was
> inspected and gawked at "in the jungle of European barbarism,"[12]
> she who displayed her steatopygia and genitalia to paying Parisian
> and London publics between 1810 and 1815; she who was discur-
> sively linked with "primitive" nature rather than "civilized" cul-
> ture; she who, in keeping with the factualized fictions of Linnaeus,
> was equated with "the monstrous" and shown in the company of
> exotic birds, animals, and plants; she who supposedly embodied

ape-like qualities and thereby confirmed European racial superiori-
ty; she whose "allegedly peculiar" sexual parts were "likened to
those of the orang-utang" and "cited as proof positive of the claim
that black people were the product of a separate—and, of course,
inferior, more primitive and bestial—line of descent"; [13] *she who*
was written and talked about extensively in Europe; she whose
dehumanizing circumstances therefore very well may have come
to the attention of Badin, quite feasibly causing his stomach to
wrench, his eyes to blur and tear, his mind to race during another
sleepless night; she who was promised a share of each gate but died
a destitute prostitute in 1816, only to face an afterlife of further hu-
miliation; she who was reduced to a scientific specimen; she whose
brain and genitalia were preserved in formaldehyde and, along
with a cast of her (in)famous body, placed on exhibit in Paris at
the Musée de l'Homme, where they remained accessible for public
"edification" until 1974, when "growing complaints and a sense
of shame" about the European past led to their being stored away
in the museum's basement; she who, in the late 1990s, became
somewhat of a South African icon, a figure pivotal to the politics of
identity, a source of "inspiration for several plays, films, artworks,"
and a highly influential poem by Diana Ferrus. [14]

———

The itinerant wax cabinets of Europe surely numbered in the
hundreds. Did the merry fair public also finance death patrols in
Europe's colonies to shoot real natives and [then] skin and nail
them to boards for delivery by post order?

Or were the skins only a byproduct of the colonial states' normal extermination of native populations?

And was the distribution of the nailed skins to fair exhibition
tents a means for white men of power to boost European morale
at home, so that everybody learned how a native should best be
treated?

Or is the history of the nailed-down man simply one of a
captured native who, for a fee, was shown at the fairs living in
a cage? And when he died of food poisoning, did the commercial
entertainment industry, as usual, remove his skin to display it
and get back the money that the food cost?

Perhaps by studying the genetic pattern of this foreigner from
another continent it can be determined [exactly] where he comes

from. Perhaps he has relatives there who are still waiting to bury him. In that case I think we should help.

Per Simon Edström, current owner of the materials on exhibit, in an extended text attached to the skin-containing display case

If the curator chose to evade the (in)delicate issue, if she chose to contradict her own publicly broadcast principles, the owner of the exhibited objects felt it absolutely necessary to voice his understandings and sentiments, felt compelled to remark upon one of the most remarkable of his displayed possessions.[15] Was this an uncalculated attempt to counter considerable cognitive dissonance, to allay ambivalence, to rationalize the questionable, to justify the showing of a most monstrous property? Did his unsubstantiated reference to numerous "nailed skins" serve to reduce the burden weighing on his mind? Was there a subconscious effort to combat guilt behind the suggestion that modern science might relieve him of "this foreigner," behind the wistful wish that DNA tests could pinpoint the skinned African's geographical origins, behind the forlorn hope that—one or more centuries after the fact—relatives remained waiting for remains? Did he really believe that among all the millions of Africans who long ago were either slaughtered or enslaved and removed to another continent, it was just his "naileddown man" who lived on in the memory of distant descendents, who had acquired enduring symbolic significance, who was specifically longed after, who had relatives "still waiting to bury him"? Did he truly believe that somewhere "out there" was a person passionately committed to historical justice, a person championing a national icon, a counterpart to Brigitte Mabandla (South Africa's Deputy Minister of Arts, Culture, Science, and Technology), the woman who was "the driving force behind the complex [government-level] negotiations, initiated in 1995" that resulted in the return of Sarah Baartman's remains from France?[16] Was the absence in Edström's remarks of any reference to the barbarically severed sex organ, to the most extraordinary of his belongings, an expression of his own repressed thoughts or doubts?[17] Did he consciously or unconsciously suspect himself of barbarously breaking some taboo? Or? Or did both the said and the unsaid involve nothing more than the verbalization of good intentions? Sincere innocence put into words?

—

Seen through present-day eyes, Sarah Baartman and all the others *[whose "abnormal" bodies or body parts have been put on exhibit]* are examples of genetically grounded integrity violation,

debasement, and discrimination. . . . What is just and fair is culturally determined and varies in time and space. That is shown by
the case of Sarah Baartman. . . . When a contemporary observer
becomes upset over the treatment of Sarah Baartman and her
like, it is because human dignity is at stake.

> *Lynn Åkesson, Swedish ethnologist, writing in 2002 and avoiding*
> *any reference to the unspeakable contents of the National Historical*
> *Museum's* Itinerant Wax Cabinet *exhibit—instead commenting*
> *(and denying), "Something like [the display of Sarah Baartman] is*
> *unacceptable today."*[18] *. . . If Åkesson and countless other Swedes*
> *failed to voice outrage or at least express a critical word, some*
> *vociferous public protesting did occur in London's popular press*
> *during 1810 when the "Wild Jungle Creature" Sarah Baartman*
> *was shown to local audiences, just three years after the Bill for the*
> *Abolition of the Slave-Trade had been passed in Parliament.*[19]

—

How are the contents of an exhibition related to current research
and ongoing social debates?
> *Inga Lundström and Marja-Leena Pilvesmaa*[20]

However significant the stances of the curator and wax-cabinet owner may
be, however important the question of unspeakable-space readings given by
1999 museum visitors may be, it is the public silence greeting the exhibit's
most stunning elements that most begs interrogation.[21] Especially since the
controversy threshold is not particularly high in Stockholm when it comes
to the contents of museum exhibitions. Especially since a mass media storm,
a gale-force moral panic, blew over the city (and nation) but eight months
earlier, when a one-artist photography exhibit consisting entirely of portrait shots of naked, prematurely well-endowed early-teenage boys opened
at the National Historical Museum. (The winds of shrill reportage—state-
legitimated child pornography!—and more reasoned culture-page debate
subsided only after the exhibit was completely trashed by a gang of
avowedly homophobic skinheads who had been steered to the museum by
all the mass media commotion.) . . . Why no SENSATION in this instance?
Why, when the Then-and-There of 1895–1898 and the Here-and-Now of
1999 were brought into constellation, was there no visible flash of lighting,
no illumination, no awakening with a startled shout (from the fantasy-filled
[bad] dreamworld of nineteenth-century racism), no fleeting revelation
converted into written expression, no shock of re-cognition followed by a

critical explosion of words, no dialectical image worth speaking about,[22] but instead a dialectics of not seeing? Why did even informed academics and public intellectuals choose to muzzle themselves? What is it that made the museum's unspeakable space so elsewhere unspeakable? What were the sources of this discursive silence? What were the strategies of silence and politics of forgetting here at work? What goes-without-saying taken-for-granteds were in operation?

—

> Silence itself . . . is less the absolute limit of discourse, the other side from which it is separated by a strict boundary, than an element that functions alongside the things said, with them and in relation to them within overall strategies. . . . There is not one silence but many silences, and they are an integral part of the strategies that underlie and permeate discourses.
>   *Michel Foucault*[23]

—

While definitive answers are definitely unavailable, while anything as widespread as this phenomenon is almost inevitably multiply (over)determined, at least one thing is abundantly clear to a long-term observer, to an inside-outsider deeply steeped in everyday Stockholm life and the daily contents of its mass media.[24] This silence did not emerge out of a void. It did not spring up out of nothingness. It was not born of a vacuum. It instead was a resounding sound. A reverberation that reverberated. An unsilent silence. A silence that could be heard distinctly—rattling, rumbling, and roaring as it echoed a larger field of identity-sustaining discourse, as it resonated with the denials, projections, and displacements characteristic of the way so many Swedes individually and collectively coped with the (re)burgeoning of racisms in their country during the late 1980s and 1990s.

> Swedish national identity has been [long] organized around the idea that Swedes are more, not less, "democratic," "progressive," and "egalitarian" than other nations.
>   *Lars Trädgårdh, historian*[25]

> It is fundamental to the self-image held by many native Swedes that Sweden is a tolerant, rational, and generous society.
>   *Christian Catomeris, journalist*[26]

For a great many Swedes there was a vast discrepancy between the ways in which they liked to think of themselves and their nation, and the circumstances increasingly endured by residents of non-European and Muslim background—by those from Africa, Asia, Latin America, and the former Yugoslavia collectively slurred as "blackheads."[27] On the one hand, people of color and Muslims, regardless of whether or not they were born in the country, were subject to extreme forms of labor-market discrimination despite frequently being highly educated;[28] housing conditions that were becoming ever more segregated (not least of all in certain high-rise Stockholm suburbs) as processes of racialization, (under)class-ification, and spatial exclusion fed into one another;[29] almost total (de facto) social apartheid; and frequently encountered state-bureaucratic paternalism.[30] These circumstances were largely, but not entirely, attributable to discourses and practices of cultural racism that were widespread throughout the country. To discourses and practices wherein negative ethnic stereotyping readily led to marginalization and other racist effects; wherein skin pigment, hair color, and other bodily markers could be unreflectedly translated into highly charged cultural markers; wherein outward biological difference and (essentialized) cultural difference could become automatically (con)fused with one another and entire groups thereby racialized. To discourses and practices whereby the particular female or male body could be (pre)seen immediately as bearer of Universal attributes: as hypersexual (threat), as hopelessly macho (male) or passive (female), as childlike (and unable to assume responsibility or "really understand" everyday social or workplace situations), as incapable of being modern (and like Us), as culturally incompetent and incapable of ever becoming "truly Swedish." And so on.[31] On the other hand, most adult Swedes, whether deeply committed to Social Democratic notions of solidarity and social justice or to liberal humanitarianism, had long viewed themselves as the most egalitarian of egalitarians, as truly True believers in tolerance, while regarding their country as a champion of the elsewhere oppressed, as a moral superpower on the world stage, as the world's most fearless voice against racism, as the world's most active opponent to its practice in South Africa and the United States.

> We still believe that our standards for treating people are higher than those held by others. We haven't become accustomed to our actually being just as racist, for example, as Americans.
> *Stig Hanno, chief integration and labor-market administrator for the Municipality of Stockholm*[32]

Swedes are [still] convinced they have no prejudices.

Immigrant voice on The Journey to Swedishness (Resan till svenskhet),
a 1997 radio documentary[33]

If Sweden was the best country invented by man, how come the
public and private ideals [regarding equality and solidarity] do
not cohere any longer? Swedes often believe in ideal versions of
themselves, and these do not always match their contradictory
realities.

A Malawi-born academic, resident in Sweden[34]

———

Made uneasy by the incongruity between these central elements of identity and whatever knowledge they had of the labor-market and housing
experiences of non-Europeans and Muslims, confronted by a confusion of
sentiments arising from their own unease about the Difference of others,
from their own discursive practices and on-the-spot emotional or practical responses to Difference, many, if not a substantial majority, apparently
had attempted to resolve their identity conflicts through denial, projection,
and displacement.[35] Through comforting themselves with the belief that the
country's racists are somebody other than themselves. Through convincing
themselves—with the help of highly redundant mass media imagery—that
only the physical violence and fascist symbolics of skinheads and right-wing
extremist groups have racist consequences. Through blinding themselves
to the fact that, however unquestionably hideous they may be, those same
small-numbered groups cannot—by the wi(l)dest stretch of the imagination—be blamed for the employment discrimination, residential segregation, and social apartheid that continues to pervade the Stockholm metropolitan area and Sweden as a whole. Through also projecting upon other
locations as well as other groups. Through adhering to a mass media–fired
popular geographical imagination. Through regarding racism as "really"
restricted to a small number of places associated with atrocious acts of violence or other manifestations of neo-Nazism or extremist activity.[36]

We can never tolerate hostility toward foreigners and racism. Not
in any form.

*Marita Ulvskog, then Social Democratic Minister of Culture, in a
1996 statement*[37]

With individually and collectively practiced racism being displaced as a question of somebody else, as something perpetrated somewhere else, would it have been possible for the exhibited skin and sex organ to have been seriously debated in public, to have been critically discussed in the mass media, without reintensifying internal contradictions, without reawakening repressed thoughts, without shoving tottering elements of identity over the precipice, into an abyss where only rocks of crushingly painful admission awaited? Would it have been possible to have openly considered the exposure of those unspeakable objects, their willful display in the National Historical Museum, without undermining nationally held myths, without admitting that there were racisms other than those practiced by National Socialist Front members and their like, without confessing that variants of racist discourse are not monopolized by the far right, without being forced into self-*recognition*? Would it have been possible for public controversy to emerge without abandoning the commonsense notion that "we don't think *that* way," without addressing stubbornly lingering ideas about the cultural inferiority and (hyper)sexuality of the African black, without sacrificing visions of the country as the ultimate in progressiveness, as the very quintessence of enlightened social modernity? Would it have been possible to voice questions or dissent publicly without descending blinder-free into the past? Without having to undo collective amnesia? Without having to remember that Sweden actually had a racist past extending back into the late nineteenth century—and well beyond? Without in the process being forced to remember that which was not to be remembered about the here and now outside-the-museum present? Without thinking the unthinkable? Without stepping beyond taboo limits? Without speaking the unspeakable? Without eventually pointing to the contradictions of so much political and mass media discourse, to the enormous chasm separating its constant calls for the "acceptance of diversity" and the cultural racism that it persistently promotes[38]—in among a number of other ways, through occasional news-account allusions to the excessive sexual desires of blacks (and "blackheads" more generally), to their sexual abuse or rape of "real" Swedish women? (Throughout the 1990s, including the summer of 1999, the press and broadcast media periodically precipitated an extended moral panic around isolated cases of gang rape and in the process equated virtually all rape of Swedish women with the actions of youths of Middle Eastern and African background, with the actions of young men who were culturally inclined to violate the bodies of women, with the actions of young men whose aggressive hypersexuality and abnormal/callous disrespect for women was part of their immutable culture.[39] In stark contrast, 1993 data indicate that only 21 percent of the 314 men arrested for rape were of non-Northern European extraction.[40])

> [Only] the sexual crimes . . . committed by men of immigrant background [are regarded as culturally determined] while the same deeds always have a psychological or social explanation if committed by Swedish men.
>   Paulina de los Reyes and Irene Molina[41]

—

Afrika

Not Europa. Not Nord Amerika. But Afrika. The name of a male fragrance and deodorant widely sold in Sweden at the very same moment that a shroud of silence had been dropped over the unspeakable case exhibited at the National Historical Museum. And at the very same moment that everyday participation in the perpetuation of cultural racism was being denied and displaced by a substantial portion of the Swedish population. Packaged in a black phallic-shaped container, as if a freely standing or detached member, Afrika was a product of the utmost suggestion, a product whose label and design went well beyond the usual thought titillation employed by other brands, well beyond the usual visual hints of an enhanced ability to seduce and satisfy. For here was a name, a color, and a form that tapped into unspeakable stereotypes commonly held in Sweden and elsewhere in Europe, into stereotypes resting on what was "well known," but hardly need be said. A name, a color, and a form that promised the purchaser all that it stood for: taboo-laden sexual attractiveness, hypersexual performative capacity, "wild" sex, "savage" or "animal-like" love making. A name, a color, and a form that said: irresistible object of desire, wish image realized, dreams of totally uninhibited sexual conquest come true. Buy me and they will come back for more. And more.

The commodity form and the racialized (and gendered) stereotype.

Totally fused.[42]

The "new" product as the ever again the same. Only Different.

Exhibit 2: The Unspeakable Space of Sergel's Square

[T]he omission of a particular memory, like that of part of a
sentence we are reading, leads sometimes not to uncertainty, but
to the birth of a premature certainty.
    Marcel Proust[43]

Forgetting takes place—or "a" place, but where precisely no one
seems to be certain, except by the evacuated trail it leaves.
    Norman M. Klein[44]

———

Allow me, one last time, to transgress multiply, to speak of an unspeakable
space in multiple ways. Allow me to remain in the just-yesterday present, and
to spotlight another space where racism has been on exhibit, displayed though
simultaneous efforts to dismantle and to forget, through simultaneous efforts
to remake that which is concrete and to dis-place those who are socially present. And, in so doing, allow me finally to address the unaddressable.

Sergel's Square *[Sergels Torg]* is . . . well known far beyond
the capital city's boundaries. Even if one has never set foot
in the place, everybody knows Sergel's Square, perhaps from
newspapers or TV, perhaps through relatives or acquaintances.
Nobody escapes Sergel's Square and Sergel's Square escapes
nobody. This place, whether we like it or not, is the heart of
Sweden. Nobody could even arrive at the idea of questioning the
Square's obvious role in the dissemination of free speech through
political meetings, demonstrations, and other gatherings. This is
the place where we *[en masse]* celebrate our Swedish heroes for
their Olympic gold in hockey. Here we cross over the bare surface of "Plattan" in order to see the Leonardo da Vinci exhibit
at the Culture Hall *[Kulturhuset]*. Here we go in order to shop
at nearby department stores. . . . Tens of thousands of people
pass over this square every day, people of different ages and of
different nationalities. Therefore Sergel's Square also stands out
as a multicultural meeting place at which a large number of the
world's countries are represented.
    Nicolas Jändel[45]

Everybody in Sweden has an opinion about Sergel's Square.
John Chrispinsson commenting during a prime-time television program[46]

Sergel's Square has been described as a huge hole right in the middle of the heart of Stockholm.
Newspaper photograph caption[47]

A square literally at the center of Stockholm. Figuratively at the center of the nation. Stockholm's Times Square. A square onto which the Central Station of the metropolitan area's subway system exits. A two-level square: above, an elliptical traffic roundabout encompassing a multispouted pool and an enormous glass-sculptured phallus; below, and to the west, a completely open plaza whose surface, patterned harlequin-like with black and white diamonds, is readily approached from the street by an extremely wide bank of stairs. A square, a municipally owned piece of property, whose official name, Sergels Torg, actually applies only to its upper level. A square whose official name honors Johan Tobias Sergel (1740–1814), the famed sculptor—he who was the last to sketch Badin.[48] A square whose sunken pedestrian portion is officially unnamed, officially unspeakable, although almost universally referred to by Stockholmers as either *Sergels Torg* or *Plattan* (The Flat[-surface]).[49] A square bordered above not only by the Culture Hall (Stockholm's forerunner to the Centre Pompidou in Paris), but also by nineteen-story-high office buildings, a major department store, bank headquarters, and other structures that signify a pivot point for the global circulation of capital, goods, and information. A square whose lower plaza fades into a maze of dark passageways and shops beneath the roundabout, into an around-the-clock darkness lending itself to all kinds of transactions. A square that came into being in the mid-1960s as part of "The Great Demolition Wave," as part of the most comprehensive urban renewal program in Swedish history, as part of a massive remaking of what had been an "unmodern" downtown area comprised of narrow streets, small-scale shops and businesses, and low eighteenth- and nineteenth-century buildings.[50] A square created as part of a modernist planning project, as a concretization of Social Democratic rationality working in tandem with finance capital and business interests. A square, a phallus-dominated public space, produced by way of governmental (hyper)rationalities and capitalist strategies—an "abstract space" in Lefebvre's fullest sense of the term.[51] A square that came into being as a centerpiece for the new cityscape built up around it, as the center of gravity for those new surrounding buildings whose largely uninspired modernist architecture has come to make certain Conservative Party politicians and some of their neoliberal supporters see red. A square that frequently serves as a site for political rallies, including hunger strikes and other attention-grabbing demonstrations by refugees from a variety of Middle Eastern, African, and Latin American countries (such as the actions taken by hundreds of Chilean exiles during March 2000 in protest of the British release of General Augusto Pinochet). A square whose steps are a gathering place for youths, a large portion of whom are males of non-European parentage from the city's segregated suburbs. A gathering place where those same suburban youths can frequently be seen mixing with young "white" Swedish women. A gathering place where some passing majority Swedes cannot prevent themselves from looking on with disapproval, cannot avoid the unreflected triggering of a *certain* field of vision, cannot but help summoning forth taken-for-granted stereotypes that readily lead them to imagine the eventual occurrence of unspeakable sexual contact.

—

It is probably so that change or "Swedification" is apt to take longer with matters involving sexuality and relations than with other culturally marked matters. . . . Studies of blacks in the USA have shown that sexual and family patterns in particular continue to survive from Africa. . . . It is therefore likely that essential features of homeland sexual behavior will remain after three or four generations.

Statement made in an official government report, 1991[52]

They write with a matter-of-fact tone, believing that the distinguishing characteristics of humans are bound up with blood ties and place of birth. This is racism even if the intent is noble. One can wonder how many Swedes are "pure" Swedes at least four generations back. What does Swedish sexual behavior look like? And to what usage are all these assertions to be put?

Comment regarding the above, clearly well-intentioned report— made in 2000 by Edna Eriksson, a young journalist of "mixed background" who had tired of being (hyper)sexually stereotyped and labeled an "immigrant" despite having spent most of her life in Sweden[53]

———

The rulers feel public space to be an extension of their own personal one: They belong there because it belongs to them. For the politically oppressed (a term which this century has learned is not limited to class) existence in public space is more likely to be synonymous with state surveillance, public censure, and political constraint.

Susan Buck-Morss[54]

[P]ublic space is closed and/or redesigned when hidden and "undesirable" elements of a culture become too visible.

Setha M. Low[55]

—

With the constitution of a new right-wing majority in Stockholm Town Hall *[in the autumn of 1998]*, Sergels Torg, the most cen-

tral public square in the Swedish capital, stunningly became the
most contested place in all Sweden.
   Mats Franzén[56]

The Square stirs up strong feelings, which has been evident in
the years of debate about it.
   Dagens Nyheter, *August 13, 1999*

By focusing on Sergel's Square and following what has been
expressed at that place, one can get a fair picture of Sweden as
a country and the important questions that have engaged its
people over time.
   Nicoläs Jändel[57]

In the summer of 1999, when the *Itinerant Wax Cabinet* exhibit was in the
middle of its run, when the National Historical Museum was still providing
an opportunity for racisms past and present to be displayed, contemporary
cultural racism was simultaneously and unwittingly being placed on exhibit
in conjunction with Sergel's Square. On August 12 six architectural proposals for a radical remaking of the square were put forth to the public with
considerable fanfare, including large color reproductions of the alternatives
in the country's major newspapers. Following directives conceived by two
powerful neoliberal municipal council members,[58] all of the proposals
shared several features in common. Some portion of the plaza's space was
given over to a residential structure. And the square was drawn up to exist
on one plane rather than two. As a consequence of the latter trait, there
were also no underground passageways, and the broad bank of steps so
congenial to sit-down socializing was totally eliminated.

[T]he open square . . . is below ground—which does not enhance
its status, but facilitates all kinds of associations with low life.

[T]he shadowy labyrinth immediately connected to the square . . .
is quite simply too good for all kinds of *black business,* according
to a representative from the police force.

Plattan has become a metonym for the drug phenomenon.

Sergel's Square and *[the entire surrounding area]* thus become
matter out of place, something disturbing the order of Stockholm's
inner city, *a reminder of the suburbs.*
   Mats Franzén[59]

You are standing 76 meters from Sweden's largest drug center. If
you turn around, take the escalator down and step through the
doors to Sergel's Square, within a few minutes you can purchase
whatever kind of drug you wish.

Wall text accompanying a photography exhibit shown at the
Culture Hall, May 31 to August 18, 2002

A tangle of open intentions and shut taken-for-granteds, of overt political
struggles and more oblique expressions of dis-ease, had led to these proposed forms of creative destruction, to suggestions of radical surgery upon
that which was but three decades old. Almost from the outset of its existence,
Plattan, and especially its shadowy extensions beneath the roundabout,
had been made synonymous with crime in general and drug-trafficking,
shoplifting, and stolen-goods dealing in particular.[60] Since the 1980s the
imagery employed in mass media accounts had increasingly suggested, by
direct and indirect means, that the bulk of Plattan's unspeakable deals were
the doing of Africans.[61] (At the same time mass media and political discourses had, without serious analysis or statistical justification, succeeded
in precipitating a long-term moral panic, in making both "crime" and
"criminality" codewords for suburban youths of non-European or Muslim
background.)[62] And then—say no more, say no more—there was the matter of what went on in open view, of the suburban-youth congregating and
social intermixing that transpired on the steps, of what people "knew" of
"blackhead" hypersexuality and its inevitable, unspeakable consequences,
of what they understood of the "blackhead" Other's masculinity and its
threat to Swedish (heterosexual) women (and thereby the nation).[63]

Why is it so that the suburb has begun to be regarded as a jungle
and immigrant youths as primitive natives?
Per-Markku Ristilammi[64]

There is a widespread fear for areas such as [the segregated
Stockholm suburbs of] Flemingsberg, Tensta, and Fittja. They
are a kind of black spot. Like southern Sudan or eastern Zaire
on a map of Africa.
Per Wirtén[65]

Somebody I know knows a policeman in Stockholm, and he says
98 percent of the crime there is committed by immigrant youths
from the suburbs.
Myth in popular circulation, first overheard 1996

Normally Stureplan *[another popular open-air meeting place in
downtown Stockholm]* is packed with people, and it's best not to
mix them up. The dopeheads are those who sit around shabbily
dressed, panhandling passersby for donations for cheap wine,
pills, and playing the pinball machines, until the Turks arrive in
gangs from all over the Stockholm area. They come to pick up
foxy women—that's the way their gangs get together—but usually
they are not particularly successful. And that's understandable.
Who would be stupid enough to answer them. So at the end of the
day they stand there, all worked up and filled with hormones that
must find an outlet. Which means picking a fight with whomever
doesn't seem to approve of them.

> *A fictional reworking of the otherwise unspeakable, of (f)actually
> imagined sexual threat, of (f)actually feared "blackhead"
> hypersexuality—from a short story appearing two years prior
> to 1999 in the weekend entertainment section of Sweden's most
> widely circulated newspaper* [66]

In political discourse, unspeakable activities an unspeakable space make.
Thus, for those neoliberal members of the Stockholm Municipal Council
whose efforts resulted in the architectural competition, Sergel's Square had
to be replaced in order to make the city's downtown core more "human," in
order—by extension—to rid it of the inhuman, the disorderly, the Different.
For them, Sergel's Square was an impure place that was a pure crystal-
lization of all they despised about Social Democratic planning and social
engineering, an impure and disgusting place that was a concretization of
the failures of the Social Democratic state and its welfare policies in general
(and, implicitly, its migrant welfare policies in particular). For them it was,
moreover, an impure and disgusting place that was the very embodiment of
all-too-high and consumption-inhibiting taxes misspent, an impure and disgusting place that had come about because market forces had not been allowed to operate completely unrestrained, because total freedom of choice
had not prevailed. [67]

> They have the stomach to equate Sergel's Square, that enormous-
> ly pronounced sign of political mania and bad taste, with the old
> Klara District. . . . And to believe that any of the six proposals is
> going to provide vitality and harmony for the city is like believing
> that you can wake a dead person to life with a pacemaker.
>
> *Christopher O'Regan, walking-tour guide and reader of* Dagens
> Nyheter, *in the August 14, 1999, issue of that newspaper*

The square was wrongly built from the start, from the very
moment they tore down old Klara—people like things on a
small scale.

> *Kalle Andersson, another reader given voice in the August 14, 1999,
> issue of* Dagens Nyheter

—

Nostalgia is not an innocent sentiment.
Lisa Rofel[68]

Nostalgia is unproductive.
> *Louise Bourgeois, in a wall caption accompanying an exhibit of her
> works in the heart of the Klara District, at the Culture Hall imme-
> diately adjacent to Sergel's Square, May 18 to September 1, 2002*

—

In the process of carrying out "The Great Demolition Wave," of clearing
the ground for Sergel's Square, the westernmost portion of Harbor Street
(Hamngatan) was obliterated, creatively destroyed and removed from the
map, along with much of the surrounding Klara District. Not a few of those
who were annoyed in 1999 about Sergel's Square as it was, and many of
those who were displeased with the architectural alternatives proposed,
readily waxed nostalgic about the Klara District of many decades past.
Feelings of loss compensated for. Past spaces romanticized and remythologized. Not always uncontradictory stories dusted off. Remembrances revised. The no longer reinvented and exaggerated. Fictions factualized and
facts fictionalized. Elements of decay and dilapidation displaced. Images
conjured up of a more "human" place. Of the city's true soul and an atmosphere throbbing with life. Of charming buildings and intimate shops. Of
printing establishments and newspaper offices. Of handicraft workshops
and artist studios. Of small hotels and residential units.[69] . . . At the end of
the nineteenth century Hamngatan was referred to in male working-class
slang, in the vocabulary of an often politically charged popular geography, as Linkstret. This substitute signifier, this expression of polysemous
folk humor, not only involved an obvious corruption of the English Link
Street (Hamngatan was the downtown area's principal east-west link)
and a reference to the prostitution occurring along part of its length (*link*
was male working-class slang for pimp). It also apparently alluded to a
"hobbling struggle," to limping along while striving to get by, to the difficult realities of making an economic go of it in Stockholm's industrial

and financial core.[70] Along that thoroughfare where the contradictions of capitalist modernity existed in practice—where bustling commerce was closely juxtaposed with degrading commodification of the female body and "underclass" men in search of an underpaid day's labor[71]—Hartkopf's Wax Cabinet and Anatomical Museum occupied a building between 1895 and 1898. Its address was number 38. Hamngatan 38 exists no more. It is, in multiple senses, a dis(re)membered space.[72] A space whose history has been eradicated. A space where collective amnesia reigns. If it still existed, it would be found somewhere on Sergel's Square, not far from the center of Plattan. . . . And but one minute's walk from another space of collective forgetting, from a space once readily associated with Badin and "ape-like" hypersexuality, from Drottninggatan (Queen Street) 23, the former site of Apoteket Morianen (The Blackamoor Pharmacy).

————

[Lefebvre's abstract space, the space of contemporary capitalism and concretized governmental rationalities] is supposed to be a space from which previous histories have been erased.
  Derek Gregory[73]

[In abstract space] economic space and political space . . . converge towards an elimination of all differences.
  Henri Lefebvre[74]

At Last: The Unaddressable Addressed

The unaddressable addressed.
The muffled fiction of history unmuffled.
The noise of the nineteenth century made to intrude.
The ruptures of memory disrupted.
The nailed-down hide and the severed penis nailed down in place.
The wax cabinet, past and present, spatially coupled with Sergel's Square.
Three unbecoming (dis)junctures
brought into illuminating conjunction.
Exhibitions of racism in triple constellation.
Trialectical image.
Lightning bolts released.
Heretical empiricism conducted.
Interrogation almost completed.

————

Memory, as we all know, is a fragile thing, subject to simplifications, distortions, and the tricks played upon it by distance.
Peter Englund, Swedish historian[75]

Nations are built on great rememberings and great forgettings. Getting history wrong is an essential part of being a nation.
Ernest Renan[76]

———

For the time being at least, as of late 2003, any radical rebuilding of Sergel's Square has been taken off the agenda. Removed, in effect, by plunging stock values, by crises of overcapacity in the information-technology and dot-com industries, by the dissemination of economic turmoil throughout the network of globally interdependent capitalisms, by the local manifestations of global recession. For the resultant fiscal difficulties confronting the Stockholm municipal government have made the project infeasible. At least in the immediate future . . . But what of the politicians, the mass media discourse producers, and others among that majority of Swedes who refuse to confront their own cultural racism directly, who cannot accept their own role in racializing non-European or Muslim Others and thereby condemning them to extreme forms of social and economic exclusion, who insist upon attempting to sustain identity through denial and projection, who remain content with the histories they (don't) know, who thereby remain in Foucault's "place of tranquilized sleep," who thereby remain locked into, unawakened from, Benjamin's "dreams"?

What are they—and their counterparts elsewhere—to make of the unspeakable (geographical hi)stories correlated in this text?

What remains for them to unsilence, to remove from the realm of the taken-for-granted, to unforget and re-member, to unveil and re-view, to recall and rename, to de-taboo, to leave no longer unspeakable?

What remains for them to *recognize*?

That it is not only the racism displayed a century ago at the current site of Sergel's Square that has been forgotten, consigned to a historical blackout, banned from collective memory, unspoken of?

That the failure to openly debate the resurrection of Hartkopf's Wax Cabinet, to publicly question the reshowing of its unmentionable objects, involved an effort to forget the present as well as the past?

That the planned physical erasure of Sergel's Square also involved an effort to forget the present? Not least of all because it sought to terminate crime and unapproved forms of social intermingling through forcing young men of non-European or Muslim background from the core of the city (and the nation), through dis-placing them, through deporting them back to the segregated suburbs, through putting them out of sight and out of (uncomfortable, discontented) mind, through acting in congruence with various national and local policies promoting the repatriation of resident refugees?[77]

That the yearning for the Klara District of the past was less a yearning for another space than a yearning for another time, than a yearning for a time when (racialized) difference didn't make such a (local) difference, than a desire to bleach out the present, to whitewash the here and now?

That collective amnesia does not grant collective amnesty to those who perpetuate racialization and under-classification?

That the unspeakable is often unpardonable?

And that?

———

It is no accident that Atget's photographs [of deserted Parisian streets] have been likened to those of a crime scene. But isn't every square inch of our cities a crime scene? Every passer-by a culprit?

Walter Benjamin[78]

Stockholm is a particular instance of enduring stereotypes that are re-worked and given distinctive contemporary forms of denial and displacement. A particular case of situated practices, discourses, and power relations at simultaneous (un)becoming work. A particular nexus of shifting, variously scaled relations and webs of interconnection—many of which currently stretch, and have previously stretched, well beyond Sweden. And, as such a nexus, Stockholm is, by definition, not alone. Of course . . . Every other major European city, every "Western" city, has its unspeakable spaces. Its spaces where racisms past and present are on exhibit, enfolded within one another, but silenced, rendered unspeakable. Its spaces where the absolutely appalling is still collectively forgotten, where the unaddressable remains unaddressed, where memory excavation is yet postponed. Its spaces where past and present have yet to be brought into mutually illuminating constellation, where awakening has yet to occur. Its spaces where the taken-for-granted is concretized. Its spaces where stereotypes of threatening hypersexuality and other negatively charged images of the Other are still activated more or less instantaneously—lightning-speed reactions that bolt to the surface automatically from the depths of the long ago learned and discursively inscribed.[79] Its spaces where the dialectics of not seeing are still operative, still privileging the modern Us over the never-can-be-modern Them. Its spaces where the (con)fusions of fact and fiction demand to be refused, to be reimag(in)ed. Its spaces where the forenow lives on, where the past is not dead—but discursively and relationally recontextualized, rearticulated with new circumstances and social formations. And, with a new twist(edness), put into practice.

———

The interval that we assert between ourselves and the past may be much less than we assume. We may be more bound up with its categories than we think. Culture and race developed to-gether, imbricated within each other: their discontinuous forms of repetition suggest, as Foucault puts it, "how we have been trapped in our own history." The nightmare of the ideologies and categories of racism continue to repeat upon the living.
    Robert J. C. Young[80]

[T]oday it is more important than ever to remember.
    Peter Englund[81]

—

Abraham Bäck, bosom friend of Linnaeus, contributed what was clearly a new method of investigation in his 1748 paper, "On the Black Skin of Negroes." During a research trip to Paris he had the opportunity to examine a dead negro and obtained a piece of his skin *[which he later submerged for a week in order to prove it would turn water black]*.
    Gunnar Broberg[82]

—

To articulate the past historically does not mean to recognize it "the way it really was" (Ranke). It means to seize hold of a memory as it flashes up at a moment of danger.
    [E]very image of the past that is not recognized by the present as one of its own concerns threatens to disappear irretrievably.
    Walter Benjamin[83]

[S]ometimes, in the service of truth, Benjamin's own words must be ripped out of context with a "seemingly brutal grasp."
        Susan Buck-Morss[84]

Notes

It is advised that the notes not be read in tandem with the text, but one entire numbered sequence at a time after the completion of each section or chapter.

Past and Present Tense

1. Walter Benjamin, "Theses on the Philosophy of History" (completed 1940, first published 1951), in *Walter Benjamin: Illuminations*, ed. Hannah Arendt (New York: Schocken Books, 1969), 253–64 (257).

2. On the notion of articulation and the historically and geographically specific reactivation of racializing images and ideas, see Stuart Hall, "Gramsci's Relevance for the Study of Race and Ethnicity," in *Stuart Hall: Critical Dialogues in Cultural Studies*, ed. David Morley and Kuan-Hsing Chen (Routledge: London and New York, 1996), 411–40. For historical details on national variations in the stereotyping of blacks, see Jan Nederveen Pieterse, *White on Black: Images of Africa and Blacks in Western Popular Culture* (New Haven, CT: Yale University Press, 1992), especially 152–65.

3. Walter Benjamin, *The Arcades Project* (Cambridge: Harvard University Press, 1999), convolute [N1, 1], 456, as translated by Howard Eiland and Kevin Mclaughlin from *Gesammete Schriften*, vol. 5, *Das Passagen-Werk* (Frankfurt am Main: Suhrkamp Verlag, 1982).

4. Paul Rabinow, characterizing Fredric Jameson's take on postmodernism ("Representations Are Social Facts: Modernity and Post-Modernity in Anthropology," in *Writing Culture: The Poetics and Politics of Ethnography*, ed. James Clifford and George E. Marcus [Berkeley: University of California Press, 1986], 234–61 [249]).

5. Esther Leslie, *Walter Benjamin: Overpowering Conformism* (London: Pluto Press, 2000), 66.

6. Walter Benjamin, "The Work of Art in the Age of Mechanical Reproduction" (1936 version), in *Illuminations*, ed. Arendt, 217–51 (236).

7. On the tactics and textual politics of "heretical empiricism" and its affinities with the paintings of Francis Bacon, see Michael J. Watts and Allan Pred, "Heretical Empiricism: The Modern and the Hypermodern," *Nordisk Samhällsgeografisk Tidskrift* 19 (September 1994): 3–26. The term is derived and reworked from Pasolini

(*Heretical Empiricism/Pier Paolo Pasolini*, ed. L. Barnett [Bloomington: Indiana University Press, 1988]).

8. John Berger, *About Looking* (New York: Pantheon Books, 1980), 112.

9. Benjamin, *Arcades Project*, convolute [J28a, 4], 279.

10. Walter Benjamin, "Little History of Photography" (1931), in *Walter Benjamin: Selected Writings*, vol. 2, ed. Michael W. Jennings, Howard Eiland, and Gary Smith (Cambridge: Harvard University Press, 1999), 507–40 (520).

11. For details, see Mekonnen Tesfahuney, *Imag(in)ing the Other(s): Migration, Racism, and the Discursive Construction of Others* (Uppsala: Uppsala University, Department of Social and Economic Geography, Geografiska Regionstudier 34, 1998); Allan Pred, *Even in Sweden: Racisms, Racialized Spaces, and the Popular Geographical Imagination* (Berkeley: University of California Press, 2000); and the literature cited in those works.

12. Michel Foucault, "Lives of Infamous Men" (1977) in *Michel Foucault: Power*, ed. James D. Faubion, vol. 3 of *Essential Works of Foucault, 1954–1984*, ed. Paul Rabinow (New York: New Press, 2000), 157–75 (162).

13. Gerhard Richter, *Walter Benjamin and the Corpus of Autobiography* (Detroit: Wayne State University Press, 2000), 168.

14. Susan Buck-Morss, rephrasing Benjamin in *The Dialectics of Seeing: Walter Benjamin and the Arcades Project* (Cambridge: MIT Press, 1989), 221.

15. Buck-Morss, again reformulating Benjamin, in ibid., 251.

16. Benjamin, "Theses," 255.

17. In granting Badin his political potential I do not believe I am speaking *for* him in the sense of speaking in his place, in the managerial way that Spivak so roundly criticizes (Gayatri Chakravorty Spivak, "Can the Subaltern Speak?" in *Marxism and the Interpretation of Culture*, ed. Cary Nelson and Lawrence Grossberg [Urbana and Chicago: University of Illinois Press, 1988], 271–313; and *A Critique of Postcolonial Reason: Toward a History of the Vanishing Present* [Cambridge: Harvard University Press, 1999], 269 ff.). Badin's voice appears in the text in three different guises. Sometimes the words are actually his, extracted from those few handwritten documents that survive. Sometimes his statements or thoughts are taken from novels, in which case they help illuminate the intricate fusings of fact and fiction associated with the (re)production of stereotypes. Most unconventionally, Badin speaks through interior monologues that I have composed, *but that rest upon indications made in his sparse written record and upon situated practices he is known to have engaged in.* However modern-sounding the wording I sometimes deploy, these are thoughts the record suggests he very possibly could have had, albeit in the categories and terminologies of late eighteenth- and early nineteenth-century Swedish. These fact-based counterfictions are designed to gain present force from their strategic location within the montage, from emplacements meant to correspond to the complex webs of social relationality in which Badin existed, from the tensions generated by what precedes and succeeds them. Whatever the case, these counterfictional monologues could not have been written without Badin's assistance, without the documented details and circumstances of his life speaking through me in some real—albeit highly mediated—sense.

18. Benjamin, "Theses," 263.

19. Buck-Morss, *Dialectics of Seeing,* 218.

20. On the presence of Benjamin's specter elsewhere in contemporary scholarship, see *Benjamin's Ghosts: Interventions in Contemporary Literary and Cultural Theory,* ed. Gerhard Richter (Stanford, CA: Stanford University Press, 2002). Also note the earlier, yet still salient, assessment of depoliticized deployments of Benjamin in Janet Wolff, "Memoirs and Micrologies: Walter Benjamin, Feminism, and Cultural Analysis," *New Formations* 20 (1993): 113–22.

21. Benjamin, *Arcades Project,* convolute [O°, 71], 863.

22. Graeme Gilloch, *Walter Benjamin: Critical Constellations* (Cambridge, England: Polity Press, 2002), 16.

23. Wolff, "Memoirs and Micrologies," 114.

24. This aspect of Benjamin's presence is not without affinity to the work of the so-called new historicists who have built upon E. P. Thompson, Raymond Williams, and Michel Foucault, among others. For the work of such literary scholars has sought to disrupt the practice of "history as usual," to deploy anecdotes and their "seemingly ephemeral details" to "undermine" the "epochal truths" contained in the "coherent" event sequences of conventional historical narratives, to use anecdotes "to chip away at the familiar edifices and make plastered-over cracks appear" (Catherine Gallagher and Stephen Greenblatt, *Practicing New Historicism* [Chicago: University of Chicago Press, 2000], 51–52). A dialectical constellation of past and present, however, does not appear on the agenda of new historicism.

25. Benjamin, *Arcades Project,* convolute [N1a, 8], 460. Emphasis in the original, which has been translated alternatively by Buck-Morss as: "Method of this work: literary montage. I have nothing to say, only to show" (*Dialectics of Seeing,* 73).

26. Walter Benjamin, *One-Way Street* (1928), in *Walter Benjamin: Selected Writings,* vol. 1, ed. Michael W. Jennings (Cambridge: Harvard University Press, 1996), 444–88; Walter Benjamin, *A Berlin Chronicle* (1932), in *Selected Writings,* vol. 2, ed. Jennings, Eiland, and Smith, 595–637; Walter Benjamin, *Berlin Childhood around 1900* (1938), in *Selected Writings,* vol. 3, ed. Jennings (2002), 344–86.

27. It is inappropriate to regard or judge *The Arcades Project* or any of its component convolutes as a montage, for that is a term suggesting a finished work rather than the collected ingredients for such a work. In various pieces of correspondence Benjamin himself lamented that he was laboring on a yet unrealized work, a book that was still in the works, however well thought out some of its elements may have been (Howard Eiland and Kevin McLaughlin, "Translator's Foreword," in Benjamin, *Arcades Project,* ix–xiv).

28. Cf. Susan Buck-Morss, "The Flaneur, the Sandwichman, and the Whore: The Politics of Loitering," *New German Critique* 39 (fall 1986), 99–140.

29. Benjamin, *Arcades Project,* convolute [N2, 6], 461.

30. However film-like, the textual montage may be deployed to show in a manner that is not possible with film montages. In the cinema, the audience member's attention is held by the *uninterrupted* flow of images and sounds—there is no way in which she can halt the procedure, pause for reflection, or turn back to check an earlier image. The reader of the textual montage, by contrast, is free to break off at any

point, to think about a point, to flip back through the pages and reread. The textual-montage producer is thereby in a position to show by encouraging interruptions for (re)consideration and the re-viewing of previous quotes or passages, to show by more or less subtly demanding that the meaning of each fragment be enhanced and shifted repeatedly as a consequence of preceding-fragment echoes and subsequent-fragment contents.

31. Gilloch, *Walter Benjamin: Critical Constellations,* 2.

32. My sources of inspiration and influence—other than Benjamin—are too entangled with one another for me to fully unravel. Most prominently they include Michel Foucault, Edward Said, Stuart Hall, Jonathan Crary, and Donna Haraway and a host of other contemporary feminist scholars.

33. Howard Caygill, *Walter Benjamin: The Colour of Experience* (London and New York: Routledge, 1998), 152.

34. Gail Ching-Liang Low, *White Skins/Black Masks: Representations and Colonialism* (London and New York: Routledge, 1996), 2.

Foremontage

1. Sander L. Gilman, *Difference and Pathology: Stereotypes of Sexuality, Race, and Madness* (Ithaca, NY: Cornell University Press, 1985), 27.

2. Stephen Greenblatt, *Marvelous Possessions: The Wonder of the New World* (Chicago: University of Chicago Press, 1991), 121.

3. O. B., "Litet om zulukaffrerna: Små notiser från en vistelse i Afrika," *Allers Familj Journal,* no. 40 (October 7, 1917): 13–14.

4. Those like Peter Gay (*Savage Reprisals* [New York: Norton, 2002]) who insist that scholars should avoid using novels of the past as "factual" historical sources—who insist that the writings of Dickens, Flaubert, and others did not capture things and circumstances as they actually were—fail to recognize that such works in themselves constituted historical facts that in various ways contributed to a network of effects. Novelists and other authors of fiction, as well as historians and other academic writers, are inescapably situated actors, embodied and emplaced in multiple ongoing (geographical-hi)stories, whose narrative texts both emerge out of and contribute to those ongoing (geographical-hi)stories, or con-texts (cf. Paul Ricoeur, "The Narrative Function," in his *Hermeneutics and the Human Sciences,* ed. and trans. John B. Thompson [Cambridge: Cambridge University Press, 1981], 274–96). Or, as Lennard J. Davis has put it in arguing that the English novel arose in the eighteenth century "partly as a complex reaction" to restrictions placed on news journalism: "Ballads, criminal tales, news reports, and novels all insisted on a connection to reality which was finally illusory since the reality they reported was largely one they were in the process of creating" (*Factual Fictions: The Origins of the English Novel* [Philadelphia: University of Pennsylvania Press, 1997], 222, 221).

5. Stuart Hall, "The Spectacle of the 'Other,'" in *Representation: Cultural Representations and Signifying Practices,* ed. Hall (London: Sage Publications, 1997), 223–79 (249). On the history of visual representations contributing to the persistence of racial stereotypes, see Pieterse, *White on Black.*

6. Nikolas Rose, *Inventing Our Selves: Psychology, Power, and Personhood* (Cambridge: Cambridge University Press, 1996), 3.

7. Michel Foucault, "Truth and Power," in *Power/Knowledge: Selected Interviews and Other Writings, 1972–1977* (New York: Pantheon Books, 1980), 109–33 (133).

8. Cf. David Theo Goldberg on fields of racist discourse in *Racist Culture: Philosophy and the Politics of Meaning* (Oxford, England: Blackwell, 1993); and "The Social Formation of Racist Discourse," in *Anatomy of Racism*, ed. Goldberg (Minneapolis: University of Minnesota Press, 1990), 295–318.

9. Judith Butler, "Endangered/Endangering: Schematic Racism and White Paranoia," in *Reading Rodney King, Reading Urban Uprising*, ed. R. Gooding-Williams (New York and London: Routledge), 15–22 (15–16).

10. Insofar as seeing and hearing operate in tandem, any "dialectics of not seeing" may have a counterpart "dialectics of not hearing"—a way of hearing that mutes anything incongruent with the previously "heard," and thereby enables the already "known" to be rediscovered and irrefutably substantiated. A growing body of psychological literature suggests that "truths" about the racialized Other may be fortified by "false memories" or the recollection of behaviors that never actually occurred—that are precipitated by the tandem operation of (pre)vision and the verbal terminology of negative stereotypes (Tadesse Araya, *Stereotypes: Suppression, Forgetting, and False Memory* [Uppsala: Acta Universitatus Upsaliensis, 2003], and the literature cited therein).

11. Bryan D. Palmer, *Cultures of Darkness: Night Travels in the Histories of Transgression* (New York: Monthly Review Press, 2000), 5.

12. For a synthesis of the considerable relevant literature on processes of social-spatial exclusion, including the work of Mary Douglas and Julia Kristeva, see David Sibley, *Geographies of Exclusion: Society and Difference in the West* (London and New York: Routledge, 1995).

13. Judith Butler, as quoted in Minelle Mahtani, "Racial ReMappings: The Potential of Paradoxical Space," *Gender, Place, and Culture* 8 (2001): 299–305 (301).

14. Derek Gregory, *The Colonial Present* (Oxford, England: Blackwell, 2004).

Entrances, Beginnings, Namings

1. *Webster's Third New International Dictionary of the English Language,* unabridged ed. (Springfield, MA: Merriam-Webster, 1999), 161.

2. Lars Wikström, "Fredrik Adolph Ludvig Gustaf Albrecht Badin-Couschi," *Släkt och hävd,* no. 1 (1971): 272–314 (274). During the latter half of the eighteenth century, 25,000 or more black Africans and Afro-Caribbeans resided in Europe, mostly in capital cities such as London, Paris, and Copenhagen, where they were employed not only by royalty and the aristocracy, but also by members of the bourgeoisie wishing to "emphasize their social status" (Kaija Tiainen-Anttila, *The Problem of Humanity: The Blacks in the European Enlightenment* [Helsinki: Finnish Historical Society, 1994], 69).

3. Par Bricole archive, DIj:1, *Biografiska uppgifter, 1796–1910,* no. 3, inventory 1451, SSA, *Egenhändig biografi av Badin* (transcribed copy, 1971). Although

no date is indicated, the document's contents suggest it was authored sometime between late 1807 and early 1810 (Wikström, "Badin-Couschi," 275).

4. Strindberg's *Queen Christina, Charles XII, Gustav III,* translations and introductions by Walter Johnson (Seattle: University of Washington Press, 1955), 205. *Gustav III* was first published in 1904 (Stockholm: Hugo Gebers Förlag), eighteen months after its completion.

5. Michel Foucault, *The Order of Things: An Archeology of the Human Sciences* (New York: Random House, 1971 [1966]), 136.

6. Mary Louise Pratt, *Imperial Eyes: Travel Writing and Transculturation* (London and New York: Routledge, 1992), 32.

7. Sten Lindroth applies the latter observation not only to *Systema naturae* but to all of Linnaeus's major works ("Linné: Legend och verklighet," *Lychnos* [1965–66]: 56–122), noting that it was in keeping with the "physico-theological thinking of the age."

8. It was not until toward the end of the eighteenth century that the already existent term "race" began to replace the terms "variety" and "nation" in European usage and to take on a new set of meanings, to refer to "an innate and fixed disparity in the physical and intellectual make-up of different peoples," to assume its more modern sense of visible biological and cultural difference (Nicholas Hudson, "From 'Nation' to 'Race': The Origin of Racial Classification in Eighteenth-Century Thought," *Eighteenth Century Studies* 29 (1996): 247–64 [258]).

9. Linneaus, *Systema naturae* (Leipzig, 1758), 21–22). Cf. Gunnar Broberg, *Homo Sapiens L.: Studier i Carl von Linnés naturuppfattning och människolära* (Uppsala: Almquist & Wiksell, 1975), 206 ff.; Broberg, "*Homo sapiens:* Linneaeus's Classification of Man," in *Linnaeus: The Man and His Work,* ed. Tore Frängsmyr (Berkeley: University of California Press, 1983), 156–94; and George L. Mosse, *Toward the Final Solution: A History of European Racism* (New York: Howard Fertig, 1978), 20. Especially since Linnaeus wrote in his own peculiar Latin, his characterization of *Homo afer* is subject to a range of translations; thus, for example, "dishonest" may also be read as "wily," and "governed by caprice" as "incapable of ruling themselves." Whatever the translation chosen, one cannot escape an imagery strongly suggesting *Europaeus* superior to *afer,* an imagery strongly resonating with less "scientific" claims then in circulation—even though Jordan and Handlin have attempted to argue that Linnaeus, since working outside the tradition of the Great Chain of Being, "was under no temptation to rank the various kinds of men" or to hierarchize in any way (Winthrop D. Jordan, *White over Black: American Attitudes toward the Negro, 1550–1812* [Chapel Hill: University of North Carolina Press, 1968], 222; Oscar Handlin, *Race and Nationality in American Life* [Boston: Little, Brown, 1957], 57–59). Regardless of Linnaeus's intentions, his classificatory scheme was a social fact that act-ually contributed to, and legitimated, ongoing and subsequent processes of stereotype production and racialization. Popkin suggests that the scheme played a major role during the Enlightenment in judging nonwhites as "inferior in terms of their 'philosophy' and 'way of life'" (Richard H. Popkin, "The Philosophical Basis of Eighteenth-Century Racism," in *Racism in*

the Eighteenth Century, ed. Harold E. Pagliaro [Cleveland: Press of Case Western University, 1973], 248).

10. Cf. Colette Guillaumin, *Racism, Sexism, Power, and Ideology* (London and New York: Routledge, 1995) and the introduction thereto by Danielle Juteau-Lee. For Britain, at least, Roxann Wheeler maintains that it was not until "the third quarter of the eighteenth century," in the wake of Buffon's *Histoire Naturelle* (1749) and the tenth edition of Linnaeus's *Systema naturae,* "that skin color emerges as the most important component of racial identity." Prior to that transition, she argues, "the ideology of human variety" was "articulated primarily through religious difference, which included such things as political governance and civil life," with much emphasis being placed on the categorical distinction between "*Christian* and *savage.*" Borrowing from Foucault's *Order of Things,* Wheeler also acknowledges that scientific practices that had gained a foothold by 1800 were placing an emphasis on structure rather than surface, thus enabling natural historians to draw a correspondence between "the more obvious signs displayed on the surfaces of bodies" and "the invisible structure beneath." "This paradigm shift," she adds, "rehearses a new way Europeans conceived of human differences and helps account for the emerging conviction that a person's exterior appearance spoke volumes about their mental capacity or, conversely, that skeletons or cranial measurement . . . revealed proclivities for entire groups of people" (*The Complexion of Race: Categories of Difference in Eighteenth-Century British Culture* [Philadelphia: University of Pennsylvania Press, 2000], 9, 289, 46, 32). But, she fails to recognize, Linnaeus's tenth-edition categorizations had already opened the door to such metonymical moves, to an unreflected viewpoint that collective Difference ran more than skin-deep.

11. On the faith placed in Enlightenment taxonomic systems, see Dorinda Outram, "On Being Perseus: New Knowledge, Dislocation, and Enlightenment Exploration," in *Geography and Enlightenment,* ed. David Livingstone and Charles Withers (Chicago: University of Chicago Press, 1999), 281–94; and Derek Gregory, *Dancing on the Pyramids: Orientalism and Cultures of Travel* (Minneapolis: University of Minnesota Press, forthcoming).

12. Foucault, *Order of Things,* 132.

13. Linnaeus spoke of his taxonomic system as a "map of nature" (Matthew H. Edney, "Reconsidering Enlightenment Geography and Map Making: Reconnaissance, Mapping, Archive," in *Geography and Enlightenment,* ed. Livingstone and Withers, 165–98 (186).

14. Pratt, *Imperial Eyes,* 30, 15, 31.

15. Lisbet Koerner, *Linnaeus: Nature and Nation* (Cambridge: Harvard University Press, 1999), 94.

16. Ibid., 166.

17. Broberg, *Homo Sapiens L.,* 224.

18. Jordan, *White over Black,* 216; cf. Pratt, *Imperial Eyes,* 15–37. In drawing up his fourfold classification, Linnaeus was clearly not alone in acting "to 'naturalize' the myth of European superiority" (Donald Worster, *Nature's Economy: A History of Ecological Ideas* [Cambridge: Cambridge University Press, 1977],

553). Hume, to take but one example, had already observed: "I am apt to suspect the negroes and in general all the other species of men (for there are four or five different kinds) to be naturally inferior to the whites" (David Hume, "Of National Characters" [1748]; quoted in Popkin, "Philosophical Basis of Eighteenth-Century Racism," 245–46). And, among other things, his categorizations were consonant with Rousseau's simultaneously developed system of differences: "One that identifies non-European people with nature and then places nature in opposition to culture" (Hugh Ruffles, "'Local Theory': Nature and the Making of an Amazonian Place," *Cultural Anthropology* 14 [1999]: 330), which is not to say that Rousseau exerted any significant influence on him. Popkin (245–62) identifies four overlapping and evolving discourse-embedded views whose circulation during the Enlightenment served as a "philosophical basis of racism," as "a basis for racist ideology": (1) nonwhites have a significantly different mental life; (2) nonwhiteness is "a sign of sickness or degeneracy," an environmentally precipitated loss of whiteness and human nature that is one with a diminished capacity for "cultural advance"; (3) some apparent human beings are really "a link between man and apes," are really "lower on the great chain of being"; (4) Caucasians were created separately and best, while those humans who were the result of "pre-Adamite creations never contained the stuff of genuine men" (n.b., Linnaeus was a monogeneticist rather than a polygeneticist; and, whatever his negative ascriptions to *Homo afer*, he at one point held "the unusual opinion" that the "common parent [of all men] was black" [A. Owen Aldridge, "Feijoo and the Problem of Ethiopian Color," in *Racism in the Eighteenth Century*, ed. Pagliaro, 273]). For a significant elaboration on the second discursive element see Phillip R. Sloan, "The Idea of Racial Degeneracy in Buffon's *Histoire Naturelle*," in ibid., 293–321. Also note Philip D. Curtin, *The Image of Africa: British Ideas and Action, 1750–1850* (Madison: University of Wisconsin Press, 1964), 36–48; Tiainen-Antilla, *Problem of Humanity*, 71–78, 103–44; and Wheeler, *Complexion of Race*.

19. Linnaeus spent the period 1735 to 1738 in Holland, during which time he received a doctorate in medicine, made trips to London and Paris, and participated in a "scientific club" largely devoted to the weekly discussion of his ongoing reworkings of *Systema naturae*. Two of those years were spent near Leiden, cataloging and completing the enormous plant collection of George Clifford, a prominent merchant. Late in life he asserted that he had "worked out everything, before he returned to his fatherland" (Koerner, *Linnaeus*, 39).

20. Linnaeus, in the "Dedicatio" to his *Hortus Cliffortianus* (Amsterdam, 1737). The compilation of this catalog convinced Linnaeus of the importance of linking his taxonomic efforts to global trading ventures, as Clifford had assembled most of his collection while director of the East India Company. Back in Uppsala "Linnaeus was especially successful in building up a network of correspondents that could provide him with plant material" (Staffan Müller-Wille, "Gardens of Paradise," *Endeavour* 25, no. 2 [2001]: 49–54 [52]; for further details, see Müller-Wille, *Botanik und weltweiter Handel: Zur Begründung eines natürlichen Systems der Pflanzen, 1701–1778* [Berlin: Verlag für Wissenschaft und Bildung, 1999]).

21. In a letter of 1761 Linnaeus noted that he devoted a portion of each afternoon writing "to my botanical friends" (Wilfrid Blunt, *The Compleat Naturalist: A Life of Linnaeus* [New York: Viking Press, 1971], 167). Speaking of himself, late in life he claimed: "Linnaeus corresponded not only within the kingdom [of Sweden] but also with various foreigners, especially with the most learned and curious of Europe. . . . Thus he did not only get to know immediately what was new but also took part in it, such that most books which came out were given to him for free" (*Vita Caroli Linnaei* [Stockholm: Almqvist & Wiksell, 1957; as quoted in Müller-Wille, "Gardens of Paradise," 52]). A number of those who studied at Uppsala under Linnaeus came from Russia, Prussia, Denmark, and elsewhere. The extensiveness of his correspondence network was further enhanced through the contacts he made with foreign visitors to Sweden.

22. Koerner, *Linnaeus*, 7, 81. In his *Diaeta Naturalis* (1733), a work in which a wide range of recent and more dated continental writings are drawn upon, Linnaeus proclaimed the Sami "the most representative of 'natural' beings—such as 'apes, Turks, Persians, Chinese, Siberians, [native] Americans'" (Koerner, *Linnaeus*, 68). Having already read the late seventeenth-century writings of Olof Rudbeck the Elder, which depicted the Sami as innocent children of nature, as well as Vallerius and other Swedish commentators, Linnaeus had approached his Sami fieldwork not with a totally uninformed eye, but with a preconstructed field of vision shaped by the (con)fusion of fact and fiction. His underlining of the Sami's "laziness" suggests an (il)logical grouping with *Homo Afer*. However, he (f)actually assigned the Sami to a special racial-freak category, *Monstrosus* (*Systema naturae*, 10th ed.), thereby contributing to Oliver Goldsmith's designation of that group as the lowest of the world's six races (*History of the Earth*, 1774) and their further negative branding in European "scientific" discourse, which regarded them, along with the Hottentots, as "the stupidest and ugliest members of the human race . . . at the very borderline of the animal kingdom" (Broberg, *Homo Sapiens L.*, 243). Moreover, as Koerner has observed: "[T]he Linnean fiction of the 'happy Lapp' is an especially strained variant of primitivism, for in the eighteenth century the Sami were a thoroughly colonized people. They suffered from smallpox, measles, and alcoholism; . . . they were conscripted into Lapland's mines; they were driven from their hunting grounds, fishing creeks and grazing lands; and the Lutheran churches burdened them with tithes, catechism exams, and compulsory church attendance" (*Linnaeus*, 73–74). Finally, it should be noted that the publications resulting from Linnaeus's Lapland journey are filled with a host of other fictions; not least of all he inflated what was actually a fifteen-day summer field trip into forty-eight days of hardship in which he endured "hunger, thirst, sweat, rambles, cold, rain, snow, ice, rocks, mountains and the Lapp language" (*Flora Lapponica* [1737]; Koerner, *Linnaeus*, 63).

23. Broberg, *Homo Sapiens L.*, 220. As early as the mid-sixteenth century, Hieronymus Cardanus (Geronimo Cardano), an Italian physician and mathematician, asserted that barbarian peoples dwelling in unfavorable climates, such as the Ethiopians and Lapps, were not far from monkeys in terms of their behavior and use of reason (ibid., 244).

24. Koerner, *Linnaeus*, 72.

25. Par Bricole archive, *Egenhändig biografi av Badin*.

26. Ibid.

27. Carl Forsstrand, "Badin," a chapter contained in his *Sophie Hagman och hennes samtida: Några anteckningar från det gustavianska Stockholm* (Stockholm: Wahlström och Widstrand, 1911), 122–37 (125).

28. Wikström, "Badin-Couschi," 275.

29. Kurdo Baksi, "Välkommen till Rinkeby," *Aftonbladet*, April 9, 1996.

30. Juan Fonseca, "Det nya sverige," in *Statens offentliga utredningar* [Swedish Government Official Reports], no. 1996: 55, *Vägar in i Sverige: Bilaga till Invandrapolitiska kommitténs slutbetänkande* (Stockholm: Arbetsmarknadsdepartementet, 1996), 93–112 (95).

31. Christina Kellberg, "Rasism vardag för Afrikaner i Sverige," *Dagens Nyheter*, June 1, 1996.

32. A scene, a fictionalized (f)act, derived from Ola Larsmo's novel, *Maroonberget* (Stockholm: Albert Bonniers Förlag, 1996), 52–53.

33. M[agnus] J[akob] Crusenstolpe, *Morianen eller Holsten-Gottorpska huset i Sverige*, 6 vols. (Stockholm: Albert Bonniers Förlag, 1928 [1840–1844]), vol. 1, *1751–1772*.

34. Wikström, "Badin-Couschi," 275–76.

35. Lars Lönnroth and Sven Delblanc, eds., *Den Svenska Litteraturen*, vol. 3, *De liberala genombrotten, 1830–1890* (Stockholm: Bonnier Alba, 1988), 83.

36. Jean-Jacques Rousseau, *Émile; or, Education*, trans. Barbara Foxley (New York: E. P. Dutton, 1930 [1762]), 19–20. Tornea (Torneå) is a Finnish city sixty miles south of the Arctic Circle. At the time of Rousseau's writing Finland still belonged to Sweden.

37. Jean-Jacques Rousseau, *Émile, or On Education*, with introduction, translation, and notes by Allan Bloom (New York: Basic Books, 1979), 3.

38. Par Bricole archive, *Egenhändig biografi av Badin*.

39. Henry Nelson Coleridge, *Sex månader i Westindien år 1825*, translation and comments by C[arl] A[dolf] Carlsson (Linköping: Axel Petre, 1835), unnumbered third page of text.

40. *Strindberg's Queen Christina, Charles XII, Gustav III*, 206.

41. Badin's birthplace, Saint Croix, and the remainder of Denmark's possessions in the Virgin Islands, were operated and administered according to mercantile principles: the purpose of colonies is to produce economic benefits for the "mother country"; colonies—which are not to buy from or sell to other countries—are useless unless they yield profits. Like other colonial plantation economies of the period, Saint Croix was enmeshed in a triangular trade that nourished nascent capitalists in the "mother country": slaves were imported from Africa; rum and molasses were shipped to Copenhagen; and from there commodities were sent off in Danish bottoms either to purchase additional slaves or to supply the island (Leif Svaleson, *The Slave Ship Fredensborg* [Bloomington: Indiana University Press, 2000]).

42. Ylva Eggehorn, *En av dessa timmar* (Stockholm: Albert Bonniers Förlag AB, 1997), 13.

43. Ola Larsmo, "Skuggan av Badin-några dagboksanteckningar av Gustav IIIs morian," *BLM–Bonniers Litterära Magasin,* no. 6 (1996): 4–9 (6).

44. Some scholars observe that Rousseau never employed the notorious phrase "noble savage" in his writings. Michael Clifford, however, convincingly notes the appropriateness of that term for the focal figure employed by Rousseau in distinguishing between "wilderness" and "civilization" in his *Discourse on the Origin and Foundation of Inequality among Mankind.* For what is described in one paragraph as the desire for liberty of the savage, is in the next labeled as "the noblest faculty of man" (Michael Clifford, *Political Genealogy after Foucault: Savage Identities* [New York and London: Routledge, 2001], 1, 171; cf. Ter Ellingson, *The Myth of the Noble Savage* [Berkeley: University of California Press, 2001]). Of course, Rousseau's positive view of the "noble savage" was opposed by many of his contemporaries in France and elsewhere, including Voltaire and Buffon. Whatever the case, a favorably inclined reader of *Émile* or the *Discourse on . . . Inequality,* such as Queen Lovisa Ulrika and those around her, would very probably have learned to associate a certain set of "noble" attributes with the term "savage."

45. January 1764 entry in the diary of Count Fredrik Sparre ("Grefve Fredrik Sparres egenhändiga anteckningar," as reproduced in *Portfeuille,* ed. M. J. Crusenstolpe [Stockholm: L. J. Hierta, 1837], 93–130 [105]). Also see Wickström, "Badin-Couschi," 277.

46. Par Bricole archive, *Egenhändig biografi av Badin.* Badin did not necessarily believe that his wildness was entirely attributable to his "mother's milk." In a marginal note he observes that, "if I wasn't [already] naturally inclined," he learned to be "mischievous" and "verbally abusive" from two members of the aristocracy, one of whom served for a while as his private tutor.

47. Rehn (1717–1793) was an accomplished interior designer and architect, as well as an engraver, drawer, and painter.

48. Carl Hernmarck, "Rehn, Johan (Jean) Eric," *Svenskt Konstnärslexikon,* vol. 3 (Malmö: Allhems Förlag, 1961), 461–63 (462).

49. Rehn also may have encountered Badin as a result of intermittently undertaking various interior design projects at the court (ibid., 461–62).

50. "Grefve Fredrik Sparres egenhändiga anteckningar," 104–5. Given the pattern of Badin's much discussed behavior, it is perhaps no coincidence that the first known usage of the word *badinage* in a Swedish text is dated to 1769 (*Svenska Akademiens Ordbok,* 2: B56).

51. As a "dwarf" Badin would have been keeping with tradition. Since the Middle Ages, if not earlier, European court jesters were often dwarves or hunchbacks, a circumstance enabling both royalty and the aristocracy to feel above those who provoked their laughter and thereby unthreatened by their barbs.

52. Sparre, who had seen Badin on December 31, 1763, described him as "a little dwarf, although not unpretty" ("Grefve Fredrik Sparres egenhändiga anteckningar,"

104). The failure of subsequent contemporaries to refer to Badin's extreme short-ness or dwarflike appearance suggests that he was short for his age and that Sparre mistakenly regarded him as older than he actually was—perhaps in keeping with a stereotype of the adult African as being childish in behavior.

53. For whatever reason, one 1845 text claims Badin "was born around 1753," thereby reducing his age by three to six years (*Svenskt konversationslexikon,* vol. 1 [Stockholm: P. G. Berg, 1845], 79).

54. W[endela] H[ebbe], "Monsieur Coichi," *Hvad Nytt från Stockholm,* June 19 and 26, 1897.

55. Rousseau's *Discourse on the Origins of Inequality* as excerpted in Stéphane Bruchfeld and Ingrid Jacobsson, *Kan man vara svart och svensk? Texter om rasism, antisemitism och nazism* (Stockholm: Natur och kultur, 1999), 51.

56. C. M. Carlander, *Svenska bibliotek och ex-libris,* vol. 2, part 2 (Stockholm: Förlagsaktiebolaget Iduna, 1904), 751–55. That Carlander was merely reiterating Wendela Hebbe's tale is apparent from other evidence contained in his poorly docu-mented Badin entry (the mention of a specific book title [cf. Wikström, "Badin-Couschi," 313]).

57. Carlander, *Svenska bibliotek,* 754.

58. Carlander's purloining of Hebbe did not stop with the Jeremiah passage. For he enumerated further examples of other supposedly underlined passages by book, chapter, and verse, each of which was also mentioned by Hebbe in almost exactly the same order.

59. On the fate of Badin's entire book collection, and thereby the extreme im-probability of Carlander's otherwise knowing what was or was not underlined, see "Re Reading" note 6.

60. Forsstrand, "Badin," 136–37.

61. Wendela Hebbe, *I Skogen: Sannsagor för ungdom* (Stockholm: L. J. Hiertas Förlag, 1871).

62. Gösta Lundström, "Wendela Hebbe," *Svensk Biografiskt lexikon,* vol. 18 (Stockholm: P. A. Norstedt & Söner, 1971), 369–73 (371).

63. Stockholm *inom broarna,* literally Stockholm within the bridges, is the small island at the center of Stockholm now known as the Old Town (Gamla Stan).

64. Although it was the 1897 publication of "Monsieur Coichi" that contributed to subsequent Badin lore and the popular bourgeois imagination, there was a much earlier version that appeared in a provincial newspaper, *Jönköpingsbladet* (January 14 and 19, 1847). The two renditions are virtually identical, word for word, except for a few minor alterations (the initial article series began: "It was a raw and chilly after-noon last March"). Hebbe may have re-released the piece in order to supplement her income, knowing full well that extremely few, if any, of her Stockholm readers would have been exposed to her efforts of a half-century earlier. She also may have been con-sciously or unconsciously spurred to republish by other representations of blacks then circulating in Stockholm (see "Part II: The Unaddressable Addressed").

65. Buck-Morss, *The Dialectics of Seeing,* 140.

66. Christian Hebbe, a merchant, owned 1,200 of the company's 80,000 shares

(Ingegerd Hildebrand, *Den svenska kolonin St. Barthélemy och Västindiska kompaniet fram till 1796* [Lund: AB Ph. Lindstedts universitetsbokhandel, 1951], 311–13). For more on the West Indian Company, its slave trade, and Badin's possible knowledge thereof, see discussion in "Memory Etchings."

67. Par Bricole archive, *Egenhändig biografi av Badin.* The politics of such an identity-construction tactic would have been consistent with the effort made by Badin—elsewhere in his autobiographical statement—to brace his lineage with Nimrod, "Forefather of the Ethiopians" (see Badin's quotation in "Re Reading" associated with note 8).

68. Crusenstolpe, *Morianen,* 1: 6. Despite her initial miss, Hebbe later does correctly have Badin arriving at the court as a present from Denmark.

69. Regarding the probable origins of Hebbe's hut-burning story, see "Geography Lessons" note 21 and the text thereto.

70. Although Hebbe's romantic novels and short stories are often regarded as quite inferior to the fiction of a number of her male and female contemporaries, and although the recognition accorded her children's stories was not lasting, she is generally assigned some importance in the history of Swedish letters. Not only was she a pioneer in the field of journalism, she was the first woman to support herself (and her three children) through newspaper employment, invented Swedish "social reportage" with a series of articles on the everyday miseries of poor women in Stockholm, and in effect served as the arts and literature editor of *Aftonbladet.* She also made a significant impact on the educated public's exposure to foreign literature, exerting considerable influence on the titles selected by Lars Hierta—her employer/sponsor/eventual lover—for the popular *Reader's Library* series, and herself translating works by Charles Dickens and Eugène Sue, among others. For details of Hebbe's life and the major literary figures who were either romantically drawn to her or part of her Stockholm circle, see Lundström, "Wendela Hebbe"; Britta Hebbe, *Wendela: En modern 1800-talskvinna* (Stockholm: Natur och kultur, 1974); and Ebba Witt-Brattström, "Att vara för mycket och för litet: Om Wendela Hebbe," in *Nordisk kvinnolitteraturhistoria,* ed. Elisabeth Møller Jensen, vol. 2, *Fadershuset, 1800-talet* (Höganäs: Förlag AB Wiken, 1993), 81–87.

71. *Aftonbladet,* February 18, 1841.

72. Lundström, "Wendela Hebbe," 372.

73. The fictionalizing of facts and factualizing of fictions become all the more blurred when Hebbe recounts how Badin's second wife personally took Crusenstolpe to task for fictionalizing the name (and court position) of Badin's first wife, and how he "in vain attempted to make her understand the privileges of a novel author" (H[ebbe], "Monsieur Coichi," June 26, 1897).

74. Åke Holmberg, *Världen bortom västerlandet,* vol. 1, *Svensk syn på fjärren länder och folk från 1700-talet till första världskriget* (Göteborg: Kungl. Vetenskaps- och Vitterhets-Sällskap 1988), 38–39.

75. *Hvad Nytt från Stockholm, Julnummer* (special Christmas edition), 1898.

76. By this date *underklass* was widely employed as a proper designation for the working classes.

77. Jonas Frykman and Orvar Löfgren, *Culture Builders: A Historical Anthropology of Middle-Class Life* (New Brunswick, NJ: Rutgers University Press, 1987 [1979]); and Allan Pred, *Lost Words and Lost Worlds: Modernity and the Language of Everyday Life in Late Nineteenth-Century Stockholm* (Cambridge: Cambridge University Press, 1990).

78. The representational (con)fusion of race and class and interwoven allusions to the "apelike" were not unusual elsewhere in late nineteenth-century Europe. For example, the "dangerous classes" of Britain—including Irish, Jews, and prostitutes as well as the bottom of the working class—were sometimes referred to as "chimpanzees" or "apelike" and on other occasions portrayed as blackened by coal dust or filth (Anne McClintock, *Imperial Leather: Race, Gender, and Sexuality in the Colonial Contest* [New York and London: Routledge, 1995], 216, 211). And a much-read treatise of 1889 described London's working-class neighborhoods as "a dark continent" inhabited by "wild races" (Ian Baucom, *Out of Place: Englishness, Empire, and the Locations of Identity* [Princeton, NJ: Princeton University Press, 1999], 36). By the late 1930s, if not earlier, the racialization of the underclass in Sweden was also given spatial imagery when overcrowded working-class residential areas in Stockholm were referred to by some as *negerbyar*—Negrovilles (or perhaps even niggervilles)—thereby marking them as out-of-place places, as "unmodern" and "backward," as "dark" and "dangerous," as not unlike the home territory of African "primitives," as out of keeping with the country's modernity project, as the negatively charged opposite to areas of recently constructed modern housing. Today the term *negerbyar* has been resurrected, being occasionally used to negatively stamp the racialized suburbs of Stockholm and other major cities, to mutually stigmatize segregated areas and their largely non-European and Muslim residents (Allan Pred, *Even in Sweden*. Other cartoon representations of Africans in the late nineteenth-century Swedish press are considered more fully in "Part II: The Unaddressable Addressed."

79. For more on late nineteenth-century textbook, press, and travel literature images, see Iheanyi J. S. Mbaekwe, *The Images of Africa in Sweden before 1914: A Study of Six Types of Persuasive Ideas* (Lund: Meddelande från Statsvetenskapliga institutionen, Lunds Universitet, 1980); Holmberg, *Världen bortom västerlandet,* vols. 1 and 2, *Den svenska omvärlds bilden under mellankrigstiden* (Göteborg: Kungl. Vetenskaps-och Vitterhets-Sällskap, 1994); Lasse Berg, *När Sverige upptäckte Afrika* (Stockholm: Rabén Prisma, 1997); and the literature cited in those works. These images are also considered more fully in "Part II: The Unaddressable Addressed."

80. Mbaekwe, *Images of Africa,* 65; Berg, *När Sverige upptäckte Afrika,* 171 ff. Such cruelty and other "uncivilized" traits were presumably to be eliminated through conversion to Christ, through transforming the project of imperialism into a work of civilization. (On this and other points the late nineteenth-century Swedish missionary literature resonated with that of British and other colonial-power missionaries, who repeatedly expressed disdain for the "savagery" of "uncivilized" Africans.) "Facts" concerning the grim treatment of the elderly had already been put

in circulation in Sweden during the late eighteenth century via the influential travel accounts of Linnaeus's protégé Carl Peter Thunberg. Although apparently having nothing more than hearsay to go on, he asserted without reservation that "Old and superannuated persons are buried alive, or else carried away to some cleft in the mountains with provision for a few days, where they are either starved to death, or fall prey to some wild beast" (Carl Peter Thunberg, *Travels at the Cape of Good Hope, 1772–1775* [Cape Town: Van Riebeeck Society, 1986 (1788–89)], 317).

81. *Hvad Nytt från Stockholm*, June 22, 1895, and November 13, 1897. These in-the-flesh images must have been given widespread verbal replication via the second-hand accounts of direct observers, as it was said—at least in the first instance—that the exhibit daily attracted an "enormous stream" of visitors.

82. Raoul Granqvist, "Swedish Writers in Africa," *Umeå Papers in English*, no. 11 (1990): 57–76 (64).

83. Crusenstolpe, *Morianen*, 1: 137. Pechlin was a longtime opponent to the throne and eventually involved in the conspiracy that led to the assassination of Gustav III in 1791. This fictionalized attribution to Pechlin is but another example of the liberties taken by Crusenstolpe in his attempt to tell history as it (f)actually was. Whereas it was apparently in 1762, in the wake of the publication of *Émile*, that Badin was first allowed to behave as an uninhibited "noble savage," Crusen-stolpe here has Lovisa Ulrica already tiring of such behavior in 1760 or 1761.

84. Olaudah Equiano, *The Life of Olaudah Equiano, or Gustavus Vassa, the African* (Mineola: Dover, 1990), 4; capitalization in original.

85. Equiano, *Life*, iv.

86. Before his death in 1797, Equiano's book went through nine editions, includ-ing one in German (1790) and one each for audiences in the United States (1791) and the Netherlands (1791) (Equiano, *Life*, iv).

87. Ibid., 41–42. Equiano was roughly twelve years old when he was initially exposed to snow in Falmouth, England.

88. Carl von Linné [Linnaeus], *Bref och skrifvelser af och till*, series 1, vol. 3 (Stockholm: Aktiebolaget Ljus, 1909), 211. In the same letter he asked Bjerchén "to be so kind as to carefully observe the genitalia" of some unspecified Negroes "in *utroque sexu*." Whatever the ways, if any, in which Linnaeus's preoccupation with genitalia involved an intermingling of science and sexual desire, it should be kept in mind that his botanical taxonomic system—the foundation for his attempt to systematize all "nature" and thereby reveal Creation's basic structure—was a sexual system. Plants were sexual beings; the stamen and the pistil were fertilizing and ovarian organs, and plant classification and subclassification were a question of their respective numbers and positions vis-à-vis one another. Sexual metaphors abound in the various editions of *Systema naturae:* in the eighth class of plants there are "eight men in the same bride's chamber"; in the fourteenth class "four men—two taller and two shorter—together with the bride"; and so on (Tore Frängs-myr, *Svensk idéhistoria: Bildning och vetenskap under tusen år*, vol. 1, *1000–1809* [Stockholm: Natur och kultur, 2000], 240). It furthermore should be understood that Linnaeus's professional concern with human genitalia dated back at least to

1738, when he supported himself as a physician in Stockholm specializing in venereal diseases. In 1758, at age fifty-one and after twenty years of marriage, he also may have had a sexual imagination fueled by a less than happy domestic life, by his relationship to a wife (unjustifiably?) described by his students as haggishly "domineering" and "selfish" (Blunt, *Compleat Naturalist*, 172, 174). That Linnaeus was at the time somewhat (guiltily?) preoccupied with female sexuality, and the (im)morality thereof, is suggested by his *Nemesis Divina*, a "spiritual diary" dating from the late 1750s. In that "testimonial to God's working in history," he presented "some 200 cases of divine retribution," a number of which "linger over how unwed mothers, or 'whores,' die by scaldings and burns, as if that was the appropriate end to their inflamed passions" (Lisbeth Koerner, "Carl Linnaeus in His Time and Place," in *Cultures of Natural History*, ed. Nicholas Jardine, Anne Secord, and Emma C. Spary [Cambridge: Cambridge University Press, 1996], 145–62 [156–57]). Regardless of the actual character of Linnaeus's sexual imagination and preoccupations, in fairness to his wife it should be added that by this time he was growing into "an egocentric diva," one who was easily wounded by the slightest criticism and had the "temperament of a hysteric" (Lindroth, "Linné: Legend och verklighet," 122).

89. Carl von Linné, *Bref och skrifvelser*, 209. Since Linnaeus's letter was undated, it cannot be determined whether Bjerchén was responding to his mentor, or vice versa. Whatever the case, all evidence suggests Bjerchén never succeeded in obtaining the requested genitalia viewing. If the owner of the young woman in question was in the business of accepting payment for her display, she may be thought of as a precursor to Sarah Baartman, "the Hottentot Venus," a woman whose steatopygia and genitalia were publicly exhibited in London, Paris, and Ireland between 1810 and 1815, and who was regarded by "most Europeans who viewed her . . . only as a collection of sexual parts" (Gilman, *Difference and Pathology*, 85, 88). French "scientific" writings about Baartman, like Linnaeus's writings about the troglodyte, served to liken "the 'lowest' human species with the highest ape, the orangutan."

90. Linnaeus at one time possessed as many as eight monkeys and apes in his collection and botanical gardens, prizing them because "no joking, nobody is so amusing, so singular and different, and as comical for everyone." He was especially attached to one of his female monkeys, Diana. Upon her death in late 1756, he wrote a friend: "Think, my beautiful monkey died—where shall I now get another to replace her. I mourn her quite a bit. Offer condolences for my grief" (Broberg, *Homo Sapiens L.*, 276–77). Is it possible that—some eighteen months later—the "Troglodyte" woman was at least subconsciously regarded as a replacement? As, whatever else, also a pet? Worthy of affection?

91. Müller-Wille, "Gardens of Paradise," 49. Müller-Wille and Lindroth are referring to Linnaeus's exceptional talents as "an observer and describer of objects" and the "spirit of scholasticism" of his taxonomic writings, in which "division and denomination according to prescribed norms" became "the most important and all-but-exclusive task." That two-facedness, that rift between sensual perception and rigid categorization, however, may be assigned multiple meanings. Cf. Lindroth, "Linné: Legend och verklighet."

92. While C. E. Hoppius is sometimes listed as the author of this dissertation, it was actually written by Linnaeus. This was in keeping with the Uppsala practice whereby one obtained the Ph.D. by publicly defending a work produced by one's mentor.

93. Broberg, "Linnaeus's Classifiction of Man," 179–94. As Broberg notes, the lineage of Linnaeus's troglodyte can be pushed beyond the seventeenth century all the way back to the writings of Pliny. Whatever its multiple fictional and (f)actual predecessors, Linnaeus's Troglodyte classification was contradicted by Bjerchén's insistence that, according to herself and other people, the sixteeen-year-old was "born in Jamaica to black parents who are still alive and live there." Linnaeus, however, stubbornly ignored his student.

94. Cf. the Broberg quotation in "Memory Etchings" associated with note 48. Although "several fifteenth-century cartographers decorated parts of Africa with [highly suggestive] little naked figures," it was not until the sixteenth century that the supposed hypersexuality of black Africans was first given published authority via a Latin treatise by Leo Africanus, a work that some decades later appeared in English translation (ca. 1600) under the title *History and Description of Africa* (quoted in Jordan, *White over Black,* 158, 33–34).

95. Ernst Brunner, *Fukta din aska: C. M. Bellmans liv från början till slut* (Stockholm: Albert Bonniers Förlag, 2002), 83.

96. Lindroth, "Linné: Legend och verklighet," 118–19 (no translation; from Lindroth's own English summary).

97. Marcel Proust, *In Search of Lost Time,* vol. 4, *Sodom and Gomorrah,* trans. C. K. Scott Moncrieff and Terence Kilmartin, rev. D. J. Enright (New York: Modern Library, 1999 [1921]), 719.

98. Broberg, *Homo Sapiens L.,* 249. In the same lecture Linnaeus claimed that the breasts of Hottentot and black women were so large they could toss them over their backs and allow their babies to nurse there.

99. Lindroth, "Linné: Legend och verklighet," 121 (no translation; from Lindroth's own English summary).

Advances(?) Love(making)s? (Anti)Climaxes?

1. Johan Linder, *Tanckar om then smittosame siukdomen Fransoser, och salivation eller dregel-curen* (Stockholm, 1713), in Broberg, *Homo Sapiens L.,* 239.

2. Jordan, *White over Black,* 33, 158. Jordan more precisely notes, "In a work notorious as a collection of commonplaces, Oliver Goldsmith represented Linnaeus as having shown that the Negro's 'penis was longer and much wider'" (*An History of the Earth, and Animated Nature,* 8 vols. [London, 1774], 2: 228). If Linnaeus actually made such a claim, he certainly was not its originator. Instead he would have been scientifically legitimating a long-circulating "fact," an idea that "was considerably older" (Jordan, *White over Black,* 158), an idea that was sometimes given graphic representation. Linnaeus is known to have been familiar with the paintings of Brazilian plants, animals, and people made by the Dutchman Albert Eckhout during the 1630s and 1640s, and which came into possession of King Fredrik III

of Denmark in 1654. One of these was of a highly sexualized, nearly naked, Afro-Brazilian male. Standing somewhat taller and immediately beside this muscular figure, and unmistakably identifiable/parallel with him, is a date-palm tree shaped as an enormous swollen penis, complete with glans and bushy base.

3. Gilman, *Difference and Pathology*, 83, 109–10.

4. Christian Carlsson, "Öppen rasism är lättare att hantera," *Dagens Nyheter*, January 18, 2000.

5. Sander L. Gilman, "Black Bodies, White Bodies: Toward an Iconography of Female Sexuality in Late Nineteenth-Century Art, Medicine, and Literature," *Critical Inquiry* (Autumn 1985): 204–42 (209).

6. Cf. the readings given this engraving by David Dabydeen, *Hogarth's Blacks: Images of Blacks in Eighteenth-Century English Art* (Kingston-upon-Thames: Dangaroo Press, 1985); as well as by Ronald Paulson in *The Art of Hogarth* (London: Phaidon, 1975), 96–97; and *Hogarth's Graphic Works*, 3rd rev. ed. (London: Print Room, 1989), 79–80. Also note Jenny Uglow, *Hogarth: A Life and a World* (New York: Farrar, Strauss, and Giroux, 1997), 201–2.

7. The response of the young woman may be seen as in keeping with an eighteenth-century propensity to identify "British working-class women as inhabiting more naturally than men the dangerous borders of racial and sexual transgression" (McClintock, *Imperial Leather*, 23). In 1772 a popular English pamphlet noted: "The lower class of women in England are remarkably fond of the blacks, for reasons too brutal to mention" (Curtin, *The Image of Africa*, 46).

8. M[agnus] J[akob] Crusenstolpe, "Badin," *Medaljonger och statyetter*, no. 2 (1882): 211–14 (211 and 213); emphasis in original.

9. Crusenstolpe, *Morianen*, 4: 45. Crusenstolpe's reference to "the attitudes and behavior" of the Gustavian period falsely suggests the absence of stereotypes of African hypersexuality at the time he was writing, around 1840.

10. Ibid., 1: 166.

11. Cf. Gilman, *Difference and Pathology*, especially 79 ff. and the sources cited therein.

12. Crusenstolpe, *Morianen*, 1: 178.

13. Carl-Gustaf Thomasson, "Morianen," *Ord och Bild* 61 (1952): 615–23 (622).

14. Nanna Lundh-Eriksson, *Sophia Albertina: Historisk kavalkad* (Stockholm: Walhström och Widstrand, 1946), 94.

15. On the other hand, the assignment of the name Ramström to Badin's fictitious wife may have been a device for Crusenstolpe to rework some personally felt ambivalence about Badin's sexual appeal and accomplishments (see quotations in this chapter associated with notes 34 and 35).

16. Crusenstolpe, *Morianen*, 1: 214.

17. Ibid., 2: 77–78, 174–75, 215 (quote), 3: 98 ff.

18. *Miranda i Sverige och Norge 1787: General Francisco de Mirandas dagbok från hans resa september–december 1787*, translation and introduction by Stig Rydén (Stockholm: Nordiska Museet, 1950), 154.

19. Badin may well have been aware that THE rumor was once again circulating.

For Badin himself was an active Freemason, while Miranda's informant, an unidentified R. (who claimed to have heard the story directly from Gustav III) is quite likely to have been encountered either during the Spanish American's court tour or as a result of his interactions with local Freemasons (note Gunnar Sahlin, *Miranda i Sverige/en Suecia* [Stockholm: Latinamerika-institutet i Stockholm, 1990], 39–43). Whatever the case, the twin rumors were not a "classic" example of bourgeois elements attempting to discredit the aristocracy and the crown on moral grounds, for they appear to have been spread primarily by fractions of the aristocracy in opposition to Gustav III, by people who themselves were often promiscuous.

20. Herman Lindqvist, *Historien om Sverige*, vol. 5, *Gustavs dagar* (Stockholm: Norstedts, 1997), 462.

21. Larsmo, *Maroonberget*, 202. Larsmo's fictionalized fact, in effect, not only has Badin having child-producing sex with Sophia Albertina during a period when she was preoccupied with her mother's failing health, but also at a date that is five years later than that suggested by Miranda's reproduced rumor.

22. "A. F. Muncks berättelse den 22 mars 1779," reproduced in Oscar Nikula, *Adolph Fredric Munck: En hovgunstlings uppgång och fall* (Helsingfors: Skrifter utgivna av Svenska litteratursällskaptet i Finland, no. 570, 1991), 327–39 (338). A close examination by one scholar, Olof Jägerskiöld, leaves little doubt that this document was actually authored by Munck. Another authority, Sten Carlsson, assures that "there is no proper reason for distrusting this account" despite "Munck's disputed character" (Nikula, *Adolph Fredric Munck*, 66, 69).

23. That Munck was rumored to be the queen's lover long before she ever became pregnant, and that Badin had grounds for being concerned about how any social interaction with the princess might be read, is evidenced by the following two diary observations made by Hedvig Elisabeth Charlotta, Gustav III's sister-in-law (then Duchess of Södermanland, later queen of Sweden, 1809–1818): "The rumor [first mentioned last month] . . . concerning Munck and the Queen continues and has gained such wide circulation that everybody is now talking about it, although in greatest secrecy" (Carl Carlson Bonde, ed., *Hedvig Elisabeth Charlottas Dagbok*, vol. 1, *1775–1782* [Stockholm: P. A. Norstedt & Söner, 1902], 22). "People continue to follow the Queen's every move with the greatest attention, especially her relationship with Munck. There is much talk about the latter, and there are many who on the sly attempt to keep an eye on her every action. When she speaks with Munck, you can be sure that all eyes are concentrated on her. I think that it ought to be dreadfully trying for her; but probably she doesn't notice it, otherwise she very likely would be more careful and avoid speaking with him constantly as she does now. I am, however, anxious about the consequences of all this; for if the Queen should become in the family way, this certainly will give rise to much ado" (97–98). Although these entries were made for the months of November 1775 and December 1777, it was not until January 1778 that there was any awareness the queen might be pregnant. In the monthly letters to a trusted friend that constitute her diary, Hedvig Elisabeth Charlotta made several other references to the feverish persistence of "the defamatory rumor" in court circles and beyond (ibid., 20, 55, 76, 89).

24. Nikula, *Adolph Fredric Munck*, 70–71; and Bonde, *Hedvig Elisabeth Charlottas Dagbok*, 1: 20.

25. Lovisa Ulrika even went so far as to suggest to her daughter-in-law and others that Gustav III had "enticed the Queen into this intrigue since he knows very well that he can't get any children in any other manner." She was so certain of Munck's role that she tried to convince her second son, Prince Carl, that he ought to protest to the king in order to protect his own succession to the throne (Bonde, *Hedvig Elisabeth Charlottas Dagbok*, 1: 102–7). The assertiveness of her claims, and the problems that they precipitated, eventually led to her being forced to sign a document withdrawing her insinuations and recognizing the "legitimacy" of the soon-to-be-born child (Wikström, "Badin-Couschi," 282). Signed under duress in the presence of all three of her children, as well as six members of the Privy Council and the Royal Chancellor, that document clearly failed to fully gag the Munck rumor.

26. "A. F. Muncks berättelse," 336–38.

27. Klas Östergren, *Gustav IIIs äktenskap*, a filmed drama first shown on Swedish television (STV 1) December 25–26, 2001.

28. Since Badin's notebook is only seventy-four pages long, despite covering decades, it might be ventured that he kept a lot to himself, that there was much he would not commit to either the spoken or the written word, that he was resolutely silent on a number of issues in addition to his rumored involvement with Sofia Albertina. On the other hand, since the notebook's contents are not chronologically arranged, it may very well be that he made jottings in whatever was at hand and that other simultaneously maintained notebooks have not survived.

29. Nikula, *Adolph Fredric Munck*, 71.

30. That Badin would have had to keep his silence in 1787, that Miranda encountered the twin Munck/queen and Badin/Sofia Albertina rumors that year, is consistent with another then-circulating story that claimed that the queen had deposited a very large sum of money in Munck's name for his "free disposition" (Bonde, *Hedvig Elisabeth Charlottas Dagbok*, vol. 2, *1783–1788* [1903], 156–57).

31. Having grown out of favor with the king before his assassination, Ehrensvärd's devastating drawing may also be read as a critical counterrepresentation, as a delayed counteraction to Gustav III's repeated issuance of medals designed to represent the *legitimacy* of his absolute monarchy. Cf. Mikael Alm, *Kungsord i elfte timmen: Språk och självbild i det gustavianska enväldets legitimetskamp* (Stockholm: Atlantis, 2002). Whatever the case, Ehrensvärd is not especially kind to Queen Sofia Magdalena, for, in keeping with Lutheran patriarchal doctrine, he has reduced her to a male-obeying subject, a subordinate (sex) object, a member of the inferior/sinister sex dutifully awaiting entry of a superior's member. Also note that Ehrensvärd was given a place in Munck's account, being depicted as one of the first two people to whom Gustav III confided his intent to seek reconciliation with the queen in order to produce an heir to the throne.

32. Bengt Hildebrand and O. Nikula, "Ehrensvärd, Carl August," *Svenskt Biografisk Lexikon* (Stockholm: Albert Bonnier, 1936), 12: 440–60 (456).

33. On Badin's order memberships and the conversations he may have been ex-

posed to, see discussion in "Memory Etchings." It was said that Princes Karl and Fredrik, both active in the Freemasons, were among those who actively spread the rumor of Munck's sexual involvement with their brother's queen (Nikula, *Adolph Fredric Munck*, 73). That other Freemasons were less than positively disposed toward Gustav III, that the Stockholm lodge was at times discord-riddled and "torn by dissension," and that some Freemasons were not beyond dealing in "malicious" gossip and sexually laden rumors, is variously evident from a 1780 diary (Johan Gabriel Oxenstierna, *Journal för Året 1780*, with a foreword by Holger Frykenstedt [Lund: C. W. K. Gleerup Bokförlag, 1967]).

34. Crusenstolpe, *Morianen*, 1: 178, 179.

35. Ibid., 4: 132.

36. Ibid., 1: 173.

37. Ibid., 2: 215.

38. Ibid., 2: 215.

39. Par Bricole archive, *Egenhändig biografi av Badin*.

40. Crusenstolpe, *Morianen*, 4: 45.

41. Ibid., 4: 155.

42. Nikula, *Adolph Fredric Munck*, 62.

43. *Miranda i Sverige och Norge 1787*, 150. Miranda's comment follows an expression of regret regarding the lesbian tendencies of "the very lovable, young and good looking" Duchess Hedvig Elisabet Charlotta, the wife of Gustav III's brother, Prince Karl. While the claims about the duchess's sexuality may or may not have been nothing more than factualized fictions put into circulation by enemies of the court, she herself expressed indigation at Gustav III's "depraved taste" in a diary entry made a few months before the king's assassination (see note 45).

44. Crusenstolpe, *Morianen* 4: 165.

45. *Hedvig Elisabet Charlottas Dagbok*, vol. 3, 1789–1792 (1907), 386. While distancing herself from Gustav III's "detestable private life," "depraved taste," and "contrary to nature" sexual habits, the duchess did draw a line to what she would believe, continuing: "and it is asserted that neither soldiers of splendid appearance nor footmen are excluded [from those he seeks intimate contact with]. Although people have assured me that this is really true, I must however doubt the veracity of something so incredible." This reluctance, expressed but four months before the masked-ball assassination, probably involved a refusal to believe those with a highly venomous attitude toward the king. However, some years earlier, in the somewhat less charged atmosphere of 1784, she did complain of the open practice of "offensive," "immoral," "Italian" sexual activities at the court (ibid., vol. 2, *1783–1788*, 62). Also note her entry for June 1791 (ibid., vol. 3, *1789–1792*, 361).

46. Carl Jonas Love Almqvist, *Drottningens juvelsmycke eller Azouras Lazuli Tintomara: Berättelse om händelser näst före, under och efter Konung Gustaf IIIs mord* (Stockholm: Gedins Förlag, 1993 [1834]), 22. While Almqvist studied documents and official records pertaining to the regicide and its aftermath in detail, his project was very different from Crusenstolpe's. He did not write a politically motivated "realistic" court chronicle, but self-consciously chose to genre-label his book

a (Byronian) romaunt—a romance with mysterious and symbolic overtones as well as dreamlike fantasies (cf. Louise Vinge, "Almqvists uppgång och fall, 1828–1866," in *Den Svenska Litteraturen,* ed. Lars Lönnroth and Sven Delblanc, vol. 3, *De liberala genombrotten, 1830–1890* [Stockholm: Bonnier Alba, 1993], 89–112).

47. Almqvist, *Drottningens juvelsmycke,* 102. Given the smallness of Sweden's literary world at the time, Crusenstolpe must have known that few of his readers would not already have been familiar with *Drottningens juvelsmycke,* and thereby in a position to "see" a relationship between Gustav III's supposed son and Badin's supposed child. And, by in various other ways situating Munck and Badin in the same orbit of court sexual contacts, Crusenstolpe opened the possibility for some to place the young woman's mother in Badin's bed, to make the blackamoor "known" to her.

48. Ibid., 68. In Almqvist's plot, the king's fascination with the girl delays his departure, thereby enabling the aristocratic conspirators to carry out their plot. Parallel to Gustav III's observation, the black Badin—as here re-presented on subsequent pages—may be seen as outwardly merry (when his role at the court and elsewhere calls for it), and yet at times gloomy and depression prone.

49. Ibid., 85–87, 99. Despite the "hottentot" reference and the dancer's black attire, the role is that of a Native American.

50. Ibid., 243. On the matter of Badin's multiple names and his identity, see discussion in "Re Reading."

51. Knut Wichman, "Crusenstolpe, Magnus Jacob," in *Svenskt biografiskt lexikon* (Stockholm: Albert Bonniers Förlag, 1931), 9: 413–34; Carina Burman, *Bremer: En biografi* (Stockholm: Albert Bonniers Förlag, 2001), 524; and "Magnus Jacob Crusenstolpe Statsfånge, 1838–1841," at http://hem.passagen.se/minata/ bild_6_sep.html.

52. Göran Skytte, *Det kungliga svenska slaveriet* (Stockholm: Askelin & Hägglund, 1986), 118. The role of this former Swedish colony as a center for the Caribbean slave trade is not widely known in contemporary Sweden, is not a part of taken-for-granted public knowledge, is an unspeakable fact, is an element of socially constructed forgetting fully in keeping with the racism-related denials, displacements, and projections commonly occurring among large numbers of Swedes.

53. Ibid., 121.

54. Ibid., 128–29.

55. Crusenstolpe's trial and sentence precipitated a monthlong series of boisterous demonstrations and riots that brought military troops to the streets of Stockholm, patrolling gunboats to its central-city waters, and a temporary closure of the royal palace. These mass public outbursts of liberal discontent culminated with a bloody and fruitless effort by a crowd of two to three thousand people to free Crusenstolpe from the city jail just before his transfer to a fortress some twenty kilometers from the capital. His imprisonment was hardly a physical ordeal. He occupied a suite consisting of three furnished rooms plus a kitchen, his wife was allowed to reside with him, he ate and drank whatever he chose to have brought in from the outside, and visitors had easy access to his quarters—conditions that allowed him to comfortably author the first three volumes of *Morianen.* . . . *Morianen* itself may be read in part as a reworking of Crusenstolpe's "passionate hatred" of King Karl XIV

Johan—who briefly treated him as a favorite but eventually took actions that resulted in his imprisonment—and of his considerable distaste for Gustav III—in general
because of the inroads he had repeatedly made into the power of the aristocracy, in
particular because of the dismissal of his much-beloved paternal grandfather from a
high judicial post. Cf. Wichman, "Crusenstolpe," especially 431.

56. Ibid., 421, 427–28.

57. Theodor Sundler, *Jorden i physiskt, historiskt och politiskt hänseende be-
traktad, eller utförligt geographiskt lexikon* (Stockholm, 1841), as quoted and sum-
marized by Holmberg, *Världen bortom västerlandet*, 1: 161–62. Sundler was not
necessarily representative on matters other than sexuality, for, as Holmberg's survey
reveals (159–66), much of the popular literature available to the Swedish reading
public at this time continued to regard black Africans and their dispersed slave descendants as innately wild and stupid, as the bearers of less capable brains, as beyond
becoming educated and civilized. This was in keeping with developments in Britain
and elsewhere on the Continent, where, by 1840, dominant discourse depicted European superiority and the inferiority of Africans and other races as natural, rather
than as the *"effects* of climate or of differing stages of civilization"* (Wheeler, *Complexion of Race*, 299; emphasis in original).

58. Crusenstolpe, *Morianen*, 4: 45.

59. Crusenstolpe completed writing the fourth volume of *Morianen* shortly after
his 1841 release from prison, less than a year after Geijer's emancipation initiative.
Memoirs from the period contend that Crusenstolpe's three-year sentence exceeded
the two-year minimum in order to prevent him from participating in the parliamentary session scheduled for 1840 and thereby making problems for the crown (Wichman, "Crusenstolpe," 424).

60. In addition to older materials already held in some personal libraries, there
were at least fourteen school texts and other books published in Sweden between
1830 and 1844 that provided generalizations about the blacks of Africa and the
West Indies (Holmberg, *Världen bortom västerlandet*, 1: 582–99).

61. H[ebbe], "Monsieur Coichi," June 26, 1897. Regarding the version of this
article provincially issued in 1847, see "Entrances" note 64.

62. Hebbe's long-term affair with Hierta was itself "adventurous" by the stan-
dards of the day. She was the mother of three (her husband had fled the country),
while Hierta was a married man who had six daughters by the time Hebbe gave
birth to their son under much hushed-up circumstances in France.

63. Hebbe, "Monsieur Coichi," June 26, 1897. Here Hebbe, or even her informant, may have been inspired by Crusenstolpe's account of Queen Lovisa Ulrika's
view of the alliance between Badin and his fictional first wife, Olivia Ramström (see
quote associated with note 34 in this chapter).

64. *Nordisk Familjebok, Konversations Lexikon och Realencyclopedia*, 2nd ed.
(Stockholm, 1904), 2: 635–36. Peter Gay has written of the unconscious projections made by late nineteenth-century European bourgeois males in reworking their
sexual anxieties focusing on the racialized Other (*The Bourgeois Experience, Victoria to Freud*, vol. 3, *The Cultivation of Hatred* [New York: W. W. Norton], 68 ff.).

And Gilman notes that miscegenation was a central term in late nineteenth-century discourses of sexuality (*Difference and Pathology*, 107). . . . The notion that Badin was small as an adult likely derives from Sparre's description (see "Entrances" note 52) or from Rehn's drawing, both of which date from a time when he was in his early teens at the most. A matter thereby of Rehn nonsense? Pure nonsense?

65. Forsstrand, "Badin," 135.

66. Thomasson, "Morianen," 616. Crusenstolpe's buttressing of the hypersexual stereotype was not confined to Sweden, as his portrayal was inserted into wider networks of circulation where it could intersect with other ongoing processes of stereotype (re)production, as *Morianen* was almost immediately translated into both Danish and German.

67. O. B., "Litet om zulukafferna," 14. This was the very same article that insisted there was no distinguishing the appearance and behavior of any one black male from that of another (cf. quote in "Foremontage" associated with note 3).

68. Wikström, "Badin-Couschi," 293; Carine Lundberg, "En gustaviansk brevväxling," *Svenska Dagbladet,* March 2, 1958. The confession contained in this letter—which also attests to Badin's loyalty at a moment when the king was politically deserted by large portions of the court and the aristocracy in general—is particularly striking, for Gustav III was apparently not the best of chess losers. "It is also told that he cheated! He would trick his opponent to look off in another direction and then avail himself of the opportunity to make an extra move or upset the pieces so as to set them up again in a more advantageous manner" (Hans Alfredson, "Svart spelar vit: Gustaf Lundbergs porträtt av Badin," in *Porträtt Porträtt: Studier i statens porträttsamling* [Stockholm: Raben & Sjögren, 1987], 85–89 [87]).

69. Larsmo, "Skuggan av Badin," 5.

70. Eggehorn, *En av dessa timmer,* 58.

71. From the time of his return from Paris, in 1744, Lundberg was much sought after, for several decades achieving an "unprecedented monopoloy as the portrait painter of the court, the aristocracy, and upper[most] bourgeoisie." Despite his age, Lundberg was at the height of his career when he did Badin's portrait (Sven Eric Noreen, "Gustaf Lundberg," in *Svenskt Konstnärslexikon* [Malmö: Allhems Förlag, 1957], 3: 599–601); all subsequent text and footnote quotes pertaining to Lundberg are from this source.

72. One mid-twentieth-century art historian characterized Lundberg's rendering of Badin as a "joking portrait combined with psychological realism" (ibid.).

73. Forsstrand, "Badin," 137; Wikström, "Badin-Couschi," 291. The portrait reproduction contained in Forsstrand is accompanied by a caption whose handwriting is clearly identical with that found in Badin's preserved notebook (*Badins Anteckningsbok,* rare book collection, Carolina Rediviva [Uppsala University Library]). It reads: "Your most humble servant by the name of Adolph Ludwig Gustaf *Badin*" (emphasis in original).

74. Eggehorn, *En av dessa timmer,* 20–21, 195, 21.

75. Ibid., 100–101.

76. Ibid., 162.

77. For details, elaboration and documentation of these various contemporary circumstances, following in the wake of what was perhaps the world's most generous refugee policy and the burgeoning of the country's non-European and Muslim population between the seventies and the early nineties, see Allan Pred, *Even in Sweden*. On the media images and discourses around gang rapes, see Anna Bredström, "Maskulinitet och kamp om nationella arenor: Reflektioner kring 'invandrarkillar' i svensk media," in *Maktens (o)lika förklädnader: Kön, klass & etnicitet i det postkoloniala Sverige*, ed. Paulina de los Reyes, Irene Molina, and Diana Mulinari (Stockholm: Bokförlaget Atlas, 2002), 182–206.

78. These elements of identity are especially widespread and deeply seated—but far from universal—among those generations born during the 1950s or earlier, among those generations most intensely subjected to the Social Democratic ideology of solidarity and equality, among those generations most apt to regard the 1950s, 1960s, and early 1970s as an unproblematic golden era, to unreflectingly link the economic expansion and improving social welfare of that period with the moral internationalism of Dag Hammarskjöld and Olof Palme.

79. Eggehorn, *En av dessa timmer*, 88.

80. Nikula, *Adolph Fredric Munck*, 62. However passionate the crown prince may have been, Munck—the confidant and reputed cuckolder of Gustav III—asserts that "no ejaculation" ever occurred even though "he surely had physical contact with her several times" ("A. F. Muncks berättelse," 329).

81. Eggehorn, *En av dessa timmer*, 223.

82. Märta Helena Reenstierna, *Årstadagboken journaler från åren, 1793–1839*, vol. 2, *1813–1825*, ed. S. Erixon, A. Stålhane, and S. Wallin (Stockholm: Norstedts, 1993), 371. Badin remarried in the summer of 1799, a year after the death of his first wife. Magdalena Eleonora Norell was the daughter of a ship's carpenter and, at age twenty, was about thirty years younger than Badin.

83. Cecil Inti Sondlo, "Svårt för svart gå ut med vit," *Dagens Nyheter*, January 24, 1997.

84. Ibid.

85. Ibid.

Re Reading, Rereadings, Reading Numbers Numerously

1. Hume, "Of National Characters" (quoted in Popkin, "Philosophical Basis," 245–46).

2. Eggehorn, *En av dessa timmer*, 223. What I have here translated as "finer" appears in the Swedish as *styvare*, a word whose principal connotation is "stiffer" (harder).

3. Par Bricole archive, *Egenhändig biografi av Badin*. Badin may well have taken special pride in the size of his library, mentioning the number of books it contained in order to impress, in order to suggest that—despite his slave origins and black skin—he was every bit as intelligent as those with whom he came in contact.

4. Larsmo, *Maroonberget*, 236.

5. In comparison, Johan Fischerström, a prolific author of diverse works who was

active at the edge of Gustav III's court, possessed only four hundred books at the time of his death in 1796 (Gustaf Näsström, ed., *En gustaviansk dagbok: Johan Fischer-ströms anteckningar för året 1773* [Stockholm: Bröderna Lagerström, 1951], 140).

6. Wikström, "Badin-Couschi," 278, 303–4, 313; Par Bricole archive, *Egen-händig biografi av Badin;* Carlander, *Svenska bibliotek,* 753–55. The exact content of Badin's library—which was apparently dominated by French items—is difficult to establish. Although some titles are jotted at random in his surviving notebook *(Badins Anteckningsbok),* and although a hundred or so presumably inherited volumes are listed in the estate inventory of his first father-in-law, most of the others are unidentifiable because the full library was auctioned off after his death and no item list survives in the archive where Stockholm's book auction records are kept (Bokauktionskammarens arkiv) (Wikström, "Badin-Couschi," 313).

7. Judging from the copious, but seemingly unsystematic, weather observations contained in Badin's notebook, some of the astronomy books in his library may have dealt with meteorological phenomena (see the beginning of "Geography Lessons").

8. Larsmo, *Maroonberget,* 280.

9. Larsmo, "*Couschi,* son av Chuso." Badin's notebook also contained a few detached words from this quote *(Badins Anteckningsbok).*

10. Several of the biblical passages in question occur in the First Book of Moses, chapter 15. Larsmo was able to make this connection by decoding a notebook entry that read I:M:15. On the "curse of Ham," which by the seventeenth century became "widely accepted as the explanation of black skin colour" and a means for theologically justifying the view of Africa as a continent condemned to eternal servitude, see Pieterse, *White on Black,* 44–45; and Ephraim Isaac, "Genesis, Judaism, and the Sons of Ham," *Slavery and Abolition* 1 (1980): 3–17.

11. *Badins Anteckningsbok.* Quite appropriately, Larsmo reads this entry as further evidence of Badin's embroilment in a search for identity. It is of no little significance that the entry ends with an expression of lasting internal conflict (see "Memory" note 7).

12. See the full quote from Badin's autobiographical statement in "Entrances," associated with note 3.

13. Par Bricole archive, *Egenhändig biografi av Badin.* The string of dots with which this statement tails off is contained in the original.

14. Badin narrating in Larsmo, *Maroonberget,* 168.

15. Wikström, "Badin-Couschi," 272.

16. Documentary evidence, as well as paintings, indicate that blacks were brought to Stockholm at least from the mid-seventeenth century onward, or from about the time of Sweden's brief colonial adventure at Cape Coast and Denmark's involvement in both Africa and the Caribbean (Wikström, "Badin-Couschi," 272–73; Larsmo, "Skuggan av Badin," 5).

17. Karin Johannisson, *Nostalgia: En känslas historia* (Stockholm: Albert Bonniers Förlag, 2001), 31.

18. Th. Hansen, *Vores gamle Trope-kolonier,* vol. 3, *Slavernes øer* (Copenhagen: Gyldendal, 1970).

19. Such an informant, if he actually existed, may well have been someone Badin initially befriended during his long voyage from Saint Croix to Copenhagen.

20. Frantz Fanon, *Black Skin, White Masks,* trans. Charles Las Markmann (New York: Grove Press, 1967 [1952]), 36–37.

21. Paul Gilroy, *The Black Atlantic: Modernity and Double Consciousness* (Cambridge: Harvard University Press, 1993), 221, 46.

22. Henry Louis Gates Jr., *The Signifying Monkey: A Theory of African-American Literary Criticism* (New York and Oxford: Oxford University Press, 1988), 13. Given the wideness of Badin's reading and the discursive networks with which his everyday life intersected, it is not unlikely that he was exposed to such arguments. Especially influential in late eighteenth-century European considerations of language was Lord James Burnett Monboddo's six-volume work, *Of the Origin and Progress of Language,* which began appearing in 1774. Among other things asserted in this Scottish Enlightenment classic was a linked ranking of peoples and languages that ranged from "barbarous" to "civil" (vol. 1, facsimile ed. [New York: AMS Press, 1972]).

23. Koerner, "Carl Linnaeus," 148.

24. Gilbert Tamas, *Sverige, Sverige, Sverige: Om ungdom, identitet och främlingskap* (Stockholm: Bokförlaget Kombinera, 1995), 85.

25. Mauricio Rojas, *Sveriges oälskade barn: Att vara svensk men ändå inte* (Stockholm: Brombergs Bokförlag, 1995), 24.

26. Bruchfeld and Jacobsson, *Kan man vara svart och svensk?,* 37.

27. Ibid., 40, 42.

28. Johannisson, *Nostalgia,* 7.

29. Ibid., 20.

30. Ibid., 21. For elaboration of Rousseau's position on music as a trigger of involuntary childhood memories, see Jean Starobinski, "The Idea of Nostalgia," *Diogenes,* no. 54 (1966): 81–103 (92–93).

31. Johannisson, *Nostalgia,* 18.

32. Ibid., 56.

33. Starobinski, "Idea of Nostalgia," 95.

34. During the mid- and late eighteenth century, the image of nostalgia "as a deadly threat was spread by the mass media of that time, for example in French encyclopedia articles as well as in many popular medical handbooks," and was repeatedly "confirmed" by autopsy findings (Johannisson, *Nostalgia,* 80). According to Starobinski, "By the end of the eighteenth century, throughout all the countries of Europe, all doctors recognized nostalgia as a frequently fatal disease"; and the instilled fear was such that "people even died of nostalgia after having read in books that nostalgia is a disease which is frequently mortal" ("Idea of Nostalgia," 95, 86).

35. Par Bricole archive, *Egenhändig biografi av Badin.*

36. To the extent Badin could not bring memories of his mother into focus, to the extent he was preoccupied with what he had forgotten of his childhood, rather than with what he could recall, his circumstances were not fully congruent with nostalgia as then commonly construed. And, knowing that he lived with his parents under the

grim conditions of slavery, he must have sensed that the undefinable for which he yearned was far from a serene idyll.

37. Nigel C. Gibsen, *Fanon: The Postcolonial Imagination* (Cambridge, England: Polity Press, 2003), 66.

38. *Badins Anteckningsbok.*

39. H[ebbe], "Monsieur Coichi," June 26, 1897.

40. Åbom and his system were taken up by many of Badin's Freemason brothers, including Adolph Fredric Munck. Åbom became so popular in aristocratic circles that he was granted an audience with Gustav III, who was so persuaded of his skills that he dispatched him to Copenhagen in order to financially ruin the Danish Royal Lottery. Of course, to no avail (Nikula, *Adolph Fredric Munck,* 90). . . . If Badin so chose, there were other periodically estabished fund-raising lotteries to which he also could turn his attention.

41. Numerous items in Badin's notebook strongly suggest that he was quite familiar with all of the Books of Moses. The most recent Swedish translation of the Bible (Bibelkommissionen, *Bibel 2000* [Stockholm: Veraum Förlag, 1999]), which strives for source accuracy, refers to Moses' wife as *kushitiska* rather than *etiopiska,* that is, as Kushian, or Couschian, rather than Ethiopian.

42. Koerner, *Linnaeus,* 109–10; Lindroth, "Linné: Legend och verklighet," 104–5. If Badin was taking any cue from Linnaeus it was only partially influential, for in a rambling religious digression within his autobiographical statement he suggests that "3 : 5 : 7 : 9" will yield "absolute conviction" once one's heart is opened to "Nature's Voice" (Par Bricole archive, *Egenhändig biografi av Badin).*

Memory Etchings, Memory Diggings, Memories in Constellation

1. Esther Leslie, *Walter Benjamin: Overpowering Conformism* (London: Pluto Press, 2000), 81.

2. Walter Benjamin, *Berlin Chronicle* (1932), in *Walter Benjamin: Selected Writings,* vol. 2, ed. Jennings, Eiland, and Smith, 597, 611.

3. Ehrenstrahl's image of the unalterable and unassimilable African mimicked representations that had been circulating in Europe for nearly two centuries. "The Italian illustrator Andrea Alciati (1492–1550) depicted the same scene of whitewashing: two whites who try to change a negro's colour by scrubbing him [with a caption that began: 'You wash an Ethiopian; why the vain labor']. . . . Alciati's emblem books were quite popular and imitated throughout Europe" (Pieterse, *White on Black,* 195).

4. Broberg, *Homo Sapiens L.,* 234.

5. Ibid., 238.

6. Equiano, *Life,* 43.

7. When reporting in his notebook that "I wanted to know for what I was intended" (see quote in "Re Reading" associated with note 8), Badin names several purposes that came to mind, including that he was meant "to help my enemies." However, he added, this possible reason "for my existence on earth" proved "repugnant. It aroused a conflict within me, and that conflict still exists" *(Badins Anteck-*

ningsbok). Such an identity-related conflict in part may have involved a discordance between Badin's Lutheran indoctrination and elements of Swedenborgianism that he not improbably was exposed to, for the latter teachings insisted that "True Christian love" is not unconditional, that the good should be loved more than the bad (Jan Häll, *I Swedenborgs labyrint: Studier i de gustavianska swedenborgarnas liv och tänkande* [Stockhom: Atlantis, 1995], 432).

8. Fanon, *Black Skin, White Masks, 7*. The work by Aimé Césaire is *Discours sur le colonialisme* (Paris: Reclame, 1970).

9. Fanon, *Black Skin, White Masks*, 112, 109.

10. Steve Pile, "The Troubled Spaces of Frantz Fanon," in *Thinking Space*, ed. Mike Crang and Nigel Thrift (Routledge: London and New York), 260–77 (264).

11. Larsmo, *Maroonberget*, 86. Strömmen is a body of water adjacent to the Old Town (Gamla Stan), an island in the middle of Stockholm on which the Royal Palace is located.

12. *Svartskalle*, or "blackhead," is the most frequently employed racial epithet in Sweden. Young people of non-European background often appropriate the term, inverting its meaning by defiantly and proudly using it to label their collective identity.

13. Fredrik Strage, *Mikrofonkåt* (Stockholm: Bokförlaget Atlas, 2001), 88.

14. Wikström, "Badin-Couschi," 303. Wikström's source is the actual letter, held in the Eriksberg Archive of the Swedish National Archives (Riksarkivet).

15. Wikström, "Badin-Couschi," 299–303; August Kinberg, *Par Bricoles gustavianska period: Personalhistoriska anteckningar till den äldsta matrikeln* (Stockholm: Hasse W. Tullbers Förlag, 1903), 86.

16. Kinberg, *Par Bricoles*, 86.

17. In his account of the assault-describing letter, Wikström, a meticulous nothing-but-what-the-documents-say historian, notes: "As far as I know this is the only time Badin complains of insulting behavior based on his skin color" ("Badin-Couschi," 303). Such an observation both ignores the implications of Badin's allusion to widely held views and the potential cost to him of complaining over lesser—but equally painful—slights.

18. Oxenstierna, foreword to *Journal för Året 1780*, 6.

19. Crusenstolpe, *Morianen*, 2: 338; emphasis in original.

20. Skytte, *Kungliga svenska slaveriet*, 41.

21. Ibid., 61.

22. Larsmo, *Maroonberget*, 250. Arfwedsson, a prominent Stockholm merchant, was also one of the largest shareholders in the West Indian Company.

23. Gustav III had hoped to ameliorate domestic financial and economic difficulties by procuring a substantial presence in the Caribbean, by extracting a possession from his ally, Louis XVI. Saint Barthélemy was relinquished as something of a consolation prize after a number of Swedish approaches dating back to 1779. During that period the negotiating French ministers had refused successive feelers pertaining to Tobago, Martinique, Guadeloupe, and even Saint Martin (Ingegerd Hildebrand, *Den svenska kolonin St. Barthélemy och Västindiska kompaniet fram till 1796* [Lund: AB Ph. Lindstedts universitetsbokhandel, 1951], 2–41).

24. The island was also devoid of any watercourse. Its sole advantage was a well-protected harbor, the site of its port town, soon named Gustavia.

25. Skytte, *Kungliga svenska slaveriet,* 28–29. The discussion of slave-trading possibilities may have increased in Badin's order circles when knowledge of the island's limited agricultural potential became more widespread following the publication of Sven Dahlman's *Beskrifning om S. Barthelemy, Swensk ö uti Westindien* (Stockholm: Upfostringssällskapet, 1786).

26. Ingegerd Hildebrand, *Den svenska kolonin,* 140.

27. Among those who were both Freemasons and involved in the West Indian Company were Baron Eric Ruuth, an adviser to the king, and another frequent confidant, the much-rumored Adolph Fredric Munck, then governor of Drottningholm Palace as well as royal stablemaster (Hildebrand, *Den svenska kolonin,* 312–14; Skytte, *Kungliga svenska slaveriet,* 40, 46; Ronny Ambjörnsson, *Det okända landet: Tre studier om svenska utopister* [Stockholm: Gidlund, 1981], 95; Nikula, *Adolph Fredric Munck,* 82–83). Ruuth was a member of the company's board of directors as well as a large stockholder.

28. Par Bricole archive, *Egenhändig biografi av Badin.* Badin's comment might also have been camouflaging a more general perception he had developed of Gustav III's personality. One scholarly inquiry delving into Gustav III's childhood and youth asserts that his behavioral pattern early evinced split, or even schizoid, characteristics that were carried into adulthood (Beth Hennings, *Gustav III som kronprins* [Stockholm, 1935]). And it was during the king's teenage years that his interactions with Badin appear to have been most frequent. Wikström ("Badin-Couschi," 282) also interprets Badin's usage as consistent with the "enigmatic, complex, constantly changing and variable" qualities of Gustav III's adult "psyche." Perhaps most relevantly, an understanding of the king as Janus-like would be consistent with the ruthless "duplicity" attributed to so many of his maneuverings by his sister-in-law (Bonde, *Hedvig Elisabeth Charlottas dagbok,* 3: 385) as well as his opponents.

29. Skytte, *Kungliga svenska slaveriet,* 50.

30. Bengt Anders Euphrasén, *Beskrifning öfver svenska vestindiska ön St. Barthelemi, samt öarna St. Eustache och St. Christopher* (Stockholm: Anders Zetterberg, 1795), 51–52; quoted in Skytte, *Kungliga svenska slaveriet,* 81. Although Euphrasén expressed some doubt as to the effectiveness of "barbaric" punishments, he did manage to reduce Saint Barthélemy's nonwhite population to a scientific object. In keeping with Linnaean taxonomic practices, Euphrasén categorized that population in much the same way he classified the local flora according to stamen and pistil characteristics. In doing so he devised a seven-grade "color scale" based on parental attributes (e.g., a *mulat* was the offspring of a Negro mother and a white father, a *mestise* the child of a *mulat* mother and white father, and a *mamblou* the child of a *mestise* mother and a *mulat* father).

31. Olof Erik Bergius, *Om Westindien* (Stockholm: A. Gadelius, 1819); quoted in Rolf Sjöström, "'En nödvändig omständighet': Om svensk slavhandel i Karibien," in *Svenska överord: En bok om gränslöshet och begränsningar,* ed. Raoul Granqvist (Stockholm/Stehag: Synposium, 1999), 48.

32. Hildebrand, *Den svenska kolonin St. Barthélemy,* 220 ff. Upon the death of Gustav III, his son Gustav Adolf, but thirteen years old, became the principal shareholder of the West Indian Company, and the ultimate decision-making power thus fell to the regency. The two representatives in question were identical with the Röhl and Hansen referred to in Badin's fictionally recalled conversation with Carl Arfwedsson.

33. Euphrasén, *Beskrifning,* 52–53.

34. *The Report of Saint Bartholomew,* June 16, July 5, August 2, and October 19, 1805, and April 12, 1806. According to Skytte (*Kungliga svenska slaveriet,* 88), shipping arrival information was no longer published after the last-named date.

35. Skytte, *Kungliga svenska slaveriet,* 90–91.

36. In 1785, just after Swedish possession, Saint Barthélemy was inhabited by 281 slaves and few, if any, "freed coloreds," as well as 458 whites. Two years later the number of slaves had grown to 741 and there were now 91 "free coloreds" present. By 1812 those two numbers had grown to 2,406 and 1,128 respectively, but thereafter they diminished until the termination of slavery in 1846 (Hannes Hyrenius, *Royal Swedish Slaves* [Gothenburg: University of Gothenburg, Demographic Reseach Institute, report no. 15, 1977], 13).

37. Although an anti–slave trading decree had been signed in 1813, it was not until 1830 that Sweden fully outlawed its colony's trans-Atlantic slave trade. This legislation not only came relatively late—being enacted thirty-eight years after the French had legally terminated slave shipments to the Caribbean, and twenty-seven and twenty-three years after the Danes and English had respectively done so—it still explicitly permitted Swedes resident on Saint Barthélemy to sell slaves already in their possession.

38. Bergius, *Om Westindien.*

39. Skytte, *Kungliga svenska slaveriet,* 51.

40. *Badins Anteckningsbok.* The string of dots is as in the original.

41. Kellberg, "Rasism vardag för Afrikaner." A study issued that year indicated that "65 percent of the African men living in the three major metropolitan areas [Stockholm, Göteborg, and Malmö] report that they *were denied admission to restaurants or other nightlife premises* at least once or twice during the past year owing to their foreign background. More than a third of the African men in those major metropolitan areas . . . report that this happened to them five or more times during the past year. More than one-fourth of the African women and almost one-third of the Arabian men [actually men of Muslim background] in those same metropolitan areas had similar experiences during the past year" (Anders Lange, *Invandrare och diskriminering II: En enkät och intervjuundersökning om etnisk diskriminering på uppdrag av Diskrimineringsombudsmannen* [Stockholm: Centrum för invandringsforskning, 1996], 36); emphasis in original.

42. Strage, *Mikrofonkåt,* 191.

43. Larsmo, *Maroonberget,* 87–88; emphasis added.

44. Crusenstolpe, "Badin," 212–13.

45. *Hvad Nytt från Stockholm,* June 19, 1897.

46. Hebbe, *I Skogen*, 126–33. "The Monkey," published twenty-four years after Hebbe's first version of "Monsieur Coichi," relied on then-suggestive, sexually-laden imagery, especially for a children's book—Luli succeeds in deceiving the eagle through curling up in a pot, upwardly exposing her bare red backside to appear like a piece of meat. She acts thusly, planning entrapment, in the hope of escaping a "birching" for the eagle's theft of another piece of meat minutes earlier. . . . What, if anything, may be speculated about these multiple reversals?

47. *Hvad Nytt från Stockholm,* June 19, 1897.

48. Broberg, *Homo sapiens L.,* 241. Buffon, in his influential *Nomenclature des signes* (1766), was among those who asserted "that fertile crosses of Negroes and apes have taken place and entered both lineages" (Sloan, "Idea of Racial Degeneracy in Buffon," 310).

49. Berg, *När Sverige upptäckte Afrika,* 16. Buffon was of the mind that the orangutan was akin to the black African, that it "might simply be the most degenerate of men, one step beyond the Hottentot" (Sloan, "Idea of Racial Degeneracy in Buffon," 309). As Buffon's writings circulated in European scientific and literary networks that extended into Sweden, others reinforced his stereotype-promoting stance. For example, Edward Long claimed in his *History of Jamaica* (1774) that "the African" was closer to the orangutan than to "the white man"(Carl Frängsmyr, *Klimat och karaktär: Naturen och människan i sent svenskt 1700-tal* [Stockholm: Natur och kultur, 2000], 77). Likewise, Samuel Thomas von Soemmerring, the leading German anatomist of the Enlightenment era, insisted in 1785 that "blacks were naturally inferior to Europeans: the 'cold facts' of anatomy showed them to be 'nearer the ape'" (Londa Schiebinger, "The Anatomy of Difference: Race and Sex in Eighteenth-Century Science," *Eighteenth-Century Studies* 23 [1990]: 387–405 [395]).

50. Jordan, *White over Black,* 236. The first bracketed phrase is mine; the second from the original translation from Latin. Although Linnaeus is here quoted as questioning the "strange origin" of black Africans, Broberg notes that in his writings about Africa "he freely mixe[d] terms such as moor, negro, hottentot, ape and troglodyte"—the "confusion was almost complete" (*Homo sapiens L.,* 292).

51. Letter from Olof von Dalin to Linnaeus, in Lundh-Eriksson, *Sophia Albertina,* 29.

52. Carl Peter Thunberg, *Resa uti Europa, Africa, Asia författad åren, 1770–1779,* 4 vols. (Uppsala: J. Edman, 1788–1793); quote from Berg, *När Sverige upptäckte Africa,* 93. Among Thunberg's explicit observations is the following: "Their mouths and cheekbones were very prominent, so that they bore the strongest resemblance imaginable to apes" (Thunberg, *Travels,* 47). As far as Thunberg was concerned, "Only language separated" the blacks he had encountered "from the apes" (Sten Lindroth, *Svensk lärdomshistoria: Gustavianska tiden* [Stockholm: Norstedts, 1981], 35, paraphrasing Thunberg, *Travels,* 314). Thunberg had traveled through southern Africa, Ceylon, Java, and Japan while employed as a surgeon by the Dutch East India Company. By the time his first volume appeared, he had been serving as professor of medicine and botany at Uppsala for five years, a circumstance that granted his observations an aura of veracity and scientific respectability and thereby

increased their possible painfulness or discomfort for Badin—and blacks elsewhere in Europe, as Thunberg's multivolume work was soon translated into German, French, and English.

53. Londa Schiebinger, *Nature's Body: Sexual Politics and the Making of Modern Science* (Boston: Beacon Press, 1993), 5.

54. Koerner, *Linnaeus*, 173.

55. Gilman, *Difference and Pathology*, 11.

56. Wickström, "Badin-Couschi," 280–81.

57. Brunner, *Fukta din aska*, 308, 145. Brunner's *Carnaval de Venise* depiction embellishes source materials quoted by the editors of Bellman's collected works (Bellmanssällskapet [The Bellman Society], *Carl Michael Bellmans skrifter*, standard edition, vol. 6, *Dramatiska arbeten* [Stockholm: Albert Bonniers Förlag, 1936], komentaren, 12–13).

58. Directly heard accounts, 1997–2000.

59. Strage, *Mikrofonkåt*, 153.

60. Another circus hand in the film is an American Indian, complete with feathered headdress. His portrayal also involves the aping of racist clichés used in Hollywood films of the time, films in which the essence and the "nature" of "the Negro" are kept intact (Fanon, *Black Skin, White Masks*, 186).

61. *Dagens Nyheter*, September 11, 2002.

62. C. C. Gjörwell in a letter dated February 5, 1771 (Otto Sylwan, ed., *En stockholmskrönika ur C. C. Gjörwell's brev, 1757–1778* [Stockholm: Albert Bonniers Förlag, 1920], 35). "Every time I see that fool," the less than appreciative Gjörwell continues, "I remember Mr. Axelsson's edifying idea" that Badin study theology at Uppsala and then be sent off to Africa as a missionary in order "to convert his brothers."

63. Johan Fischerström in a diary entry (Näsström, *Johan Fischerströms anteckningar för året 1773*, 74). The Swedish word *kvickhet* is subject to all three translations—and Badin's reading may well have been quick, smart, and witty simultaneously.

64. Only one other role played by Badin is specifically identifiable—that of a soldier/guardian of the law in an entertainment arranged in 1776 to celebrate Princess Sophia Albertina's name day (Wickström, "Badin-Couschi," 280). Whether it too may have encouraged any association between Badin and sexuality is unascertainable in the absence of details. However, the part did place Badin on the stage with the king and queen and other members of the royal family, including the princess herself, at a time when sexual rumors about Munck and others were already flourishing.

65. Fanon, *Black Skin, White Masks*, 17, 63. Separating periods of first quote in original.

66. As quoted in *Jazz*, a documentary film by Ken Burns, part 3 (2001); dance critic's comment from Pieterse, *White on Black*, 143.

67. Larsmo, *Maroonberget*, 187.

68. Badin gives an account of this meeting in his autobiographical statement (Per Bricole archive, *Egenhändig biografi av Badin*), in which he both refers to a dramatic

threat to have his "head removed" and details the king's subsequent turn to heartfelt mercifulness, but makes no mention of being offered the title of Royal Assessor. For the events and intrigues leading to Badin's involvement in the document burning, see Wikström, "Badin-Couschi," 285–88.

69. Carlander, *Svenska bibliotek,* 753. Regarding Carlander's factual accuracy and reliability, see "Entrances" notes 56, 58, and 59.

70. Hebbe, "Monsieur Coichi," June 26, 1897.

71. Those appointed to an assessorship were usually members of the aristocracy, such as Crusenstolpe, who was named to such a post at the Royal Svea Court of Appeals in 1825.

72. Lars Rhodin, *Samling af Swenska Ordspråk i ordning ställde efter alfabetet* (Stockholm: Joh. Pehr Lindh, 1807), 7.

73. Pelle Holm, *Ordspråk och talesätt* (Stockholm: Bonniers, 1975), 24–25.

74. Wikström, "Badin-Couschi," 297. In the death notice published in one of Sweden's then leading newspapers (*Post och Inrikes Tidning,* April 30, 1822), Badin was referred to simply as mister (Carlander, *Svenska bibliotek,* 753).

75. *Dagens Nyheter,* April 19, 2001.

76. Cf. Buck-Morss, "The Flaneur, the Sandwichman, and the Whore," 99–140, and *Dialectics of Seeing,* 306–7.

77. *Svenska Dagbladet,* May 30, 2001, quoting a report prepared for the office of National Anti-Discrimination, or the National Anti-Discrimination Ombudsman (Diskrimineringsombudsmannen).

78. On the extreme level of labor-market discrimination existing in Sweden compared to other OECD countries, on the role played therein by cultural racism and the imagery of its associated fields of vision, and on the educational achievements of the country's African, Asian, and Latin American refugees and immigrants, see Pred, *Even in Sweden,* 142–68. On the mass media representations and scientific discourses through which cultural racism operates in Swedish labor markets, see Katarina Mattsson, *(o)likhetens geografier: Marknaden, forskningen och de Andra* (Uppsala: Geografiska Regionstudier 45, Department of Social and Economic Geography, Uppsala University, 2001).

79. From the lyrics of "Bränn BH:n" (Burn the Bra) in Feven's CD album, *Hela vägen ut* (All the Way Out), as reproduced in full in Ingemar Unge, "Vad är det dom säger," *Vi,* May 10, 2001, 58–62.

80. "Samtal emellan en Sjö Capten och en Neger," *Dagbladet,* March 16, 1783 (Gunnar Broberg, ed., *Gyllene Äpplen: Svensk Idéhistorisk Läsebok,* vol. 1 [Stockholm: Atlantis, 1995], 597–99). Among other indicators that the author was a Swedenborgian is the fact that he signed himself "Blessed Freedom of the Press." Swedenborg's religious works, written in Latin, were published in England and Holland in order to escape the discipline of Swedish censors; and his followers of the 1780s—sometimes confronted by censorship problems of their own—often championed freedom of the press.

81. Carl Bernhard Wadström, *Observations on the Slave Trade* (London, 1789). A Swedish translation was published in Norrköping during 1791.

82. C. B. Wadstrom, *An Essay on Colonization, Particularly Applied to the Western Coast of Africa, with Some Free Thoughts on Cultivation and Commerce* (London: Darton and Harvey, 1794), 9–10.

83. Karin Johannisson, *Magnetisörernas tid: Den animala magnetismen i Sverige* (Uppsala: Lärdomshistoriska samfundet, 1974), and "Förnuftets orosandar— Magnetisörer, swedenborgare och frimurare i den gustavianska tidens Stockholm," *Artes—Tidskrift för litteratur, konst och musik* 13, no. 1 (1987): 18–30. Aristocrats, and others of high station around Badin, appear to have been drawn less to the doctrine of Swedenborgianism than to the mesmerism and other occult practices pursued by many of its Stockholm followers during the 1780s and 1790s.

84. Perhaps spurred by his Masonic confreres, Badin may have actually read some Swedenborg, as excerpts of his works began to appear in Swedish in 1786, such as in the newly founded *Aftonbladet*. While it may be no more than a coincidence, Badin's notebook reference to the First Book of Moses, chapter 15, corresponds with Swedenborg's focus on the First Book of Moses in his exegetical writings (Inge Jonsson, "Swedenborgs himmelska sanningar," *Artes—Tidskrift för litteratur, konst och musik* 13, no. 1 [1987]: 33).

85. Ambjörnsson, *Det okända landet,* 115. Swedenborg and his followers insisted that the questions with which the official church was preoccupied dealt solely with appearances.

86. According to Swedenborg's doctrine, heavenly knowledge could be attained, or revealed, either as a consequence of untrammeled innocence or empirically based analytical reason (ibid., 114–16).

87. Brackets are employed so as to avoid suggesting that Badin's possible recognition of the contradictions inherent to the economic motives of Wadström's colonization scheme would have been phrased in terms of markets and capitalism. However, as others have observed, both the "Plan for a Free Community" and Wadström's *Essay on Colonization* emerged out of and contributed to ongoing slavery debates in England—where Wadström resided after 1788—which pitted the interests of industrial capitalism against those of mercantilism. See Ambjörnsson, *Det okända landet* (122–23 ff.) on the ideas embedded in the more utopian "Plan for a Free Community," especially its stance on "the baneful tyranny of money" and the relation between its glorification of agricultural and natural resource producers and the labor theory of value.

88. Ambjörnsson, *Det okända landet,* 95.

89. Hildebrand, *Den svenska kolonin St. Barthélemy,* 142.

90. Almqvist, *Drottningens juvelsmycke,* 177.

91. Carlsson, "Öppen racism."

92. Ibid.

Geography Lessons, Night and Day Weather, Navigating Darkness and Lightness

1. *Badins Anteckningsbok.* Here, unlike an earlier notebook excerpt, the ellipses are not Badin's, but inserted because of the length of his weather observations.

2. Between 1788 and 1803 Badin dwelled in a building located at the current

site of the railroad system's Central Station. According to valuation lists kept by the tax authorities, at least one of his rooms contained silk upholstered furniture as well as silk window curtains (Wikström, "Badin-Couschi," 297).

3. Historians of science have depicted the late eighteenth century as a period marked by "a rapid increase in the range and intensity of application of mathematical methods," by a "quantifying spirit," or "passion to order and systematize as well as to measure and calculate" (J. L. Heilbron, "Introductory Essay," in *The Quantifying Spirit in the Eighteenth Century,* ed. Tore Frängsmyr, J. L. Heilbron, and Robin E. Rider [Berkeley: University of California Press, 1990], 1–23 [2]). On the renewed interest in quantified weather observation in Europe during the decades following 1770, see Theodore S. Feldman, "Late Enlightenment Meteorology," in ibid., 143–77.

4. During Badin's 1771 visit to Berlin and the court of Frederick the Great, some thought was given to his remaining there in order "to begin learning the basics of astronomy." And, he notes in his autobiographical statement, "To accomplish that I was given those books which were necessary, of which I still own three." He all the same returned to Stockholm on the justification that "in Sweden there were probably those who could [help me to] pursue my already begun [study of] astronomical science. I was thinking then of Royal Secretary [of the Academy of Sciences, Per Wilhelm] Wargentin and of something else that then moved my heart more than now" (Par Bricole archive, *Egenhändig biografi av Badin*). Badin's astronomy studies, however limited, quite probably familiarized him with meteorological matters and the measurement thereof, *as from about the mid-eighteenth century onward in Europe it was astronomers and physicists who were the prime movers in the large-scale collection of scientific data pertaining to weather and climate,* a development set in motion a century earlier by the invention of the barometer and the discovery of a connection between air pressure and weather conditions. (From the Middle Ages well into the seventeenth century, astronomers and astrologists had been the presumed meteorological experts, as it was believed that weather changes were entirely determined by the position and phase of the moon plus the position of the planets vis-à-vis one another.) Although Descartes had taken Stockholm's first barometric measurements as early as 1649, and although an interest in weather observation had led the Swedish astronomer Anders Celsius to develop the first thermometer based on fixed freezing and evaporation points in 1742, it was not until 1783 that the Royal Academy of Sciences began to systematically publish thrice-daily weather observations for Stockholm and other Swedish cities (N. V. E. Nordenmark, *Astronomiens historia i Sverige intill år 1800* [Uppsala: Almqvist & Wiksells Boktryckeri AB, 1959]; Herman Richter, *Geografins historia i Sverige intill år 1800* [Uppsala: Almqvist & Wiksells Boktryckeri AB, 1967], 125–26; *Nordisk Familjebok,* vol. 18 [Stockholm: Nordisk Familjeboks Förlags Aktieboelag, 1913], 265–66). However, in his guise as Secretary of the Royal Academy, Wargentin had begun keeping a detailed and continuous meteorological journal from January 1, 1754, onward, and in this and in other critical ways he contributed to the emergence of scientific meteorology and climatology in Sweden during the 1750s (Frängsmyr, *Klimat och*

karaktär, 48–50, 96–97). Badin may well have picked up his weather recording skills directly from Wargentin, or he may have been acquainted with one or more of those taking measurements for the Academy in his adult years. If either or both of these circumstances were the case, his own observations all the more clearly would have constituted an act of identification, of identifying with other astronomers and meteorologists. Although the chances are small, perhaps even with Jean-Baptiste Lislet-Geoffrey, a black who, in 1786, became a corresponding member of the Académie Royale des Sciences in Paris (Schiebinger, "Anatomy of Difference," 401, 403).

5. Owing to unfavorable weather conditions in all three of these years, the harvests of rye, barley, and oats were especially poor in extensive areas of Sweden, including Stockholm's more immediate agricultural hinterland, where Badin's holdings were located. Despite a substantial increase in imports, shortages were widespread, leading to high grain and bread prices, very difficult times for smallholders, and the threat of famine for much of the country's urban lower classes. Coupled with the changing political climate in the aftermath of the French Revolution and the considerable diversion of grain production into highly profitable aquavit distillation by large landowners, these circumstances precipitated a series of protests and riots—especially during late 1799 and early 1800—not only in Stockholm, Göteborg, Malmö, and Norrköping, the leading cities of the time, but also in such second-tier centers as Landskrona, Karlskrona, Örebro, Karlstad, Linköping, and Kalmar (Rolf Karlbom, *Hungerupplopp och strejker, 1793–1867: En studie i den svenska arbetarrörelsns uppkomst* [Lund: Gleerups, 1967], 31–89). Each account of any of these events, whether encountered in the press or by word of mouth, may have touched Badin in at least two ways—either by highly upsetting his aristocratic and bourgeois order brothers, or by indirectly reminding him that his grain-sales profits were at the mercy of precipitation and temperature extremes, that his ability to live comfortably was subject to the forces of nature. Accounts of these popular disturbances may also have uncomfortably reminded him of the long-term commitment he had made in 1799 to donate a barrel of high-quality rye and a barrel of wheat annually to the philanthropic hospital operated by fellow members of the Order of the Carpenters (Timmermansorden). This commitment may have occupied a prominent place in his mind when he began making his meteorological entries, as the first delivery had recently come due, in November 1801, at a time when he likely had little grain to spare (Wickström, "Badin-Couschi," 300). Furthermore, Badin may well have been especially concerned with the quantity of snow that did or did not fall if he was directly or indirectly familiar with the writings of the noted Uppsala astronomer Daniel Melanderhjelm, and especially his *Afhandling om väderleken förlidne sommar år 1783* (Treatise on Last Summer's Weather, 1783 [Uppsala, 1784]). For there Melanderhjelm had proposed some connection between summer weather conditions and the springtime snow and ice melt of northern Sweden and Finland, Norway's mountains, and the polar area north of those three countries (Nordenmark, *Astronomiens historia*, 265). *As 1783 had been a crop-failure year and the first in which Badin arranged for the operation of his farm properties, he had considerable reason for taking interest in Melanderhjelm's treatise.*

6. Some weeks later, on February 12, 1802, Badin pawned a silver coffeepot for what was then a handsome sum, and on April 15 of the same year he again replenished his cash resources by taking a loan against eight spoons *(Badins Anteckningsbok).*

7. Numerous entries and comments in *Badins Anteckningsbok* and Par Bricole archive, *Egenhändig biografi av Badin.*

8. During his occupation of this residence, Badin and his wife employed as many as four young women and never had less than one maidservant (Wikström, "Badin-Couschi," 297).

9. According to the meteorological views holding sway in Sweden during the late eighteenth century, wind-direction patterns were of two types: those that were general, or constant, and dependent on the attractive force of the sun and moon; and those that were generated by temporary circumstances, such as earthquakes (according to Melanderhjelm, the extremely warm and dry summer of 1783 was primarily a consequence of numerous strong earthquakes in Sicily and Calabria and the altered character of southerly winds they brought on through releasing "previously enclosed steam, smoke and air" (Nordenmark, *Astronomiens historia,* 264–65).

10. Clarence J. Glacken, *Traces on the Rhodian Shore* (Berkeley: University of California Press, 1967), 581, 558–60, 569, 573. In the second quote Glacken is referring to the principal work of Abbé Jean Baptiste Du Bos, *Reflexions critiques sur la poesie et sur la peinture,* an attempt to explain the climatic distribution of the arts and sciences that apparently achieved wide audience, being first published in 1719 and reissued for a fourth time, in revised form, in 1740. The final comments are derived from Montesquieu's classic *De l'esprit des lois,* which initially appeared in 1748.

11. Charles de Secondat Baron de la Brëde et de Montesquieu, *De l'esprit des lois* (Paris: Société Les Belles Lettres, 1950–1961), 2: 398.

12. Frängsmyr, *Klimat och karaktär,* 9, 33.

13. Montesquieu's *De l'esprit des lois* was closely read by many Swedenborgians and other well-placed Swedes during the final two decades of the eighteenth century, especially in the years leading up to Gustav III's 1792 assassination—a period in which much of the aristocracy became increasingly displeased with the advances made by bourgeois commoners within the military and the state's administrative apparatus, a period in which there was mounting discontent with the king's despotism. Montesquieu's *Spirit of Laws* made a lasting impression upon the more "moderate" opposition in particular, in no small measure owing to the publication of lengthy quotes, summaries, and even entire chapters in such influential periodicals as *Afton-bladet, Medborgaren* (The Citizen), and *Allmänna Magazinet* (Ambjörnsson, *Det okända landet,* 107–10); Rolf Karlbom, *Bakgrunden till 1809 års regeringsreform: Studier i svensk konstitutionell opinionsbildning, 1790–1809* (Göteborg: Scandinavian University Books, Studia Historica Gothoburgensia, III, 1964).

14. Frängsmyr, *Klimat och karaktär,* 128. Neikter produced a sixteen-part work, *De efficacia climatum ad variam gentium indolem praecipue ingeniea et mores,* which appeared between 1777 and 1797 and was much influenced by Montesquieu, Buffon, and William Falconer's *Remarks on the Influence of Climate, Situation, Nature of Country, Population, Nature of Food, and Way of Life, on the Disposi-*

tion and Temper, Manners and Behaviour, Intellects, Laws and Customs, Form of Government, and Religion, of Mankind [London, 1781]). See Frängsmyr's *Klimat och karaktär* for a thorough and nuanced discussion of the ideas therein contained and the constitution of Neikter's situated knowledge. As Neikter's magnum opus appeared in Latin rather than French or Swedish, Badin's familiarity with it would have been secondhand. However, Niekter's ideas also came into circulation via his Uppsala University lectures and the subsequently published talk he gave upon being admitted to the Royal Academy of Letters (Vitterhetsakademien) in 1786 ("Smakens olikhet, uppkomst och fall hos särskilda folkslag," in *Svenska krusbär: En historiebok om Sverige och svenskar,* ed. Björn Linnell and Mikael Löfgren [Stockholm: Bonnier Alba, 1995 (1793)], 86–113).

15. Among those others enabling such an argument was Buffon, who argued in his *Histoire naturelle* (1749) that the "degenerate races" might be restored "to the purity and vigor of the original type" through a long-term transplantation to the temperate zone, a change of diet, and exposure to a European education (Sloan, "Idea of Racial Degeneracy in Buffon," 309; Popkin, "Philosophical Basis of Racism," 251). Moreover, by the time of Badin's weather notes the widely influential German natural historian Johann Friedrich Blumenbach had asserted in his various editions of *On the Natural Variety of Mankind* (1776, 1781, 1795) that the characteristics of Africans and other "degenerate races" would diminish and eventually disappear "if they were placed in the right environment" (Frängsmyr, *Klimat och karaktär,* 73; also note Wheeler, *Complexion of Race,* 250–51). In their published writings two of Badin's black counterparts, Olaudah Equiano *(Life)* and Ottobah Cugoano *(Thoughts and Sentiments of the Evil and Wicked Traffic of the Slavery and Commerce of the Human Species* [1787]), had also by then similarly "favored the environmentalist argument that all men were by nature equal and that differences in color were the product of climate" (Schiebinger, "Anatomy of Difference," 394).

16. Jean Bodin, French Renaissance scholar (1530–1596).

17. See the quote from Rousseau's *Émile, ou l'éducation* in "Entrances" associated with note 36.

18. Badin may have been further beset by doubt and vexation if he came across any knowledge of Montesquieu's critics, including Voltaire, who contended that climate was at best a secondary determinant of cultural difference. Or if any knowledge ever reached him regarding Henry Home's *Sketches of the History of Man* (1774), in which the unitary-species, or monogenetic, views of Buffon and Linnaeus were rejected in favor of a polygenetic view of human differentiation, in which it was argued that it was not climate that had shaped "degenerated" racial differences, but God who had placed each of "His" differently created races in an "appropriate climate." Or if he had become aware of the contents of Bengt Ferrner's 1780 presidential address to the Royal Academy of Sciences (Vetenskapsakademien), in which Montesquieu's and Niekter's views on the impact of climate on national and individual character were directly challenged. Or, especially, if he learned that Per Wilhelm Wargentin, who may very well have been his tutor in matters meteorological (see note 4) fully sided with Ferrner in a published response to the just

named address. Or if he became familiar with those 1793 and 1794 publications of Petrus Kölmark and Johan Fischerström that variously questioned climatological determinism. Or, most problematically, if he discovered that Neikter's position on climate and transmutability extended to skin color, allowing not only that white people grow dark in "hot climates," but also asserting, "Negroes who have been transported to Europe gradually lose some of their blackness, although it can't go away completely, just as it is usually impossible to fully wash away the coloring of dyed wool" (Frängsmyr, *Klimat och karaktär,* 76–77, 120–26, 143, 103).

19. This is a line of thought embedded in the writings of Du Bos that so influenced Montesquieu (Glacken, *Traces on the Rhodian Shore,* 556).

20. Cf., among others, Fanon, *Black Skin, White Masks,* 180 ff., regarding the long-standing symbolic connotations of black and white in French and other European languages.

21. According to a description published in 1758—the year Badin was taken off to Copenhagen—considerable amounts of land on Saint Croix had been cleared by deforestation and burning during the immediate past. The same account emphasizes that slaves who were engaged in this heavy labor endured conditions of "terrible heat and smoke" from dawn to dusk (Hansen, *Slavernes øer,* 194). It may very well be that Wendela Hebbe's highly improbable tale of Badin setting fire to his parents' hut and then delighting in the flames involves a gross distortion—after numerous tellings and the passage of about ninety years—of whatever he may have experienced of land-clearing fires.

22. Glacken, *Traces on the Rhodian Shore,* 593.

23. Such a direction-based flight of the imagination, or geographical leap, would have been possible despite the absence at that time of any conceptualization of large-scale weather systems—as it demanded cartographic knowledge and nothing more.

24. Actually, another single page of weather observations does occur somewhat later in Badin's notebook. Even though there is reference on the previous page to a loan made on September 30, 1803, there is no determining the year of this meteorological entry, as other notebook materials do not follow a strict chronological sequence (see note 35). Whether the observations in question were recorded before or after those of the 1801 Christmas season, there apparently was some significant temporal separation involved, and hence Badin was presumably in another—but not necessarily unrelated—state of mind. Whatever the case, the existence of another much shorter set of data and comments in no way undermines the identity-related arguments made here.

25. Koerner, "Carl Linnaeus," 157; cf. quote in "Entrances" associated with note 15.

26. Strage, *Mikrofonkåt,* 18. In the everyday discourses of Swedish cultural racism, the term "immigrant" is applied to people of non-European background even if they are born in Sweden. This usually unreflected usage is a clear-cut boundary marker, an indication that only white natives may be regarded as "real" Swedes.

27. Ibid., 22.

28. Ibid., 21.

29. *Dagens Nyheter,* November 11, 1991.

30. Jordan, *White over Black,* 253.

31. Lise Patt, "On Blind Spots," in *Benjamin's Blind Spot: Walter Benjamin and the Premature Death of Aura,* ed. Patt (Topanga: Institute of Cultural Inquiry, 2001), xiv–xvi (xv).

32. Nils Henrik Aschan Lilljensparre was Stockholm's first police chief and the initial organizer of Sweden's police system.

33. *Strindberg's Queen Christina, Charles XII, Gustav III,* 212.

34. Wikström, "Badin-Couschi," 296.

35. Since Badin apparently at least sometimes made entries on the first page he opened to, there is not a strict chronological order to the dated contents of his notebook. Undated items therefore often defy temporal location.

36. Wikström, "Badin-Couschi," 296.

37. Claes Lundin and August Strindberg, *Gamla Stockholm: Anteckningar ur tryckta och otryckta källor* (Stockholm: Gidlunds Förlag, 1974 [1882]), 537; Nils Wester, *Kungliga Politi- och Brand-kommissionen: Studier rörande Stockholms stads politiväsen under 1700-talet* (Stockholm: Monografier utgivna av Stockholms kommunalförvaltning, 1946), 195–202; and Wikström, "Badin-Couschi," 296. On the development of street lighting in Europe's large cities during the eighteenth and nineteenth centuries, see Wolfgang Schivelbusch, *Disenchanted Night: The Industrialization of Light in the Nineteenth Century* (Berkeley: University of California Press, 1988).

38. Lundin and Strindberg, *Gamla Stockholm,* 558. Brighter-burning Argand lamps—with their double air-supplied flames—did not begin to appear on Stockholm's streets until the end of the 1820s, long after they were first introduced in Paris and London.

39. Fanon, *Black Skin, White Masks,* 190–191.

40. Reimert Haagensen, *Beskrivelse over Eylandet St. Croix* (Copenhagen, 1758), as quoted in Hansen, *Slavernes øer,* 198.

41. Ambjörnsson, *Det okända landet,* 86.

42. Skytte, *Det kungliga svenska slaveriet,* 96, in summarizing the contents of Bergius, *Om Westindien.*

43. Lundin and Strindberg, *Gamla Stockholm,* 557. The decree stipulated that lighting was to be provided from the "onset of evening" until past midnight, during a period that extended from September 20 through March 15. The requirement did not hold on clear, moonlit nights.

44. During the second half of the eighteenth century, when heavy drinking was commonplace to all classes, Stockholm had an extremely high density of drinking establishments—a circumstance that often translated into street brawls, attempted assaults and robberies, verbal aggression directed at strangers, and other forms of unruly public behavior, particularly at night during the darker part of the year. One estimate for around 1770 puts the number of pubs, or saloons, in the city at close to seven hundred—or about one for every fifty male children and adults (Henrik Schück, "Stockholm på Bellmans tid," in *Historia kring Stockholm,* ed. Torgny

Nevéus, part 3 [Stockholm: Wahlström & Widstrand, 1965], 389). Another suggests that the number of establishments then serving distilled alcohol may have been as high as eight hundred (Claes Lundin, "Källare och kaffehus i Stockholm under senare hälften af 1700-talet," *Sankt:Eriks Årsbok*, 1902, 34–56). Although a centrally organized municipal police force took over responsibility for Stockholm's "order and security" in 1776, and although its "diligence" in clearing "thieves, perpetrators of violence and other bad people" from the streets was occasionally praised in the press, various types of aggressive accostings surged during the late 1790s in conjunction with high prices, widespread hunger and need, and general unrest among the lower classes (cf. note 5). In the fall of 1798, with the level of nighttime public disorder mounting and the days growing shorter, the governor of Stockholm attempted to restore order by once again issuing a proclamation forbidding seamen, apprentices, and journeymen from either venturing outside their residences after 10:00 p.m., or from roaming about the streets or gathering in groups after dark. This had little effect, according to one bourgeois observer, who claimed that the night after the proclamation's publication "there occurred more noise and racket than ever before." In January 1800, another well-situated commentator complained, "Never [previously] have every kind of violence, robbery, murder and the grossest burglaries and thefts been thusly committed here—and with a level of boldness that is virtually without precedent" (Nils Staf, *Polisväsendet i Stockholm, 1776–1850* [Stockholm: Monografier utgivna av Stockholms kommunalförvaltning, 1950], 286–87).

45. Cf. the discussion of Gaston Bachelard's *La flamme d'une chandelle* (Paris, 1961), in Schivelbusch, *Disenchanted Night*, 96–97.

46. Michel de Certeau, *The Practice of Everyday Life* (Berkeley: University of California Press, 1984), 91–110 (101). For a somewhat different and illustrated version, see Michel de Certeau, "Practices of Space," in *On Signs*, ed. Marshall Blonsky (Oxford, England: Basil Blackwell, 1985), 122–54. By the time of Badin's notebook entry, street lighting was not the sole observational technology deployed for maintaining public safety and security. Efforts to keep public spaces under surveillance, and to create subjects self-aware of such efforts, were intensified in 1776 in conjunction with the establishment of a more formal police force. Although Stockholm then only had a population of about seventy thousand, the city was divided into thirty-three "surveillance districts," each under the supervision of an official whose title *(uppsyningsman)* is most appropriately translated as "overseer" (Wester, *Kungliga Politi- och Brand-Kommissionen*, 117).

47. H[ebbe], "Monsieur Coichi," June 26, 1897.

48. Skytte, *Kungliga svenska slaveriet*, 17, building upon William W. Boyer, *The Virgin Islands: A History of Human Rights and Wrongs* (Durham, NC: Carolina Academic Press, 1983), 22–29.

49. Translated from the original Danish law text, as reproduced in Hansen, *Slavernes øer*, 49–51. The nineteen paragraphs of this juridical barbarism were framed shortly after the Danes had abandoned one of their smaller islands, Saint John, owing to a slave rebellion that lasted six months, and in the very same year in

which they purchased Saint Croix from the French. These laws were widely applied, among other occasions, after a purported slave conspiracy on Saint Croix in 1759, the year after Badin's departure with Governor von Pröck. Gardelin's regulations were no longer being fully applied by the time the British briefly occupied Saint Croix in 1801.

50. Haagensen, *Beskrivelse over Eylandet St. Croix* (quoted in Hansen, *Slavernes øer,* 196). During Haagensen's stay on Saint Croix there were at least two instances in which slaves were castrated and several other cases in which they were deprived of a limb. He also notes that slaves whose skin had grown leather-like from whipping were punished with neck-irons from which large hooks hung so as to insure they would become entangled if they ran off into the bushes or forest.

51. Boyer, *The Virgin Islands,* 33.

52. Recall that Hebbe's purported 1847 source was a woman who claimed to be a friend of Badin's second wife, who would in turn have heard the story from Badin himself. And that 1847 would have been more than eighty years after the "fact." . . . If Hebbe's source was actually told any story about Badin's fear of the dark, it may possibly have involved a reworking or covering up of his adult behavior—of behavior that Magdalena Eleonora Norell had herself witnessed—as his nightlong weather recording is at least suggestive of a darkness-related insomnia problem. During Badin's lifetime it was commonly thought that "nostalgia" eventually precipitated tormented insomnia (Johannisson, *Nostalgia,* 21, 55); so it is not implausible that any sleep-depriving anxieties rooted in his past—and the contradictions of his current existence—were psychosomatically compounded by a belief that he was suffering from that "illness" (cf. discussion in "Re Reading").

53. In 1758 a census indicated the presence of 11,807 slaves and 1,690 whites on Saint Croix, a ratio of seven to one (Waldemar Westergaard, "Account of the Negro Rebellion on St. Croix, Danish West Indies, 1759," *Journal of Negro History* 11, no. 1 (1926): 50–61 (52). Anxiety over a possible slave revolt presumably was compounded by verbal communication of the experiences and memories of those resident Danes who had lived on Saint John in 1733 (see note 49), those who were already in place on Saint Croix in 1746, when an uprising was aborted, or those English and Irish settlers who previously had fled rebellious circumstances in Antigua and elsewhere in the British Caribbean. Fears also may have been strengthened by more general knowledge, for in those New World plantation economies outside of the United States where blacks were in the large majority, slave revolts occurred with "explosive regularity" during the eighteenth century (Palmer, *Cultures of Darkness,* 177–78, and the literature cited therein).

54. Greater restrictions against the social intermingling of slaves were also imposed as part of the technology of insurrection prevention. Thus, according to the additional rules, or Reglement, imposed in 1755: "Slaves belonging to different masters were forbidden to assemble at weddings or other events, under pain of whipping and branding for the first offense and death for subsequent offenses" (Boyer, *The Virgin Islands,* 27).

55. The confessing slave, who provided the sole "evidence" of conspiracy, was

apprehended for questioning after wisecracking about the future to two whites disputing with one another. In keeping with the reigning perception of menace from below, and the long-practiced grisly strategies for discouraging any form of rebellion, the judicial authorities chose to "make an example of" him following his suicide. According to the "trial" judge's report: "His dead body was dragged through the streets by a horse, by one leg; thereafter hanged on the gallows by a leg, and finally taken down and burned at the stake." In the hope of reaffirming control and inhibiting future occurrences, the means of torture and execution applied to those subsequently found "guilty" surpassed those of the Gardelin Code in their savage cruelty. In candidly describing the treatment of the thirteen publicly put to death, the presiding judge noted that one, "was broken on the wheel with an iron crowbar, laid alive on the wheel, where he survived 12 hours. The head was then set on a stake, and the hand fastened on the gallows." The most gruesome, prolonged, and fear-inspiring executions were preserved for the three "ringleaders." After extensive torture on the rack, they were gibbeted—suspended by chains from the arm of an upright post in an iron cage, where they baked in the sun and were spat upon by passing whites. The most fortunate of them survived but forty-two hours, while the agony was prolonged for almost nine days in the extreme case (Westergaard, "Account," 50–61; Hansen, *Slavernes øer,* 218–19).

56. See Badin's letter excerpt in "Memory Etchings" associated with note 14.

57. Hansen, *Slavernes øer,* 217. Even if Coffi was not identical with any of the "conspiracy" participants named Coffe, the frequency of whippings and other bodily cruelities was such that Badin may have all the same seen his brother (or father) brutalized.

58. The Reglement of 1755 in theory prohibited the sexual abuse of slave women. However, this and other of its nonpunitive features—which were to be enforced as Governor von Pröck saw fit—were never implemented because of opposition from plantation owners who refused to acknowledge that slaves had any rights whatsoever (Boyer, *Virgin Islands,* 27). In Saint Croix, as in other slave colonies, it was white male sexuality that proved ungovernable.

59. Haagensen reported that Saint Croix slaves were typically awakened by "a bark" at three or four in the morning (Hansen, *Slavernes øer,* 194). The first of such rude awakenings, with its unannounced and unanticipated fright, very conceivably may have been among Badin's earliest (repressed) memories. (By forcing slaves to move in the dark to the day's appointed site, and by putting them to work at the crack of dawn, owners maximized their extraction of labor and ensured that field output did not rot before being processed. On the "feverish intensity of operations," strict scheduling coordination, and time-consciousness associated with Caribbean sugar plantations, see Sidney W. Mintz, *Sweetness and Power: The Place of Sugar in Modern History* [New York: Viking Penguin, 1985], 50–52).

60. The exact circumstances under which Badin came to accompany von Pröck to Europe are unknown. One possibility is that Badin's parents were house slaves and that somehow Badin had caught von Pröck's eye, becoming a favorite for one reason or another. Another possibility is that Badin was appropriated from his field-

slave parents as a form of punishment either for their "transgressions" or labor-performance inadequacies or for persistent "insubordination" on the part of his brother. A third possibility, not mutually exclusive of the other two, may have been a desire on von Pröck's part to take someone home to Copenhagen who was still in his formative years, someone who could still readily learn Danish and grow into the role of decorative lackey already filled by so many other young Afro-Caribbeans in Denmark's capital city. In the first or third instances, the blow to Badin's parents may have been softened by some form of payment. (Another never-implemented stipulation of the 1755 Reglement prohibited the "separation of marriage partners and minors from their parents" [Boyer, *Virgin Islands*, 27].) Whatever the case, the moment of removal from his parents is very apt to have been extremely traumatic.

61. Sven Lindqvist, *Exterminate All the Brutes*, trans. Joan Tate (1992; New York: New Press, 1996), 7.

62. Translator's note in Coleridge, *Sex månader i Westindien år 1825*, unnumbered first and third pages of text.

63. Sjöström, "'En nödvändighet,'" 53. Sjöström finds the silence and ignorance regarding the ninety-three-year occupation of Saint Barthélemy ironical given the prominent place in the popular imagination assigned to New Sweden, the country's colonization of Delaware that lasted no more than seventeen years (1638–1655).

Departure Tears, Exits, Endings

1. Equiano, *Life*, 79.

2. However, as made evident in his autobiography, Sergel (1740–1814) had no kind words for Rehn's instructional capabilities (Ragnar Josephson, "Sergel [Sergell, Särgell], Johan Tobias," *Svenskt Konstnärslexikon*, vol. 5 [Malmö: Allhems Förlag, 1967], 118–26).

3. Sergel's social and artistic network included Carl August Ehrensvärd—the creator of the infamous Munck lampooning and the simianized profile of Badin—with whom he began a close friendship in 1779. They frequently urged one another on in the creation of comic, and often obscene, sketches.

4. The Swedish word for sculptor, *bildhuggare*, literally means image (picture, representation) carver.

5. Regarding Badin's periodic need to pawn possessions in order to make ends meet, see "Geography Lessons" note 6. It is also reported that Badin attempted to borrow money in 1815 from a fellow Par Bricole and Freemason member so as to cover expenses incurred in conjunction with yet another fraternal organization (Carl Forsstrand, *Malmgårdar och sommarnöjen i gamla Stockholm* [Stockholm: Hugo Gebers Förlag, 1919], 212–13).

6. In June, 1791, the Duchess of Södermanland noted that Munck had obtained an audience with Princess Sophia Albertina in which, among other things, "he tried, as best he could, to vindicate himself for all the falsehoods he had spread about her" (Bonde, *Hedvig Elisabeth Charlottas Dagbok*, vol. 3, 358). Whether the falsehoods in question involved Badin and their purported offspring, a current court intrigue, or some other matter, Sophia Albertina's version of events twice underscores Munck's

concern that others were "attempting to blacken his reputation" (Sophia Albertina in letters dated May 27 and 31, 1791 [reproduced in an extended footnote in ibid., 358–60]). While neither the duchess nor Sophia Albertina specify Munck's falsehoods, his metaphorical preoccupation could well have been reworked, or displaced, by way of a rumor that literally involved blackness.

7. In his role as assistant to L'Archevêque, Sergel may even have been present at the scene drawn by Rehn in 1762 or 1763. In that case the young Badin would have been "making a face" for Sergel as well as Rehn.

8. Josephson, "Sergel," 121, 124. Sergel's depressions were compounded by his gout-based physical sufferings. In 1795 he composed a powerful suite of thirteen drawings, titled *Extreme Despair (Yttersta förtvivlan)*, which in part was based upon his nightmares but also built upon certain literary inspirations (ibid., 124).

9. Lord Evelyn Baring Cromer, *Modern Egypt*, as quoted in Edward W. Said, *Orientalism* (New York: Vintage Books, 1979), 38.

10. Koerner, *Linnaeus*, 181. As early as 1846, in (f)act, Linnaeus was fictionally (oil-) painted as blond and blue-eyed.

11. H[ebbe], "Monsieur Coichi," June 26, 1897. The official inventory of Badin's possessions at the time of his death indicated that he owned one flagpole and four flags (Wikström, "Badin-Couschi," 302), a circumstance lending believability to Hebbe's daily flag-hoisting claim.

12. Crusenstolpe, *Morianen*, 2: 273–74.

13. At least between 1809 and 1817, if not until his 1822 death, Badin received an annual pension from the princess that, along with the grain sales from his three country holdings, significantly helped to support his household, including his second wife, his first wife's sister, and a varying number of maidservants (Wikström, "Badin-Couschi," 298–99).

14. In illustrations accompanying travel writings, atlases, and other eighteenth-century European publications, Africa and its "savage societies" were often humanly embodied in a black figure wearing little more than a feathered headdress and a sheath of arrows (Wheeler, *Complexion of Race*, 34). Unlike the portrayed Badin, such figures also carried a bow in one hand.

15. Here Badin refers to "an already-held image," rather than a "stereotype," as the latter term did not as yet exist.

16. Statens offentliga utredningar (Swedish Government Official Reports), no. 1996: 95, *Sverige, framtiden och mångfalden: Slutbetänkande från invandrarpolitiska kommittén* (Stockholm: Arbetsmarknadsdepartementet, 1996), 15.

17. Johannisson, *Nostalgia*, 10.

18. Ibid., 57–58. In another French publication of 1821, Jean Dominique Larrey, a military doctor, portrayed nostalgia as the consequence of pathological processes in the brain that, in their most extreme form, result in a "dismantling and dissolution of the self," thereby "extinguishing resistance capacities and leaving the body wide open to the rapid and destructive progress of disease" (synopsized in ibid., 59).

19. Ibid., 20.

20. Lindroth, "Linné: Legend och verklighet," 121 (no translation, from Lindroth's own English summary).

21. From a letter to Albrecht von Haller, dated November 13, 1764 (in ibid., 122).

22. Johannisson, *Nostalgia*, 22. Jung-Stiller's usage of nostalgia was common to the religious literature of the period and very well may have enabled Badin's periodic yearnings to be doubly charged during his last years.

23. Cf. "Re Reading" note 34 and the text thereto.

24. The original attributions are made in Carlander, *Svenska bibliotek*, 753–54; and Hebbe, "Monsieur Coichi," June 26, 1897. The problematic character of these attributions is suggested by Thomasson ("Morianen," 623) and Wikström ("Badin-Couschi," 313). Also see "Entrances" notes 56 and 58. However, if the inscription (f)actually exists, it would appear that Badin recalled other slaves being shipped from Saint Croix to Copenhagen along with him.

25. *Badins Anteckningsbok*. On the same notebook page Badin also refers to the forty-fifth chapter of the First Book of Moses, wherein the returning Joseph reveals himself to his brothers and inquires whether or not his father is still alive.

26. Walter Benjamin, "The Storyteller: Observations on the Works of Nikolai Leskov" (1936), in *Selected Writings*, vol. 3, ed. Jennings, 151.

27. *Hvad Nytt från Stockholm,* June 19, 1897.

28. See quote in "Memory Etchings" associated with note 57 regarding Badin's appearance in *Le Carneval de Venise*.

29. Rhodin, *Swenska Ordspråk*, 2; *Svenska Akademiens Ordbok*, 2: A 1962.

30. Wikström, "Badin-Couschi," 305.

31. John Updike, "Both Rough and Tender: The Autobiography of an Australian Folk Hero," *New Yorker*, January 22, 2001, 80–83 (83).

32. Peter Carey, *True History of the Kelly Gang* (New York: Alfred A. Knopf, 2000).

33. Richard Flanagan, *Gould's Book of Fish: A Novel in Twelve Fish* (London: Atlantic Books, 2001), 302.

34. Monica Braw, *Främling: Roman om en svensk i fjärren land* (Stockholm: Albert Bonniers Förlag, 2002), 51–52. Cf. quote in "Memory Etchings" associated with note 52 regarding Thunberg's views.

35. Ibid., 259–60. According to Braw (13), Thunberg was eventually nicknamed "The Rattlesnake" because of the way his old carriage rattled through Uppsala's streets.

36. Ibid., 313.

37. Ola Larsmo, "Alla människor har sin egen berättelse," *Dagens Nyheter,* June 14, 2002.

38. *Aftonbladet*, April 16, 1996.

39. Carey, *Kelly Gang*, opening unnumbered page.

40. Michel-Rolph Trouillot, *Silencing the Past: Power and the Production of History* (Boston: Beacon Press, 1995), 27, 152–53.

41. The pharmacy's original predecessor opened in 1670, opposite the Royal Palace stalls, and in the course of its existence moved three times before being shifted

to Drottninggatan 23 (Viking Källström, ed., *Stockholms näringsliv,* vol. 2 [Stockholm: N. H. Lovén, 1924], 779–81).

42. Claes Lundin and August Strindberg, *Gamla Stockholm* (Stockholm: Gidlunds Förlag, 1974 [1882]), 201–2.

43. Among Stockholm's other licensed pharmacies operating during 1825 were The Lion, The Leopard, The Stag, The Swan, The Owl, The Griffin, and The Unicorn (Källström, *Stockholms näringsliv,* 2: 763–801).

44. Cf. Pred, *Lost Words and Lost Worlds.*

45. Edward W. Said, *Culture and Imperialism,* 4.

46. Walter Benjamin, *Arcades Project,* convolute [K2a, 3], 393; convolute [N4, 3], 464.

Epilogue

1. Bonde, *Hedvig Elisabeth Charlottas Dagbok,* 1: 32, 442.

2. Athanasius Kircher (1602–1680), the inventor of the magic lantern, developed a number of mechanisms for manipulating the mirrors of his device in order to create illusions, including the transformation of spectators' heads. The use of the magic lantern for entertainment purposes at Gustav III's court may well have been inspired by activities at Versailles where, during the 1770s, a showman used the forerunner to modern slide and cinema projectors to produce Shadow Plays, or "Ombres Chinoises." On the history of the magic lantern and its eighteenth-century applications, see Martin Quigley Jr., *Magic Shadows: The Story of the Origin of Motion Pictures* (Washington, DC: Georgetown University Press, 1948); Terry Castle, "Phantasmagoria: Spectral Technology and the Metamorphics of Modern Reverie," *Critical Inquiry* 15 (Autumn 1988): 26–61, especially 31–33; Jonathan Crary, *Techniques of the Observer: On Vision and Modernity in the Nineteenth Century* (Cambridge: MIT Press, 1990); and Margaret Cohen, *Profane Illumination: Walter Benjamin and the Paris of Surrealist Revolution* (Berkeley: University of California Press, 1993), 237–42.

3. Jay Parini, *Benjamin's Crossing: A Novel* (New York: Henry Holt, 1997), 62–63.

Foremontage

1. Graeme Gilloch, *Myth and Metropolis: Walter Benjamin and the City* (Cambridge, England: Polity Press, 1986), 76.

2. *Webster's Third New International Dictionary of the English Language,* unabridged ed. (Springfield, MA: Merriam-Webster, 1999), 2,511.

3. *The Shorter Oxford English Dictionary,* 3rd ed., revised with addenda (Oxford, England: Clarendon Press, 1962), 2,314.

On Exhibit: Hartkopf's Unspeakable Space, or Past Moment as Forenow

For Benjamin, the critical "materialist historian" occupies himself with "those moments in the course of history that matter most to him, by virtue of their index as 'fore-history,' because [they have] become moments of the present day and change their character according to the catastrophic or triumphant character of that day" (Benjamin, *Arcades Project,* convolute [N9a, 8], 474). In order to emphasize that the past is not past, I have chosen to use the term "forenow" rather than "fore-history."

1. Steven C. Dubin, *Displays of Power: Memory and Amnesia in the American Museum* (New York: New York University Press, 1999), 3; emphasis in original.

2. Susan A. Crane, "Curious Cabinets and Imaginary Museums," in her *Museums and Memory* (Stanford: Stanford University Press, 2000), 60–80 (61).

3. Donald Preziosi, "No Art, No History," paper presented at a symposium on *An "Authentic" City for a Modern World: Cairo in the Nineteenth Century* (Berkeley, October 29, 1999); emphasis added.

4. Benjamin, *Arcades Project,* convolutes [L1, 3], 405; [Q3, 3], 533, and [B3, 4], 69. In the last instance Benjamin is referring to Breton's surrealistic novel, *Nadja* (1928).

5. Giuseppe Olmi, "Science-Honour-Metaphor: Italian Cabinets of the Sixteenth and Seventeenth Centuries," in *The Origins of Museums: The Cabinet of Curiosities in Sixteenth- and Seventeenth-Century Europe,* ed. Oliver Impey and Arthur MacGregor (Oxford: Clarendon Press, 1985), 5–16. On the early antecedents of the wax museum, also see Richard D. Altick, *The Shows of London* (Cambridge: Harvard University Press, 1978), 5–21, 50–54; Hillel Schwartz, *The Culture of the Copy: Striking Likenesses, Unreasonable Facsimiles* (New York: Zone Books, 1996), 101–3; Vanessa R. Schwartz, *Spectacular Realities: Early Mass Culture in Fin-de-Siècle Paris* (Berkeley: University of California Press, 1998), 92–96; and Mark Sandberg, *Living Pictures, Missing Persons: Mannequins, Museums, and Modernity* (Princeton, NJ: Princeton University Press, 2003).

6. Altick, *Shows of London,* 52. Regarding the history of Madame Tussaud's Waxworks, their often unspeakable contents and their reception, see ibid., 332–49; Vanessa R. Schwartz, *Spectacular Realities,* 96–97; and Sandberg, *Living Pictures.*

7. Vanessa R. Schwartz, *Spectacular Realities,* 103. Smaller waxworks containing life-size figures actually predated Madame Tussaud by 150 years or more, usually appearing very briefly in fair booths or in rented urban rooms (Altick, *Shows of London,* 50–53).

8. Vanessa R. Schwartz, *Spectacular Realities,* 97; and Per Simon Edström, "Spåren av vaxkabinettet," in *Ett resande vaxkabinett* (Stockholm: Statens historiska museums utställningskatalog nr. 328), 15–30.

9. Edström, "Spåren av vaxkabinettet," 24.

10. Allan Pred, "Spectacular Articulations of Modernity: The Stockholm Exhibition of 1897," *Geografiska Annaler* 73B, no. 1 (1991): 45–84; Pred, *Recognizing European Modernities: A Montage of the Present* (London and New York: Routledge, 1995), 31–95; and Anders Ekström, *Den utställda världen: Stockholmsutställningen 1897 och 1800-talets världsutställningar* (Stockholm: Nordiska Muuseets Förlag, 1994).

11. Schwartz, *Culture of the Copy,* 105.

12. Tony Bennett, *The Birth of the Museum: History, Theory, Politics* (London

and New York: Routledge, 1995), 10, 6. The expression "machines for progress" was widely used in the late nineteenth century to refer to international expositions and world's fairs as well as public museums.

13. Sandberg, *Living Pictures*, 29–34. Also see Pelle Snickars, *Svensk film och visuell masskultur 1900* (Stockholm: Aura Förlag, 2001), 85–95. The term "Panoptikon," not to be confused with Foucault's usage derived from Bentham's panopticon prison, was a term used throughout the Germanic-language countries of Northern Europe and, in Scandinavia at least, underscored a class distancing from the wax cabinet (Sandberg, *Living Pictures*).

14. The Swedish Panoptikon, which first opened its doors in 1889, was viewed by local bourgeois commentators as further evidence that Stockholm had finally arrived as a true metropolis, as a cosmopolitan center that was now fully integrated into the principal network of European cultural circulation (Sandberg, *Living Pictures*). However, this purportedly sophisticated establishment was not always as distinct from Hartkopf's Wax Cabinet and other similar attractions as its catalog and other publicity asserted. While not entirely devoted to the genre, Hartkopf's did insert a few of its wax effigies in staged tableaux, in "living picture" contexts that strove for authenticity. And, for all its "specifically bourgeois positioning," for all the suggestion that social contagion was not to be feared on its premises, the Panoptikon apparently "attracted a much broader audience." Moreover, the moralistic tone of its program guides to the contrary, its basement displays of the mid-1890s at least for a brief time contained crime and punishment sequences "with stronger erotic content" (ibid.; cf. Gunnar Broberg, "Entrébiljett till en skandal," *Tvärsnitt*, no. 1–2 [1991]: 118–25). A smaller competitor to the Swedish Panoptikon, established in 1890 as the Oriental Maze Salon, Edon Salon and New Panoptikon (Orientaliska Irrgångs-salong, Eden-Salong och Nya Panoptikon), soon offered a series of wax-figure harem scenes as its principal attraction despite attempting to set itself above Stockholm's wax cabinets by way of its name (Sandberg, *Living Pictures*). Appropriately, the site of this competing entertainment was located between Hartkopf's and the Swedish Panoptikon.

15. Paul Greenhalgh, *Ephemeral Vistas: The Expositions Universelles, Great Exhibitions, and World's Fairs, 1851–1939* (Manchester, England: Manchester University Press, 1988), 18.

16. Broberg, "Entrébiljett," 118.

17. Cf. ibid. (Would-be) hegemonic discourses in late nineteenth-century Sweden, as elsewhere in Europe, were "fixated with normality," thereby encouraging institutions such as Hartkopf's to commodify deviance (Edström, "Spåren av vaxkabinett," 11).

18. It cannot be established with certainty that the hide, the detached penis, or any one of the effigies named in this and the preceding paragraph were to be actually encountered at Hartkopf's Wax Cabinet. They may, instead, have been on exhibition at Thiodolf Lütze's Wax Cabinet, or Grand Musee du Plastique, which during the period 1895 to 1898 occupied two different sites on the Stockholm island of Djurgården, about thirty-minutes' walk from Hartkopf's establishment. Confusion arises because items from the two wax museums eventually became stored together

some time subsequent to 1898 (Edström, "Spåren av vaxkabinettet," 26). The fact that some of the items in question may have been viewable at one Stockholm location rather than another does not significantly detract from the observations and arguments that will be developed here.

19. Ludmilla Jordanova, "Objects of Knowledge: A Historical Perspective on Museums," in *The New Museology*, ed. Peter Vergo (London: Reaktion Books, 1989), 25, 33.

20. Jonathan Crary, *Techniques of the Observer: On Vision and Modernity in the Nineteenth Century* (Cambridge: MIT Press, 1990), 5-6. In insisting upon the term "observer," in attempting "to delineate an observing subject who was both a product of and at the same time constitutive of modernity in the ninetenth century" Crary is, quite appropriately, making a move away from the term "spectator" and all its connotations of passive onlooking (9).

21. David Theo Goldberg, *Racist Culture: Philosophy and the Politics of Meaning* (Oxford, England: Blackwell, 1993), 43.

22. Tony Bennett, "The Exhibitionary Complex," *New Formations* 4 (1988): 92; and Bennett, *Birth of the Museum*, 78.

23. K. Kastman and T. Brunius, *Geografiska bilder från jordens skilda länder och folkslag: En bok för skolan och hemmet* (1866), 325–26, as excerpted in Luis Ajagán-Lester, *"De andra" i pedagogiska texter: Afrikaner i svenska skoltexter, 1768–1920*, Svensk sakprosa, no. 13 (Lund: Institutionen för Nordiska språk, Lunds Universitet, 1997), 33.

24. Ajagán-Lester, *"De andra,"* 14.

25. E. Carlson, J. J. Dalström, and C. Lidman, *Folkskolans geografi* (1905 edition), 87–88, as excerpted in Ajagán-Lester, *"De andra,"* 54.

26. Ajagán-Lester, *"De andra,"* 55. Some of the texts in question were simply direct translations from the German. Friedrich Ratzel, who at the time exercised great influence over Swedish academic geography, had himself written of the Ashanti in words that would not have been out of place in *Folkskolans geografi* and other textbooks of the time. He referred to them as "true, wooly-headed blacks," and noted that their shamans employed "hysterical" dances to exorcise evil spirits (*The History of Mankind*, trans. A. J. Butler [London: Macmillan, 1898], 2: 352–57, 3: 125–43, as quoted in Sander L. Gilman, *Difference and Pathology: Stereotypes of Sexuality, Race, and Madness* [Ithaca, NY: Cornell University Press, 1985], 111).

27. Sven Lindqvist, *Exterminate All the Brutes*, 7.

28. Recall that Linnaeus's various discourse-influencing works were themselves not the ultimate origin of racial stereotypes, as those writings not only emerged out of his correspondence network and commerce-facilitated networks of scientific exchange, but also were consonant with the thought of other key Enlightenment figures. Also note that only ten years after the 1758 version of *Systema Naturae* appeared, a history schoolbook published in Sweden (H. J. Woltemar, *Anwisning till hela stats-historien*) observed that most of Africa had "fairly wild [or savage] inhabitants" (Ajagán-Lester, *"De andra,"* 25).

29. Cf. Annie E. Coombes on the role of the *Illustrated London News* in

(re)producing black African stereotypes during 1897 (*Reinventing Africa: Museums, Material Culture, and Popular Imagination in Late Victorian and Edwardian England* [New Haven, CT: Yale University Press, 1994], 11–22); and M. Christine Boyer, more generally, on the power of widely replicated graphic images to gain control over nineteenth-century imaginations by "forcing them into stereotypical molds" (*The City of Collective Memory: Its Historical Imagery and Architectural Entertainments* [Cambridge: MIT Press, 1996], 526).

30. Ekström, *Den utställda världen;* and Pred, *Recognizing European Modernities*, 31–95.

31. In Sweden, as in Britain and Europe more generally at this time, the "boundaries between different forms of writing—travel narratives, adventure genres and scientific treatises—were more fluid than perhaps we have been accustomed to thinking" (Gail Ching-Liang Low, *White Skins/Black Masks: Representation and Colonialism* [London and New York: Routledge, 1996], 2).

32. Derek Gregory, *Dancing on the Pyramids: Orientalism and Cultures of Travel* (Minneapolis: University of Minnesota Press, forthcoming), and the literature cited therein.

33. Åke Holmberg, *Världen bortom västerlandet,* vol. 1, *Svensk syn på fjärren länder och folk från 1700-talet till första världskriget* (Göteborg: Kungl. Vetenskaps- och Vitterhets-Sällskap, 1988), 357–70; and Lasse Berg, *När Sverige upptäckte Afrika* (Stockholm: Rabén Prisma, 1997), 171 ff. Although the image of Africans as uncivilizable savages was occasionally called into question in Swedish print, there was not much in the way of real debate on the matter during the final years of the nineteenth century.

34. See McClintock, *Imperial Leather,* among many others.

35. Crary, *Techniques of the Observer,* 20; and *Suspensions of Perception: Attention, Spectacle, and Modern Culture* (Cambridge: MIT Press, 1999), 29–30; emphasis in original.

36. Bennett, "Exhibitionary Complex," 92; and Bennett, *Birth of the Museum,* 78.

37. Zine Magubane, *Bringing the Empire Home* (Chicago: University of Chicago Press, 2004).

38. Peter Gay, *The Bourgeois Experience: Victoria to Freud,* vol. 3, *The Cultivation of Hatred* (New York: W. W. Norton, 1993), 81.

39. Here, too, is a distorted echo of Linnaeus, who in his *Anthropomorpha* (1760) first declares that the somewhat depressed nose of the pygmy resembles that of the Hottentot, and then suggests that the hindmost quarters of the former bear a "closer alliance with the apes than with us" (Broberg, *Homo sapiens L.,* 183).

40. Franz Otto, *Bilder och berättelser ur lifvet i Sydafrika* (translated from the fourth German edition by J. R. Spilhammar, with 127 illustrations, 1886), 25, 34, as excerpted in Ajagán-Lester, *"De andra,"* 36, 38. Ajagán-Lester notes: "It is difficult to determine the extent to which it was distributed in the schools, even if the contents in themselves can be judged as typical of then prevailing representations of Africa" (15).

41. *Katalog öfver A. Eisfeldts konst- och vax-kabinett bestående af mekaniskt rörliga figurer i kroppsstorlek* (Sundsvall: Boktryckeri-Aktie-Bolaget, 1877), 7.

42. Because of the anatomical explicitness of some its displays, Hartkopf's Wax Cabinet, and other establishments like it, were normally not visited by men and women at the same time. Newspaper advertisements usually specified one or two days per week when "the entire museum would be open only to ladies."

43. Cf. Coombes, who notes that guidebooks to British museums and simulated African villages during the 1890s frequently emphasized the physical attributes of black males and females in such a manner as to infer them "more closely connected with animals than humans" (*Reinventing Africa*, 101).

44. Gilman, *Difference and Pathology*, 11–12, 88; and Gilman, "Black Bodies, White Bodies: Toward an Iconography of Female Sexuality in Late Nineteenth-Century Art, Medicine, and Literature," *Critical Inquiry* 12 (Autumn 1985): 237.

45. Newspaper advertising text (Edström, "Spåren av vaxkabinettet," 24). Once again, for reasons given in note 18, it should be emphasized that it is not entirely certain whether the skin and detached penis were actually on exhibit at Hartkopf's or another relatively nearby wax cabinet. If they were seen at the other establishment, here-speculated associations still could have been made, either because of repeated exposure to Hartkopf's newspaper advertisements and street posters, or because people had been to both exhibits.

46. This quoted selection resembles "guidebook" entries for the more upscale Swedish Panoptikon, where the narrative voice "quite literally led visitors through the display, told them where and when to look, and what they should be sure to notice, most often referring to the scenes as real places and events" (Sandberg, *Living Pictures*).

47. This translation is not actually from the Swedish catalog in use between 1895 and 1898, but from the Danish catalog employed when some of the Hartkopf holdings were shown in Copenhagen during 1902 (*Hartkopfs Musaeum* [Copenhagen: Triers Bogtrykkeri, 1902], 14–15; emphasis in original). The wording is more or less identical with that of a (Swedish-language) catalog employed during 1894 at a wax museum in Gävle, a city 125 miles north of Stockholm (*Katalog öfver H. Duringers Museum* [Gefle: Ahlström & Cederborgs boktryckeri, 1894]). This suggests the Hartkopf operators either were also behind the Gävle enterprise or had purchased the display in time for their 1895 opening in Stockholm.

48. By 1913, when Hartkopf's assemblage of exhibits was scheduled for an appearance in the university town of Lund, it was announced that one could now see two gorillas carrying off two girls (*Arbetet*, November 8, 1913).

49. To the extent that fin-de-siècle fantasies of African genitalia were the product of discursive stereotyping, to unities of accepted vision, to visions of the black as "pure" race and "pure" sexuality, Gilman refers to them as "publicly repressed sexual fantasies" (*Difference and Pathology*, 111). Elsewhere he notes, "By the eighteenth century, the sexuality of the black, both male and female, [already had become] an icon for deviant sexuality in general; . . . Buffon [and subsequently others]

commented on the lascivious apelike sexual appetite of the black" ("Black Bodies, White Bodies," 209, 212).

50. Cf. Bhabha on Fanon, "Western sexuality" and "fear and desire for the Negro" (Homi K. Bhabha, *The Location of Culture* [London and New York: Routledge], 41).

51. On nineteenth-century discourses pertaining to miscegenation, "racial" intermixture, and hybridity, see Robert J. C. Young, *Colonial Desire: Hybridity in Theory, Culture, and Race* (London and New York: Routledge, 1995); and Ann Laura Stoler, *Race and the Education of Desire: Foucault's History of Sexuality and the Colonial Order of Things* (Durham, NC: Duke University Press, 1995), 12, 26–27, 43–52, 105–7, 181–83. Focusing on the Dutch East Indies, Stoler pushes the existence of these discourses—and their associated practices—in Europe back into the seventeenth century.

52. According to Gay (*Bourgeois Experience*, 68 ff.), Darwinian-buttressed racial thinking among the European bourgeoisie during the latter decades of the nineteenth century served as a ready justification for aggression. As he would have it, overtly negative images—bolstered by an unconscious male projection of anxiety regarding the sexual potency of the racialized Other—provided an alibi for aggression, a license for patronizing, ridiculing, bullying, or exterminating, *and in so doing provided pleasure*. Cf. observations on lynchings and the castration of black men in the post–Civil War United States in Heidi J. Nast, "Mapping the 'Unconscious': Racism and the Oedipal Family," *Annals of the Association of American Geographers*, 90 (2000), 215–55. On the most general level, Nast argues that "the psyche, within which the psychoanalytic "unconscious" reposes . . . [was] an interiorized repository within which the violent acts and desires of colonization were secreted or made *legitimately secret* and *unspeakable*" (215; emphasis in original).

53. *Katalog öfver H. Duringers Museum,* inside cover. See note 47 for details. Such rhetoric was, among other things, in keeping with the more general resonances existing in 1890s Sweden between popularization of the natural sciences and notions of national progress (Ekström, *Den utställda världen,* 102–3).

54. Jonas Frykman and Orvar Löfgren, *Culture Builders: A Historical Anthropology of Middle-Class Life* (New Brunswick, NJ: Rutgers University Press, 1987 [1979], 235, 239).

55. Israel Holmgren, *Mitt liv,* vol. 1 (Stockholm: Natur och kultur, 1959), 39, as translated in Frykman and Löfgren, *Culture Builders,* 239. The Swedish counterpart to Victorian bourgeois morality is usually labeled as Oscarian, after kings Oscar I and Oscar II, who sequentially reigned from 1844 to 1907.

56. Ludmilla Jordanova, *Sexual Visions: Images of Gender in Science and Medicine between the Eighteenth and Twentieth Centuries* (Madison: University of Wisconsin Press, 1989) 50, 55.

57. Apparently women were actually allowed into this risqué area on those days when admission to Hartkopf's in its entirety was restricted to "ladies" (*Ett resande vaxkabinett,* 13).

58. These objects may be seen both as a device for frightening supposedly "im-

moral" working-class men into a more chaste and orderly line, and as a reminder to those middle-class men who had been been given an Oscarian sexual education from childhood, who had been lengthily schooled in the dangers of masturbation and otherwise steered toward repressed sexuality. For most middle-class men, at least, there was a contradiction-ridden "standard of morality, which made prostitution a necessary evil. Whores allowed men to relieve their frustrations at regular intervals with no untoward social consequences. Scientific discourse even emphasized the physiological benefits to be derived from regular evacuations" (Frykman and Löfgren, *Culture Builders*, 239–40).

59. For the complex of anxieties around the prostitute, venereal disease, and race existing in Europe at this time, see Sander L. Gilman, "'I'm Down on Whores': Race and Gender in Victorian London," in *Anatomy of Racism*, ed. David Theo Goldberg (Minneapolis: University of Minnesota Press, 1990), 146–70.

60. The female wax anatomical models in question, like others widespread in Europe during the late nineteenth century, were all the more likely to be emotionally powerful and sexual-fantasy evoking because of the meticulous accuracy of their eyebrows, eyelashes, and pubic hair, because these details yielded "a verisimilitude so relentless" that the realism intended became "hyper-realism" (Jordanova, *Sexual Visions*, 47). Hillel Schwartz (*Culture of the Copy*, 107) speaks of such models as perpetuating a "gravid pornography, private parts teased out, the lovely naked woman manhandled." Cf. Jordanova, "Objects of Knowledge," 36–37; and Altick, *Shows of London*, 338–42.

61. Crary, *Techniques of the Observer*, 11.

62. Mikhail Bakhtin, *Rabelais and His World* (Bloomington: Indiana University Press, 1984).

63. Both Sandberg *(Living Pictures)* and Vanessa R. Schwartz *(Spectacular Realities*, 2, 37–43, 108–18) argue that the daily experience of reading late nineteenth-century newspapers was not unlike that of visiting a wax museum, because the mass-circulation press simultaneously spotlighted celebrity personages, "represented a sensationalized version of contemporary life," rendered the banal spectacular, and randomly juxtaposed subject matter from around the world. They also variously claim that moving about a wax museum bore a certain similarity to walking past "the vast [mannequin-filled] window displays" of department stores, or to the fly-by of faces and concrete phenomena experienced in navigating the traffic of crowded metropolitan streets. But none of these general parallels are especially suggestive as to the readings particular men and women gave to the phenomena here under discussion.

64. The cartoon referred to is by Albert Engström, Sweden's most famous artist-cartoonist and is reproduced in his *Kolingen: Dess släkt och vänner* (Stockholm: Albert Bonniers Förlag, 1945), 87. The caricatured black stevedore may have been one Jean-Louis Petterson, who was sketched and painted by several other Stockholm artists around 1900–1903. In perhaps the best known of these depictions, by Oscar Björck, his exposed upper body and exotic attire clearly identify him as an uncivilized and inferior Other, while the handheld sword-like object extending from his crotch confirms his dangerous (hyper)sexuality.

65. The heavy use of irony in Stockholm working-class humor of the period was particularly evident in the nicknames and other elements of everyday language employed by dockers. Such usages on occasion played upon the word *neger* (variably meaning Negro, black, or nigger). One dockworker whose hair, eyebrows, and moustache were albino-like was dubbed *Svenska negern* (the Swedish Negro/black/nigger); and, with an added touch of social inversion, (ink-stained?) journalists were collectively referred to as *bladnegrer* (newspaper Negroes/blacks/niggers) (Allan Pred, *Lost Words and Lost Worlds*, 146, 159).

66. Stockholm's population grew from about 260,000 in 1895 to over 280,000 in 1898. Given those totals, and no more than a single-digit presence of male blacks, the likelihood of any particular Stockholm resident encountering somebody from Africa was extremely small unless they frequented the docking areas with some regularity.

67. Between 1881 and 1900 over 27,000 Stockholm residents migrated to the United States (Fred Nilsson, *Emigrationen från Stockholm till Nordamerika, 1880–1893: En studie i urban utvandring* [Stockholm: Monografier utgiva av Stockholms Kommunalförvalting 31, 1970], 283). Moreover, as almost 60 percent of Stockholm's population was born elsewhere in Sweden, there were many who had friends and relatives in the United States who had never dwelled in the Swedish capital (Gösta Ahlberg, *Stockholms befolkningsutveckling efter 1850* [Stockholm: Almqvist and Wiksells, 1958], 86, 159).

68. Coombes, *Reinventing Africa*, 215. On the content of such exhibitions, see ibid., 85 ff.; and Gilman, *Difference and Pathology*, 111–20. Also cf. note 43; and Altick, *Shows of London*, 268–87, on mid-nineteenth-century London displays of Bushmen and Hottentots.

69. This spectacle moved from Strömparterren to two other variety-show venues in Stockholm before leaving the city in mid- or late April (*Stockholms-Tidningen*, April 6, 13, 1895).

70. Pieterse, *White on Black*, 179.

71. *Hvad Nytt från Stockholm*, June 22, 1895; *Stockholms Dagblad*, June 20, 26, 1895. In keeping with their long racialization, Swedish-born Samis, or Lapps, were also commodified and exhibited in "caravans," or road shows, that toured Scandinavia and the Continent during the latter part of the nineteenth century and well into the twentieth century. They, too, were displayed in a dehumanizing and often pornographic manner that emphasized their inferiority—thereby confirming what was already "known" about them, thereby reinforcing an already constructed field of vision (Gunnar Broberg, "Lappkaravaner på villovägar: Antropologin och synen på samerna fram mot sekelskiftet 1900," *Lychnos*, 1981–82, 27–85).

72. *Hvad Nytt från Stockholm*, November 13, 1897; *Dagens Nyheter*, November 1, 1897; *Fadernesbladet*, November 6, 1897; *Nya Dagligt Allehanda*, November 30, 1897; *Svenska Dagbladet*, October 31, November 9, 17, 1897. When criticized for providing four liters of alcohol per day to be shared by the seventy adult members of his "troupe," the village's "impresario" defended himself by noting he was contractually obligated to do so and observing, "Everybody who knows

anything about the negro way of life ought to know that it is altogether unthinkable for these people to perform their completely primitive dances without the aid of hard liquor" (*Svenska Dagbladet*, November 9, 1897). This and other references to the alcohol dependency of the visiting blacks simultaneously reinforced bourgeois stereotypes of Swedish working-class males as "savage" and of "another race" owing to their alcohol dependency (cf. cartoon referred to in "Entrances" associated with note 75).

73. *Hvad Nytt från Stockholm*, November 13, 1897; *Social-Demokraten*, November 9, 12; *Svenska Dagbladet*, November 26, 1897.

74. *Svenska Dagbladet*, November 1, 1897; *Dagens Nyheter*, November 1, 1897.

75. Gilman, *Difference and Pathology*, 116, 111. This subtext emerges even though *Ashantee* is "on the surface . . . a liberal protest against the exploitation of the blacks by a European public with a taste for the exotic" (111).

76. *Hvad Nytt från Stockholm*, November 13, 1897.

77. *Hvad Nytt från Stockholm*, February 16, 1895.

78. *Söndags-Nisse*, June 2, 1895.

79. *Söndags-Nisse*, November 17, 1895. Given the racist and anti-Semitic tone of materials often appearing in this humor magazine, the ending of the first sentence may just as well have been translated as "nigger stories," since the meaning of the Swedish word *neger* varies with context. . . . Among the Stockholm newspapers reporting the Payne rumor were *Stockholms Dagblad* (November 11, 1895) and *Hvad Nytt från Stockholm* (November 16, 1895).

80. *Dagens Nyheter*, January 12, 14, 19, 31, February 1, 20, May 29, 1895; *Hvad Nytt från Stockholm*, February 16, November 16, 1895; *Nya Dagligt Allehanda*, January, 11, 12, 14, 1895; *Söndags-Nisse*, January 27, 1895; *Stockholms-Tidningen*, January 29, February 1, 21, May 30, 1895; and *Svenska Dagbladet*, February 4, 1895.

81. Lars M. Andersson, "Bilden av juden i svensk skämtpress," *Historisk Tidskrift*, 28–64 (from the author's own English summary, 60). Also note Andersson's mammoth work, *En jude är en jude är en jude . . . Representationer av "juden" i svensk skämtpress omkring, 1900–1930* (Lund: Nordic Academic Press, 2000), which pushes the role of humor magazines in national identity formation back to the fin-de-siècle.

82. *Söndags-Nisse*, April 28, 1895.

83. See discussion of Pears' soap advertising in McClintock, *Imperial Leather*, 32–33, 210–14, 225 (quote from 214). McClintock regards the marketing of Pears' soap as emblematic of the "commodity racism" characterizing "the culture of imperialism in the last decades of the nineteenth century" (33). Advertisements for another then-popular British soap product, Monkey Brand, featured an anthropomorphized monkey who fulfilled multiple symbolic and mediating purposes regarding gender, race, and class; not least of all, as an "icon of metamorphosis" the monkey "perfectly [served] soap's liminal role in mediating the transformations of nature (dirt, waste and disorder) into culture (cleanliness, rationality and industry)" (217). Cf. Pieterse, *White on Black*, 196–98.

84. During the final years of the nineteenth century such "comical" (mis)representations also occasionally appeared in other elements of the press (for example, the cartoon referred to in "Entrances" associated with note 75), as well as in advertising posters and sheet-music covers.

85. Andersson, "Bilden av juden," 60. Stockholm's "comic press had a very wide circulation, not the least because every barbershop subscribed to comic magazines" (ibid.). Its publications "were read everywhere," not only in barbershops but also "in clubs, restaurants, and cafés," as well as in "hotels and theatres" (Andersson, *En jude är en jude*, English summary, 589). According to Andersson's judiciously determined estimates of publication totals and number of readers per copy, the total national audience during the 1895–1898 period surely numbered in the hundreds of thousands, a substantial fraction of which resided in Stockholm (75–76).

86. *Söndags-Nisse*, May 9, 1897. In another instance, the cannibalism-depicting text and drawings of "The Sun-Broiled Missionary" appeared under the headline "Exotic Song III" and thereby once again encouraged associations with the Fisk Jubilee Singers, who had completed their second Stockholm stay a few months earlier (*Söndags-Nisse*, November 3, 1895). . . . While cartoons that depicted Africans as cannibals apparently did not become commonplace until the late nineteenth century, European geographies published during the eighteenth century "generally include[d] cannibalism as part of the African disposition," even though many travel accounts "dismiss[ed] the possibility" (Wheeler, *The Complexion of Race*, 331). On the resurgence of cannibalism images in late nineteenth-century Europe and the work performed by those images, see Pieterse, *White on Black*, 116–21.

87. *Söndags-Nisse*, July 2, 1895. Such infantile depictions of black Africans clearly served to justify colonial paternalism. On the European colonial-power press imagery being mimicked in this cartoon, see Pieterse, *White on Black*, 88–89. On the "absence of reason" as a rationale for governing colonized Africans without their consent, see Zine Magubane, "Simians, Savages, Skulls, and Sex: Science and Colonial Militarism in Nineteenth-Century South Africa," in *Race, Nature, and the Politics of Difference*, ed. Donald S. Moore, Jake Kosek, and Anand Pandian (Durham, NC: Duke University Press, 2003), 99–121.

88. *Söndags-Nisse*, February 17, 1895.

89. Gilman, "'I'm Down on Whores,'" 166–67.

90. Double work was further encouraged by an image of the male Jew as a "sex-obsessed racial defiler" and "exploiter" of Swedish working-class women. Such representations had appeared periodically in the Swedish press since the 1850s and were now being further imprinted in the popular imagination by other humor magazine contents (although a contradictory set of comic-press images portrayed Jewish men as "sexually disinterested, physically timorous cuckold[s] obsessed with business and money" [Andersson, *En jude är en jude*, 126–32, 590]).

91. *Svenska Akademiensordbok*, vol. 13 (1935).

92. *Söndags-Nisse*, June 23, 1895.

93. Cf. more general arguments on the emergence and construction of European nationalisms in that trio of classics, Benedict Anderson's *Imagined Communities:*

Reflections on the Origin and Spread of Nationalism (London: Verso, 1983); Ernst Gellner's *Nations and Nationalisms* (Oxford: Blackwell, 1983); and E. J. Hobsbawm's *Nations and Nationalism: Programme, Myth, Reality* (Cambridge: Cambridge University Press, 1990).

94. Pred, *Recognizing European Modernities*, 31–95; Ekström, *Den utställda världen.*

95. If, as Lars Andersson so thoroughly and convincingly contends, the racially stereotyping anti-Semitic cartoons frequently contained in Stockholm-based humor magazines "played a not insignificant role" in national identity construction over a period of several decades, then the same may be argued regarding the comic representations of blacks during the final years of the nineteenth century—especially since the comic press then targeted Africans at least as often as Jews. Despite the exhaustiveness of his dazzling scholarship, Andersson has not a word to say on the parallel caricaturing of blacks in either his "Bilden av juden" or *En jude är en jude.*

96. Cf. Andersson *(En jude är en jude)* on the "Once a Jew always a Jew" message repeatedly contained in cartoons and the impossibility of Jewish assimilation that it conveyed. Among other things, cartoons emphasized that Jews could not wash away their Jewishness, that they had "a pronounced aversion to soap," that there was no removing the filth derived from their degeneracy and unwholesomeness, and from the "dirty business" that they conducted (590).

97. Cf. Stuart Hall, "The Spectacle of the 'Other,'" in *Representation: Cultural Representations and Signifying Practices*, ed. Hall (London: Sage Publications, 1997), 223–79 (262); and Pieterse, *White on Black*, 180.

98. W[endela] H[ebbe], "Monsieur Coichi," *Hvad Nytt från Stockholm*, June 26, 1897.

99. Hebbe's decision to dust off an article she had published fifty years earlier in a provincial newspaper, her decision to bring the much-begummed image of Badin back to life, did not occur in a vacuum. Her rewrite was a situated practice, and as such was almost surely in part precipitated by the high volume of negatively charged African representations then in circulation within Stockholm. And by her perception of a capital opportunity, a chance to issue a potboiler at a moment when Africans were cartooned as pot-boiling cannibals?

100. Although the argument is not worked out here, the constellation of images and chains of sexual fantasy evoked by the skin and penis may have been linked with sublimated homoerotic desire on the part of some male heterosexual observers (cf. Low, *White Skins/Black Masks*, 53 ff.).

101. Badin would also have been known to those who had read the 1880 edition of Crusenstolpe's *Morianen.*

102. Walter Benjamin, "Theses on the Philosophy of History" [1940], in *Illuminations*, ed. Arendt, 256.

103. William J. Glover, "Making Lahore Modern: Urban Form and Social Practice in Colonial Punjab, ca. 1849–1920" (Ph.D. diss., University of California at Berkeley, Department of Architecture, 1999).

104. S. A. Andrée, *Konsten att studera utställningar*, 2nd ed. (Stockholm, 1897).

See also Anders Ekström, "Industriexpositionen: En 'läroanstalt'?" *Tvärsnitt*, no. 1 (1997): 104. Also note Ekström, *De utställda världen*, 233–40.

105. The pedagogic technique of "object lessons" was highly popular during the final decades of the nineteenth century, being employed in international expositions and world's fairs, museums, and a variety of colonial governmental projects as well as in schools. Derived from the writings of Johann Pestalozzi (1746–1827), a Swiss educator and social reformer much influenced by Rousseau, the technique called for unifying "objects" and "lessons" through visual (or other sensual) means in such a way as to prove revealing, as to call forth specific perceptions or moral capacities, as to define the (ab)normal, as to form subjects along desired lines (Glover, *Making Lahore Modern;* cf. Bennett on the "object lessons in power" associated with museums and other elements of "the exhibitionary complex" [*Birth of the Museum*, 59–88]). Whether or not the operators of Hartkopf's intentionally set up object lessons, whether or not they even only subconsciously imitated that didactic technique from other institutions, whether or not they were simply putting their own unspeakable taken-for-granteds into practice, they all the same were in the business of teaching racial lessons by way of exhibited objects, they all the same employed objects in such a manner as to help (re)produce racialized subjectivities while producing profits for themselves.

106. Note Gilman, *Difference and Pathology*, 11–35, on the conditions under which stereotypes emerge and become reinforced or transformed—even in the virtual absence of the stereotyped group (cf. Sander L. Gilman, *On Blackness without Blacks: Essays on the Image of the Black in Germany* [Boston: G. K. Hall, 1982]). If stereotypes of the African black helped bring personal stability to residents of a turbulent Stockholm, they certainly were not the only racialized stereotypes that did so at the end of the nineteenth century. Especially if one looks beyond the brief 1895–1898 period, a much more important role was played by racialized stereotypes of the Jew and the Sami, or Lapp, both of whom, while not numerous, were much more likely to be actually seen repeatedly in Stockholm (Andersson, "Bilden av juden" and *En jude är en jude*; Andrea Amft, "Att skapa en 'autentisk' minoritet: Om makt relationen mellan svenskar och samer från slutet av 1800-talet till 1970-talet," *Historisk tidskrift*, no. 4 (1998): 585–615; and Broberg, "Lappkaravaner"). As previously noted, Lapps, like Africans in other European capitals, were not infrequently exhibited as living examples of a "primitive" race; on the Continent they were even sometimes shown in zoological parks in much the same way as wild animals.

On Exhibit: Unspeakable Spaces of 1999, or Forenow and Present in Constellation

1. Jay Parini, *Benjamin's Crossing: A Novel* (New York: Henry Holt, 1997), 226.

2. Bhabha, *Location of Culture*, 66.

3. Barbara Kirschenblatt-Gimblett, *Destination Culture: Tourism, Museums, and Heritage* (Berkeley: University of California Press, 1998), 6.

4. Allan Pred, *Even in Sweden: Racisms, Racialized Spaces, and the Popular Geographical Imagination* (Berkeley: University of California Press, 2000), 231;

based on Lars Melvin Karlsson, "Att tvingas möta fördomar och rasism," *Pocket-tidningen R* 26, no. 3 (1996): 8.

5. Cecil Inti Sondlo, "Hur tolerant är Söder egentligen?" *Dagens Nyheter,* June 10, 1994.

6. In the exhibition catalog's foreword (*Ett resande vaxkabinett,* 5).

7. Inga Lundström and Marja-Leena Pilvesmaa, *Kunskap som kraft: Handlings-program för hur museerna med sitt arbete kan motverka främlingsfientlighet och rasism* (Stockholm: Kulturdepartementet, DS 1996:74, 1996), 31.

8. The National Historical Museum exhibit consisted of a personally inherited collection, only a part of which had been shown at Hartkopf's. The remainder of the collection had been displayed at another Stockholm wax cabinet (see "On Exhibit, Hartkopf" note 18). When the present owner initially unpacked his collection, a large bag marked "Gorilla" was found empty (Edström, "Spåren av vaxkabinettet," 28).

9. Lundström and Pilvesmaa, *Kunskap som kraft,* 35, 39, 48.

10. *Ett resande vaxkabinett,* 13–14.

11. *Sunday Independent* (South Africa), August 11, 2002; *Dagens Nyheter,* August 1, 2002. The final sentence of this quote may not be entirely accurate, as it represents a translation of the Swedish version of Mbeki's original statement.

12. Mathatha Tsedu, "So Painful, but Also So Sweet, because We Aren't Crying for Her Return," *Sunday Independent* (South Africa), August 11, 2002.

13. Bennett, "Exhibitionary Complex," 90. Baartman's outer labia were repeat-edly described and drawn as long and "dangling," forming what racial scientists of the period termed a "Hottentot apron." This, it will be recalled, was exactly the feature Linneaus was hoping to find on the supposedly "orang-utang"-related "Troglodyte" woman he was unable to purchase (see quote in "Entrances" associ-ated with note 88).

14. Caroline Bauer, "Battle for Sarah Baartmann," *Sunday Times* (South Africa), August 11, 2002. For details on the degrading commodification and "scientific" objectification of Sarah Baartman, see Percival R. Kirby, "The Hottentot Venus," *Africana Notes and News* 6, no. 3 (1949): 55–62; Kirby, "More about the Hottentot Venus," *Africana Notes and News* 10 (1953): 124–34; Altick, *Shows of London,* 269; Bernth Lindfors, "'The Hottentot Venus' and other African Attractions in Nineteenth-Century England," *Australasian Drama Studies* 1 (1983): 83–104; Gil-man, *Difference and Pathology,* 85–90; and Carmel Schrire, "Native Views of West-ern Eyes," in *Miscast: Negotiating the Presence of the Bushmen,* ed. Pippa Skotnes (Cape Town, South Africa: University of Capetown Press, 1996), 343–54. Also note the facts fictionalized in Suzan-Lori Parks's play, *Venus* (New York: Theater Com-munications Group, 1997).

15. While the owner did provide an article for the catalog (Edström, "Spåren av vaxkabinettet"), nowhere else at the exhibit itself did he openly identify himself as the author of accompanying display-case labels.

16. Caroline Hooper-Box, "The Minister Who Brought Her Home," *Sunday Independent* (South Africa), August 11, 2002. Negotiations were hindered, among other reasons, because the director of Musée de l'Homme was concerned about

"the integrity" of his collection and because politicians "feared that giving up Sarah Baartman's remains to her country of origin would open the floodgates on demands for the return of countless relics by all whose countries, cultures and people had been plundered during the colonial era" (Bauer, "Battle for Sarah Baartmann").

17. Was there even some significance to the caption being placed on the display-case face farthest away from the penis?

18. Lynn Åkesson, "Individens frihet ställs mot människans värdighet," Axess 1, no. 4 (June 2002): 23–25. Although Åkesson is totally silent about the 1999 exhibit, certain turns of phrase reveal that she was fully aware of my previously published article regarding the matter (a much shorter version of this montage—"Unspeakable Spaces: Racisms Past and Present on Exhibit in Stockholm, or the Unaddressable Addressed," City and Society 23, no. 1 [2001]: 119–59).

19. Schrire, "Native Views," 348.

20. Lundström and Pilvesmaa, Kunskap som kraft, 53.

21. While 1999 audience readings and conventions of observation are not directly considered here, to deal with the public-silence issue is in large measure to deal with some of the key filters through which most readings presumably were made—with taken-for-granted cultural reworkings brought to the site of display.

22. I am here, of course, playing upon Benjamin's "dialectical image," especially as presented in "Convolute N: On The Theory of Knowledge, Theory of Progress" of his Arcades Project (456–88), and as discussed in Susan Buck-Morss, The Dialectics of Seeing.

23. Michel Foucault, The History of Sexuality, vol. 1, An Introduction, trans. Robert Hurley (New York: Vintage Books, 1990 [1976]), 27.

24. The author has spent an average of four months per year in Sweden since first coming to that country in 1960 to conduct dissertation research. Since becoming an Internet user, he has been able to regularly keep track of Stockholm's daily press while in Berkeley.

25. Lars Trädgårdh, "European Integration and the Question of National Sovereignty: Germany and Sweden," Working Paper 2.50, Center for German and European Studies, University of California at Berkeley, 4.

26. Statens offentliga utredningar (Swedish Government Official Reports), no. 1998:100, Har rasismen tagit slut nu? Bilaga till betänkande från den nationella samordningskommittén för Europaåret mot racism (Stockholm: Inrikesdepartementet, 1998), 29.

27. This widely employed epithet, which on occasion even has been known to slip into the vocabulary of mainstream politicians, may also encompass swarthy southern Europeans as well as Bosnian and Kosovar Muslims.

28. Throughout the mid- and late 1990s, the unemployment rate for those of non-European nationality or parentage fluctuated between 33 and 45 percent, or six to seven times the rate of those "real" Swedes whose family history had been associated with the country for many generations. By 1994 the labor-force participation rate for those of African birth had fallen to 19 percent, and Sweden, along with Norway and Denmark, had the worst record among all OECD countries for labor-

market discrimination against the foreign-born (Pieter Bevelander, Benny Carlson, and Mauricio Rojas, *I Krusbärslandets storstäder: Om invandrare i Stockholm, Göteborg och Malmö* [Stockholm: SNS Förlag, 1997], 264).

29. "A 1997 OECD report indicates that the immigrant share of the total population of poor suburban areas is higher in Sweden than in other OECD countries. The same is true of the ratio of immigrants respectively living in poor and other residential areas. In this respect ethnic segregation is more severe in Sweden than in, for example, France or Great Britain" (Per Wirtén, *Etnisk boendesegregering: Ett reportage* [Stockholm: Boinstitutet, 1998], 9).

30. For background to all of the circumstances named in this sentence, discussion of the processes involved, as well as further details and numerous sources, see Pred, *Even in Sweden.* Also note the much more abbreviated account given in Pred, "Memory and the Cultural Reworking of Crisis: Racisms and the Current Moment of Danger in Sweden, or Wanting It Like Before" *Society and Space* 16 (1998): 635–64, especially 638–41.

31. Put otherwise, the workings of cultural racism in Sweden may be conceptualized and empirically specified in terms of ontological and metonymical "dirty tricks." Ontological dirty tricks operate through socially constructed categories and concrete circumstances being repeatedly transformed into each other; while metonymical dirty tricks involve making the individual analytically synonymous with the entire group, transferring the Universal upon the Particular, thereby making the distinguishing characteristics of any specifically encountered individual disappear. See Pred, *Even in Sweden,* for treatment at length.

32. Bevelander, Carlson, and Rojas, *I krusbärslandets storstäder,* 127.

33. Program ett, Sveriges Radio, June 2, 1997.

34. Nuruddin Farah, *Yesterday, Tomorrow: Voices from the Somali Diaspora* (London: Cassell, 2000), 169.

35. Public pronouncements and other evidence also indicate that some fraction of the population had experienced a further destabilization of identity because what was arguably the world's most generous refugee policy during the 1970s and 1980s had been terminated in 1994. Because Sweden's current strict policy, including frequent denial of admission to torture victims—had come under periodic criticism from the UN High Commission for Refugees, the UN Committee against Torture, Human Rights Watch, and Amnesty International. Because it had now become almost impossible for people of color or Muslim background to migrate to Sweden unless, by means of ever more narrowly defined criteria, they could prove themselves dependent upon previously admitted migrants.

36. The popular geographical imagination largely propagated by the mass media also demonizes the segregated and highly multiethnic suburbs of the country's three largest metropolitan centers as "problem areas," allowing that term to become synonymous with "problematic" non-European and Muslim people, while further allowing the name of any one segregated suburb to serve as a stand-in for all such suburbs—and, by extension, for the entire sum of their residential populations (Pred, *Even in Sweden;* Urban Ericsson, Irene Molina, and Per-Markku Ristilammi,

Miljonprogram och media: Förställningar om människor och förorter [Stockholm: Riksantikvarieämbetet and Integrationsverket, 2002]).

37. Lundstöm and Pilvesmaa, *Kunskap som kraft,* 6.

38. For a lengthy consideration of these contradictions, see Pred, *Even in Sweden,* 265–87.

39. A lengthy and nuanced feminist analysis of the discursive content of these moral panics is contained in Anna Bredström, "Maskulinitet och kamp om nationella arenor: Reflektioner kring 'invandrarkillar' i svensk media," in *Maktens (o)lika förklädnader: Kön, klass & etnicitet i det postkoloniala Sverige,* ed. Paulina de los Reyes, Irene Molina, and Diana Mulinari (Stockholm: Bokförlaget Atlas, 2002), 182–206.

40. Statens offentliga utredningar, no. 1996:55, *Sverige, framtiden och mångfalden: Slutbetänkande från Invandrarpolitiska kommittén* (Stockholm: Arbetsmarknadsdepartementet, 1996), 150.

41. Bredström, "Maskulinitet och kamp," 197.

42. Advertising and other mass media images frequently appearing throughout much of contemporary Western Europe continue openly to link the bodies of African men and women with hypersexuality, with "wild" or "animal-like" sex. Black bodies are more or less nakedly employed to promote commodities, to associate products with the ultimate in sexuality and the fulfillment of desire. On the occurrence of such images in Germany and their everyday-life consequences for the stereotyped, see Damani Partridge, "Making Un-Geman Bodies: Citizenship, Nationalism, and Technologies of Exclusion after the Wall" (Ph.D. diss., University of California at Berkeley, 2003). On Italy, see Heather Merrill, "Speaking Subjects: Remaking Feminism, Race, and Gender in the New Migrant Europe" (Ph.D. diss., University of California at Berkeley, 2000). N.b., Afrika was still being marketed in Sweden during 2003.

43. Marcel Proust, *In Search of Lost Time,* vol. 2, *Within a Budding Grove,* trans. C. K. Scott Moncrieff and Terence Kilmartin, rev. D. J. Enright (New York: Modern Library, 1998 [1919]), 553.

44. Norman M. Klein, *The History of Forgetting: Los Angeles and the Erasure of Memory* (London and New York: Verso, 1997), 301.

45. Nicolas Jändel, *Sergels torg: En plats för Sverige i tiden* (Uppsala: Arbetsrapport 62, Kulturgeografiska Institutionen, Uppsala Universitet, June, 1994), 5.

46. Kunskapens kronan, broadcast on TV2, July 13, 2002.

47. *Metro,* July 4, 2002.

48. The square is proximate to the former site of Sergel's studio. Badin must have been highly familiar with the buildings and streets once occupying the square, as his residence of the late 1780s and early 1790s was but two blocks away.

49. Nils-Gustaf Stahre, Per Anders Fogelström, Jonas Ferenius, and Gunnar Lundqvist, *Stockholms gatunam* (Stockholm: Monografier utgivna av Stockholms kommun, no. 50, 1984), 172–73.

50. Demolition was facilitated by specially passed parliamentary laws pertaining to the municipal expropriation of real estate. For an analysis of this ambitious

undertaking—which extended from about 1950 to 1980—and its associated land-rent dynamics, see Eric Clark and Anders Gullberg, "Long Swings, Rent Gaps, and Structures of Building Provision: The Postwar Transformation of Stockholm's Inner City," *International Journal of Urban and Regional Research* 15 (1991): 492–504. Regarding the planning and political struggles associated with "The Great Demolition Wave," see Göran Sidenbladh, *Planering för Stockholm, 1923–1958* (Stockholm: Monografier utgivna av Stockholms kommun, no. 22, part 5, vol. 3, 1981); Sidenbladh, *Norrmalm förnyat, 1951–1981* (Stockholm: Monografier utgivna av Stockholms kommun, no. 66, 1985); and Anders Gullberg, *City-Drömmen om ett nytt hjärta: Moderniseringen av det centrala Stockholm, 1951–1979,* 2 vols. (Stockholm: Stockholmia Förlag, 2001).

51. In his *Production of Space* (Oxford: Blackwell, 1991 [1974]), Henri Lefebvre characterizes the abstract space of capitalism in a number of ways, often emphasizing its embodiment of visual-phallic-geometric power. His various usages are contextualized and unpacked in Derek Gregory's extended commentary on "modernity and the production of space" (*Geographical Imaginations* [Oxford: Blackwell, 1994], 348–416). Of particular relevance here is Eugene J. McCann, "Race, Protest, and Public Space: Contextualizing Lefebvre in the U.S. City," *Antipode,* 31 (1999), 163–84.

52. Statens offentliga utredningar (Swedish Government Official Reports), 1991: 60, *Olika men ändå lika: Om invandrarungdomar i det mångkulturella Sverige* (Stockholm: Civildepartementet, 1991), 57.

53. Birgitta Albons, "Vi vill hejda den välvilliga rasismen," *Dagens Nyheter,* November 11, 2000.

54. Susan Buck-Morss, "The Flaneur, the Sandwichman, and the Whore," 118.

55. Setha M. Low, "The Secret, the Unspeakable, the Unsaid: Spatial, Discourse, and Political Economic Analysis," *City and Society* 13, no. 1 (2001): 161–65 (164). Also see Low, *On the Plaza: The Politics of Public Space and Culture* (Austin: University of Texas Press, 2000).

56. Mats Franzén, "As Useful as Disgusting: Sergels Torg, Stockholm—An Exceptional Politics of Place" (paper delivered at "Space and Cities," a symposium held at the Swedish Collegium for Advanced Studies in the Social Sciences, Uppsala, May 26–27, 1999), 1.

57. Jändel, *Sergels torg,* 22.

58. Mikael Söderlund of the Conservative Party and Stella Fare, leader of the much smaller Stockholm Party.

59. Franzén, "As Useful as Disgusting," 4, 16, 6, 17; emphasis added.

60. Much of the drug dealing popularly attributed to Plattan does not actually occur there, but on the abutting Drottninggatan (Queen Street) and at other proximate downtown locations (Franzén, "As Useful as Disgusting," 14–15).

61. Whether or not the incidents in question have occurred at Plattan, the purported drug crimes of men of African origins are not infrequently reported or problematized in the press, more often than not in a manner that reinforces prejudice—especially since the nationality, ethnicity, or geographical background of other drug criminals

is generally not specified. Ethiopians, Somalis, and other Africans are thusly understood as a bad "cultural" influence, while the exposure of youths of non-European background to endemic forms of Swedish drug culture are ignored (Edda Manga, "Knark, globalisering och invandrarskräck," in *Sverige och de Andrea: Postkoloniala perspektiv*, ed. Michael McEachrane and Louis Faye [Stockholm: Natur och Kultur, 2001], 218–44). Cf. Mekonnen Tesfahuney on the "hermeneutics of suspicion," which in his non-Ricoeurian usage refers to the various means by which the nonwhite immigrant becomes a priori regarded as suspect, to the ways in which such suspicion both emerges out of and informs the discourses of cultural racism (*Imag(in)ing the Other(s): Migration, Racism, and the Discursive Construction of Migrants* [Uppsala: Uppsala Universitet, Geografiska Regionstudier 34, 1998]).

62. On the contents and impacts of these discourses, see Pred, *Even in Sweden*, 131–42; Ylve Brune, *Stereotyper i förvandling: Svensk nyhetsjournlistik ominvandrare och flyktningar* (Stockholm: Utrikesdepartementet, Regeringskansliet, 2000); Brune, "'Invandrare' i mediearkivets typgalleri," in *Maktens (o)lika förklädnaner*, ed. Reyes, Molina, and Mulinari, 150–81; Bredström, "Maskulinitet och kamp"; and Urban Ericsson, "Förortens diskursiva topografi: Bilder av de/det Andra," in Ericsson, Molina, and Ristilammi, *Miljonprogram och media*, 51–101.

63. Cf. Bredström, "Maskulinitet och kamp."

64. Per-Markku Ristilammi, "Betongförorten som tecken," in *I stadens utkant: Perspektiv på förorter*, ed. Karl-Olov Arnstberg and Ingrid Ramsberg (Tumba: Mångkulturellt centrum, 1997), 81.

65. Wirtén, *Etnisk boendesegregering*, 7.

66. Yaniv Friedman and Catrin Ormestad, "Äppelmörderskan and hudflängaren," *Dagens Nyheter*, June 20, 1997. These two authors also helped reinforce the pathologization of non-European-background suburban residents, also helped perpetuate various negative stereotypes, through an extensive series of short "humorous" fiction pieces that ran in *Dagens Nyheter* in 1996 and more sporadically thereafter.

67. This argument is developed by Franzén ("As Useful as Disgusting") who appropriately points out that, all their criticisms of the Social Democrats to the contrary, the neoliberal proponents of redeveloping Sergel's Square still obviously chose, in their own execution of power, to "put trust in the rationality of social engineering and its capability to design social life through the planning of space." He also notes that neoliberal promoters of the scheme had gained the support of local retailers and the Stockholm Chamber of Commerce who triply envisaged a reduction in crime, the insertion of more high-price boutiques and other up-scale usages into the area, and the capturing of customers who might otherwise frequent outlying shopping malls. At the same time many Stockholm residents were opposed to any rebuilding of Sergel's Square, feeling that "it is the taxpayers who will be hit," that "when Stockholm can't afford to take care of the poor and vulnerable, the physically and mentally ill, they shouldn't be constructing a monument to themselves" (readers expressing themselves in *Dagens Nyheter*, August 14, 1999).

68. Lisa Rofel, *Other Modernities: Gendered Yearnings in China after Socialism* (Berkeley: University of California Press, 1999), 135.

69. On the actual residential characteristics as well as retailing, industrial, office, and entertainment activities of the Klara District in 1895, 1910, and 1930, see William William-Olsson, *Huvuddragen av Stockholms Geografiska Utveckling, 1850–1930* (Stockholm: Monografier utgivna av Stockholms kommun, no. 1, 1964 [1937]); and H. W:son Ahlmann, I. Ekstedt, G. Jonsson, and W. William-Olsson, *Stockholms inre differentiering* (Stockholm: Meddelande från Geografiska Institutet vid Stockholms Högskola, no. 20, 1934). On the physical appearance of the district in the 1950s, see Bosse Bergman, *Klara 1950: Gator och näringar i en city stadsdel* (Stockholm: Stockholmia Förlag, 2001); and Gullberg, *City—Drömmen,* vol. 1.

70. The Swedish verb *linka* means to hobble, or walk with a limp; while the verb *streta* means to strive or struggle. For sources, further elaboration, and a more general discussion of the symbolic discontent and ideological counterpunching associated with this and other elements of Stockholm's popular geography during the 1890s, see Pred, *Lost Words and Lost Worlds,* 92–142.

71. "Underclass" is not a recent linguistic borrowing in Swedish. In nineteenth-century parlance distinctions were already drawn between the "overclass," the "bourgeois" or "middle" class, and the "underclass."

72. See the illuminating theoretical discussion of presence, erasure, and spatial signification contained in Michael Landzelius's *Dis[re]membering Spaces: Swedish Modernism in Law Courts Controversy* (Göteborg: Göteborg University, Institute of Conservation, 1999).

73. Gregory, *Geographical Imaginations,* 360. Cf. note 51.

74. As quoted in McCann, "Race, Protest, and Public Space," 169.

75. Peter Englund, *Brev från nollpunkten: Historiska essäer* (Stockholm: Atlantis, 1998), 8.

76. As quoted in Martha Minow, *Between Vengeance and Forgiveness: Facing History after Genocide and Mass Violence* (Boston: Beacon Press, 1998), 118.

77. On Swedish efforts to induce the return migration of racialized groups during the late 1990s see Pred, *Even in Sweden,* 54–55.

78. Walter Benjamin, "Little History of Photography" [1931], in *Selected Writings,* vol. 2, ed. Jennings, Eiland, and Smith, 527.

79. Psychological research conducted in Sweden, Great Britain, Australia, and the United States testifies to the speed with which negative racial stereotypes may be activated, even among those who declare themselves unprejudiced (for Swedish evidence and references to the international literature, see Tadesse Araya, *Stereotypes: Suppression, Forgetting, and False Memory* [Uppsala: Acta Universitatus Upsaliensis, 2003]).

80. Young, *Colonial Desire,* 28.

81. Englund, *Brev från nollpinkten,* 9.

82. Gunnar Broberg, *Homo Sapiens L.,* 235.

83. Benjamin, "Theses," 255.

84. Buck-Morss, "The Flaneur, the Sandwichman, and the Whore," 101.

Index

Allan Pred is professor of geography at the University of California, Berkeley. He is the author of numerous books, most recently *Even in Sweden: Racisms, Racialized Spaces, and the Popular Geographical Imagination* and *Recognizing European Modernities: A Montage of the Present.*